DEMOCRATIC NORMS OF EARTH SYSTEM GOVERNANCE

Deliberative democracy is well suited to the challenges of governing in the Anthropocene. But deliberative democratic practices are only suited to these challenges to the extent that five prerequisites – empoweredness, embeddedness, experimentality, equivocality, and equitableness – are successfully institutionalized. Governance must be created by those it addresses; applicable equally to all; capable of learning from (and adapting to) experience; rationally grounded; and internalized by those who adopt and experience it. This book analyzes these five major normative principles, pairing each with one of the Earth System Governance Project's analytical problems to provide an in-depth discussion of the minimal conditions for environmental governance that can be truly sustainable. It is ideal for scholars and graduate students in global environmental politics, earth system governance, and international environmental policy. This is one of a series of publications associated with the Earth System Governance Project. For more publications, see www.cambridge .org/earth-system-governance.

WALTER F. BABER is Professor in the Environmental Sciences and Policy Program and the Graduate Center for Public Policy and Administration at California State University, Long Beach. He is also Affiliated Professor at the Raoul Wallenberg Institute of Human Rights and Humanitarian Law in Lund, Sweden. He has published many research articles and five previous books, including four coauthored books with Robert V. Bartlett. Most recently this has included *Environmental Human Rights in Earth System Governance: Democracy Beyond Democracy* (Earth System Governance Elements series, Cambridge University Press, 2020). He has been a Lead Faculty of the international Earth System Governance research alliance since 2012, and has had Fulbright scholar appointments in Italy, Sweden, and Austria.

ROBERT V. BARTLETT is the Gund Professor of the Liberal Arts in the Political Science Department and the Environment Program at the University of Vermont, where he is also a fellow in the Gund Institute of Environment. He has published many research articles and eleven previous books, several of which have won prizes. He has been a Lead Faculty of the international Earth System Governance research alliance since 2012, and has had Fulbright scholar appointments in New Zealand, Ireland, Italy, and Austria.

DEMOCRATIC NORMS OF EARTH SYSTEM GOVERNANCE

Deliberative Politics in the Anthropocene

WALTER F. BABER
California State University, Long Beach

ROBERT V. BARTLETT
University of Vermont

CAMBRIDGE
UNIVERSITY PRESS

University Printing House, Cambridge CB2 8BS, United Kingdom

One Liberty Plaza, 20th Floor, New York, NY 10006, USA

477 Williamstown Road, Port Melbourne, VIC 3207, Australia

314–321, 3rd Floor, Plot 3, Splendor Forum, Jasola District Centre, New Delhi – 110025, India

79 Anson Road, #06–04/06, Singapore 079906

Cambridge University Press is part of the University of Cambridge.

It furthers the University's mission by disseminating knowledge in the pursuit of education, learning, and research at the highest international levels of excellence.

www.cambridge.org
Information on this title: www.cambridge.org/9781108831222
DOI: 10.1017/9781108923651

© Walter F. Baber and Robert V. Bartlett 2021

This publication is in copyright. Subject to statutory exception
and to the provisions of relevant collective licensing agreements,
no reproduction of any part may take place without the written permission
of Cambridge University Press.

First published 2021

A catalogue record for this publication is available from the British Library.

Library of Congress Cataloging-in-Publication Data
Names: Baber, Walter F., 1953– author. | Bartlett, Robert V., author.
Title: Democratic norms of earth system governance : deliberative politics in the anthropocene /
Walter F. Baber, Robert V. Bartlett.
Description: Cambridge, United Kingdom ; New York, NY : Cambridge University Press, 2021. |
Includes bibliographical references and index.
Identifiers: LCCN 2020046807 (print) | LCCN 2020046808 (ebook) | ISBN 9781108831222 (hardback) |
ISBN 9781108926577 (paperback) | ISBN 9781108923651 (epub)
Subjects: LCSH: Environmental policy–International cooperation. | Environmental policy–Citizen participation. |
Democracy and environmentalism. | Earth System Governance Project.
Classification: LCC GE170 .B367 2021 (print) | LCC GE170 (ebook) | DDC 363.7/0526–dc23
LC record available at https://lccn.loc.gov/2020046807
LC ebook record available at https://lccn.loc.gov/2020046808

ISBN 978-1-108-83122-2 Hardback
ISBN 978-1-108-92657-7 Paperback

Cambridge University Press has no responsibility for the persistence or accuracy
of URLs for external or third-party internet websites referred to in this publication
and does not guarantee that any content on such websites is, or will remain,
accurate or appropriate.

Contents

List of Tables		*page* vii
Acknowledgments		viii
1	Democratic Governance in the Anthropocene: Equivocal, Experimental, Equitable, Empowered, Embedded	1
2	Toward Consensual Earth System Governance	23
3	Empowered Democratic Agency in the Anthropocene: Reconciling People to Nature and Each Other	47
4	Embedded Governance Architecture in the Anthropocene: The Structure of Institutionalized Ecological Rationality	77
5	Experimental Adaptiveness in the Anthropocene: Reconciling Communities and Institutions to Environmental Change	104
6	Equivocal Democratic Accountability in the Anthropocene: Where Effective Legislatures Do Not Exist	123
7	Equitable Access and Allocation in the Anthropocene: Reconciling Today and Tomorrow	138
8	Earth System Democracy: Governing Humanity in the Anthropocene	152

Afterword: Governance by Uncommon Global Environmental Law?   164

Notes   173
Bibliography   176
Index   205

Table

2.1   A deliberative policy matrix   *page* 25

Acknowledgments

This volume, our fifth book-length collaboration, has been gestating since 2014. We thank the three anonymous reviewers who provided feedback to us on behalf of Cambridge University Press. Most of the chapters have been presented at conferences and workshops on two continents, and we thank the many participants and discussants who contributed to improving our thinking and writing with their comments on those early drafts and our presentations. An early version of part of Chapter 1 was previously published as "Deliberative Democracy and the Environment" in *The Oxford Handbook of Deliberative Democracy*, edited by André Bächtiger, John S. Dryzek, Jane Mansbridge, and Mark E. Warren, Oxford University Press, 2018, pp. 755–767. We particularly thank John Dryzek and André Bächtiger for comments that improved that earlier work. An early version of part of Chapter 2 was previously published as "Consensual Environmental Policy in the Anthropocene: Governing What Humanity Hath Wrought" in *Public Policy, Governance and Polarization: Making Governance Work*, edited by David K. Jesuit and Russell Alan Williams, Routledge, 2018, pp. 87–105. An early version of Chapter 6 was previously published as "Democratic Accountability in the Anthopocene: Toward a Non-Legislative Model" in *Environmental Governance in the Anthropocene: Institutions and Legitimacy in a Complex World*, edited by Philipp Pattberg and Fariborz Zelli, Routledge, 2015, pp. 167–183. We thank Philipp Pattberg for valuable suggestions on that work.

Our research and writing has been consistently sustained by our home institutions. Bartlett's work is supported by the Gund Chair of the Liberal Arts at the University of Vermont.

Baber particularly thanks the Austrian-American Educational Commission (Fulbright Austria) and the Diplomatic Academy of Vienna for the 2016 Fulbright-Diplomatic Academy Visiting Professorship of International Studies, and the Swedish Fulbright Commission and the Raoul Wallenberg Institute for Human Rights and Humanitarian Law for the 2017/18 Fulbright Lund Chair of Public

International Law. He also thanks the US Commission for the International Exchange of Scholars for both of these appointments that provided support and conducive circumstances to make his work on this project possible.

Bartlett thanks the US Commission for the International Exchange of Scholars, the Austrian-American Educational Commission (FulbrightAustria), and the Diplomatic Academy of Vienna for the time, quiet space, and stimulating environment that made possible the completion of a draft of this manuscript during an appointment as 2019 Fulbright-Diplomatic Academy Visiting Professor of International Studies.

At Cambridge University Press, we are grateful for the professionalism and good humor of Emma Kiddle and Sarah Lambert, and for the always-valuable advice and support of Frank Biermann, series editor of the Earth System Governance series.

1

Democratic Governance in the Anthropocene

Equivocal, Experimental, Equitable, Empowered, Embedded

The complexity and interpenetration of the environmental problematique, the impact severity of some crucial environmental trajectories, and the unfathomable diversity of humans and human cultures combine to make governing interaction with earth's natural systems the most daunting challenge humans will ever face. The challenge is doubly daunting because of its urgency: Many of the most frightening and irreversible trends in the environment – as seen globally, regionally, and locally – are driven by deeply imbedded forces that cannot be altered, stopped, or reversed in the short term of a few years or even a few decades. Time is of the essence for beginning and accelerating the obviously needed transformations, even as knowledge about the world remains grossly inadequate to light very much of any path that global society must start down (Linnér and Wibeck 2019). The processes that must be confronted and reflexively transformed lie at the heart of modernity, notably the forces and relations of economic production, the ways that risk is managed, and the processes of knowledge generation and dissemination (Christoff and Eckersley 2013, 30; Dryzek 2014; Dryzek and Pickering 2017; Eckersley 2017). If it is ever going to be possible for humans to undertake successful environmental governance simultaneously at multiple levels as required, it must be by embracing principles and adopting rules for complex institutions that can effectively and justly exercise responsibilities for protecting the rest of nature (in all its complexity) from humans, and humans (in all their diversity) from themselves.

In the Anthropocene, environmental governance must be effective both within and across identities, while the inescapable *equivocality* of democratic governance means that discussions can never be closed; they can merely be transformed as old problems and concerns give way to new. This means that the *experimental* quality that effective environmental governance must possess cannot be a transient quality but, rather, must be a permanent feature of the landscape of democratic decision-making in which success is realized in a context of identity politics. For these processes to take place without distortion and without posing systemic disadvantage on parties who identify as minorities, and for intergroup differences to be accommodated, substantial *equality* of access to decision-making and *equitable* allocation of fundamental capabilities are essential prerequisites. They are prerequisites that can only be ensured by institutional arrangements that provide for *empowerment* of those whose identities are otherwise ill-favored by the political and economic status quo and for the *embeddedness* of environmental decision-making in the communities of fate where people actually determine their shared life experiences. Moreover, the circumstances of the Anthropocene call for building some considerable measure of ecological rationality into the processes and structures responsible for environmental governance (Dryzek and Pickering 2019).

More than just democracy in the form of aggregation of votes, deliberative democratic practice is a prerequisite for the learning, local knowledge, and engagement required by enlightened environmental governance under the conditions associated with the concept of the Anthropocene.[1] Effective governance institutions and rules must be grounded in widely shared understandings, created by those they address, applicable equally to all, capable of learning from (and adapting to) experience, rationally grounded, and internalized by those who adopt and experience them (Baber and Bartlett 2015, 1–11). Deliberative democratic practices are especially well suited to these challenges.

The underlying premises of this claim and their conceptual history point us to the environmental governance promises of democratic deliberation (Gunderson 1995, 46) but also to the very real perils of deliberation – both as a form of politics generally and as a strategy for environmental protection. Both conceptually and in practical experimentation, deliberative environmental democracy has evolved significantly in recent decades, yet further progress is urgently needed in our understanding of this marriage of democratic theory and real-world, global-to-local problem-solving in a world that is getting smaller while some political and social distances increase (Baber and Bartlett 2005, 2009a, 2015; Dryzek 2017a; Dryzek and Pickering 2017).

1.1 Promise

The environmental promise of deliberative democracy was born, and continues to be borne, by the realization that under purely aggregative mechanisms of democracy, environmentalists do their cause little favor when they frame it in moral or ethical rather than political terms (Gunderson 1995). The moral insight that "we are all in this together" is obviously a valid one and certainly implies a level of mutual environmental obligation (Feinberg and Willer 2013). But nothing about that obligation suggests that nominally democratic forms of interest aggregation (polling, referenda, representative elections) either capture its normative content or identify its most appropriate institutional form. Deliberative environmental democracy, however, is more promising in several specific ways.

First, as a general matter, deliberative democracy is thought to have both an inclusive and rationalizing influence on environmental politics. Its open and participatory character promises a form of knowledge mobilization that is potentially inclusive of all knowledge systems and, through reciprocal dialogue, allows for the negotiation of knowledge quality in terms of credibility, salience, and legitimacy (Baber and Bartlett 2005; Bremer 2013; Curato et al. 2017). Even though the most diverse deliberative body is unlikely to contain within its participant group the entire range of potentially meaningful discourses regarding any given environmental issue, the presence within a deliberative body of a variety of individuals provides a far wider conduit for the complexities of the real world to influence policy outcomes than can any form of elite decision-making (Baber and Bartlett 2015; Dryzek and Pickering 2017). A poster child for this promise is the prevalence of deliberative partnerships in the area of watershed management (Baber 2010; Hardy and Koontz 2009; Leach and Pelky 2001; Lubell et al. 2002). In this context, deliberative democracy's potential for giving voice to historically neglected populations has been commented on in particular (Cronin and Ostergren 2007; Curato et al. 2017). This aspect of deliberative democracy's promise is centrally related to the fact that it conceives of political representation in discursive terms rather than as a matter of demographics, interest groups, or ideology (Dryzek 2017a; Dryzek and Niemeyer 2008).

Second, deliberative environmental democracy offers an opportunity for environmental decisions to profit from the uptake of local knowledge. Especially in the international context (Baber and Bartlett 2009a; Dryzek 2017b), it is vitally important that centrally adopted policies reflect the understandings of the people living in the ecosystems that those policies are intended to protect. In the area of climate adaptation, for example, local communities are likely to be uniquely valuable sources of information regarding issues such as land and water management, physical infrastructure, livelihood strategies, and social institutions (Lebel 2013). This insight about the capacity of deliberative environmental democracy to provide for a decentered form of policy-making has been deployed in the rangelands of Arizona (Arnold and Fernandez-Gimenez 2007), the mangrove forests of Brazil (Glaser and Oliveira 2004), the plains of Kenya (Mburu and Birner 2007), the coastal zones of the Asia-Pacific (Lebel 2013), and the global climate arena (Bäckstrand 2011). Moreover, this form of deliberative environmental democracy is potentially self-reinforcing, because decentered democracy is strengthened when multiple linkages are created to connect local forms across time and space (Curato et al. 2017; Hayward 2008). The decenteredness of deliberative environmental democracy, which can be thought of as a second form of inclusiveness, also leads naturally to a third promise of deliberative environmental democracy – that it produces policies that are more just than those of mere aggregative democracy.

As a third potential advantage to environmental deliberation, the idea of justice carries considerable freight. For example, environmental policies are sometimes a form of normative pre-commitment, employing a deliberative procedure to specify in advance the just course for a society to take if certain environmental challenges arise. For instance, the US Endangered Species Act uses a species listing procedure to trigger a robust standard for species protection when the threat level reaches a specified threshold (Baber and Bartlett 2005).

However, frequently the question in environmental politics arises as the result of an inequitable distribution of environmental goods or harms. Whether environmental injustices arise from racsim or poverty, the strongly inclusive character of deliberative environmental democracy makes it an especially welcoming form of governance for those who would seek to redress such grievances (Baber and Bartlett 2009b). Advocates for environmental justice are able to exploit the dialogic character of deliberative environmental democracy by using their "storylines" to shift the dynamics of deliberative systems and to advance their own interpretations of environmental problems and policy-making processes. Specifically, these storylines can be used to set (or reset) the agenda on environmental hazards, to construct the form of public deliberation, to change the rules of the game, to construct the normative content of public deliberation, to shape meanings related to environmental policy, and to couple or align forums, arenas, and courts across the system (Curato et al. 2017; Dodge 2014).

A fourth important promise of deliberative environmental democracy is, to put it bluntly, better environmental decisions. Elite decision-makers sometimes flatter themselves to think that they produce the best environmental decisions when they can pursue their highly sophisticated work without much interference from others. This ignores two fundamental problems. The first is that environmental policies that fail to enjoy broad-based support cannot achieve ecological sustainability because they will fail to be politically sustainable (Baber and Bartlett 2005). Perhaps more important, the underlying premise of elite environmental decision-making is mistaken. Elite decisions are, more often than not, inferior to decisions made by deliberative environmental democracy, as an example will show. Environmental politics increasingly faces human-made risks in many domains (technology, environment, energy, food, health, security, etc.) that pose new challenges of risk governance – involving as they do variables whose values are irreducibly indeterminate. The resulting conditions of uncertainty and ambiguity impose evaluative, cognitive, and normative problems. Solving those problems requires an interplay between the state, experts, stakeholder groups, and the public at large. This environment of risk governance confronts us with a question: How can societies develop political institutions and processes for governing risk more effectively and how can members of a society be better involved in risk governance? A deliberative system (Dryzek 2017a; Parkinson and Mansbridge 2012) with a functional division of labor that assigns specific tasks to and recognizes the specific competencies of experts, stakeholder groups, and citizens can facilitate an appropriate integration of scientific and experiential substance. The integration of expertise and experience can be promoted by such a process of differentiated deliberation by experts, stakeholders, and the public, which can produce better outcomes than the classical risk analysis approach found in many regulatory systems (Klinke and Renn 2014).

Finally, deliberative environmental democracy holds the promise of environmental decisions that are more consensual and, for that reason, more legitimate. The relationship between consensus and legitimacy has long been a topic of contention within the community of deliberative democratic theorists (Baber and Bartlett 2015, 2020). Some have argued that consensus is an essential byproduct of epistemic deliberation, in cases where the issues at stake are epistemic, and that we have reason to regard a broad range of political issues as epistemic because doing so is crucial to explaining the value of deliberative contestation about political matters (Fuerstein 2014). Others have suggested that the defining objective of democratic deliberation should be "meta-consensus," which is to say a consensus about the nature of the issue at hand and an agreement on the domain of relevant reasons or considerations (involving both beliefs and values) to be taken into account in the decision process (Niemeyer and Dryzek 2007). Still others have argued that the ideal of consensus (as agreement based on reasons that all could accept) should be abandoned in favor of a form of deliberation guided by a framework of civility that takes account of the complexity of every tradition and of every *actual* person's views in pursuit of tenets that all believe will provide a basis for agreement (Bohman and Richardson 2009). This debate can be counted on to continue, because the concept of consensus is central to the understanding of what it means to claim that governance decisions are legitimate because they represent the consent of the governed (Moore and O'Doherty 2014, Baber and Bartlett 2015, Curato et al. 2017).

1.2 Perils

Dissents from the deliberative democracy orthodoxy are "perils" because outright rejections of this form of democratic practice are few (consisting mainly of agonistic democrats and democracy rejectionists). Critics of deliberative democracy find it difficult to defend aggregative democracy as somehow preferable to the more deliberative forms of governance. With the growing literature on successful deliberative democracy experiences, rejectionist arguments sound increasingly like claims that bees should be aerodynamically incapable of flight. Little is lost by ignoring the rejectionist fringe because few of their substantive arguments have found their way into more measured appraisals of deliberative democracy.

Perhaps the most central peril of deliberative environmental democracy is that public deliberation can turn out to be less inclusive than it hopes and pretends to be. At the simplest and least theoretically interesting level, subgroups within the population whose views are substantively important to the issue under deliberation can be excluded in some way. This is the same problem of group representation that plagues both polling and aggregative voting, but it cuts deliberative democrats more deeply because their aspirations are higher. As an example, many have argued that political discourse generally privileges the beliefs, experiences, and speaking styles of Western, white, well-educated men at the expense of others. Moreover, by associating ideal deliberative procedure with the virtues of autonomy, self-determination, rationality, and a clear boundary between public and private life, deliberative environmental democracy has adopted a masculinist perspective (Lövbrand and Kahn 2014). Empirical research, however, suggests a more complex picture. For instance, using experimental data with many groups to investigate the links between individuals' attitudes and speech, Karparowitz, Mendelber, and Shaker (2012) find a substantial gender gap in voice and authority. But the gap disappears under circumstances of a unanimity rule and the presence of a few women participants, or under majority rule with many women participants. Deliberative designs can, therefore, avoid inequality by fitting institutional procedures to the social context of the situation. The gender inequities of which we are all aware do not present an insurmountable obstacle for deliberative environmental democracy. In fact, deliberative theory provides a procedural solution for precisely that sort of problem, a solution inherent in the realization that the point of inclusiveness in deliberative democracy is discursive rather than demographic. People are empowered, not by being in a particular room in particular numbers but by hearing their own stories told within a larger narrative.

A second form of deliberative peril has to do with the promise of integrating local knowledge into environmental decision-making. There is evidence to suggest that technical experts are prone to a particular pattern of conceptualizing the value of public knowledge. In the context of local air quality management, for example, expert understandings of the potential benefits of technological citizenship and what status they accord to lay knowledge relative to their own roles suggest a continuing expert-deficit model of lay knowledge. Experts suspect that the public misunderstands environmental issues. Although they recognize the need for public "buy-in" to the solutions to problems such as air pollution, this does not translate into a more proactive engagement of lay knowledge in the assessment of such issues. In fact, experts seem to be personally challenged by such notions (Petts and Brooks 2006). This obvious need for a cultural shift in expert understanding of the value of lay knowledge, supported by a move away from an oversimplification of the need for (and value of) public participation, is not a product of deliberative environmental democracy. It is, rather, a reflection of preexisting attitudes that have actually been picked up and problematized by deliberation. As orthodox approaches to environmental decision-making (relying solely on ecological expertise) continue losing legitimacy, greater attention will be given to integrated and participatory approaches (which draw on multiple sources of knowledge in order to accurately describe complex socioecological processes). There is growing recognition that environmental management requires a strategy that can accommodate the multiple and often competing needs of contemporary and future stakeholders. These conceptual advances suggest a number of cognitive criteria that deliberative environmental democracy must meet, including (1) accurately understanding complex socioecological system processes, (2) focusing on "slow" variables, (3) integrating multiple scales of analysis, (4) integrating multiple stakeholder perspectives and values, (5) ensuring that future generations are fairly represented, (6) ensuring that less powerful stakeholders are fairly represented, and (7) integrating local and scientific knowledge (Whitfield, Geist, and Ioris 2011). Deliberative democracy's critics do not argue that merely aggregative, agonistic, or participatory forms of democratic politics stand a better chance than deliberative environmental democracy of achieving this degree of embeddedness in environmental decision-making.

A third criticism of deliberative democracy claims that it does not live up to the normative standards of political equality and fairness – environmental justice – because members of socially disadvantaged groups (even though represented) are often incapable of effectively participating in deliberations. It is often suggested that deliberative democracy reproduces inequalities of gender, race, and class by privileging calm rational discussion over passionate speech and action. But this criticism ignores the considerable extent to which passionate argument is already an integral part of deliberative democracy practice (Hall 2007). For example, empirical data from a study of six citizen conferences fails to support the thesis that deliberative practices invariably replicate social inequalities (Lin 2014). Investigators used six dimensions of discursive interaction to measure deliberative inequality, including frequency and time of speech, dialogic capacity, initiating new topics, making rational arguments, and influencing conclusions. They found that, because of procedural factors instituted to approximate the ideal situation of speech, deliberative inequalities were not significant in the deliberative dimensions of making rational arguments and influencing conclusions. Inequities in the four other dimensions of discursive interaction depended on the nature of issues under discussion. For less complex issues that had greater impacts on citizens' daily lives, most citizens showed that they possessed the "situated knowledge" needed to participate effectively in discursive interactions. Deliberative inequalities were not significant for these kinds of issues (Lin 2014). If additional studies continue to indicate that members of previously disadvantaged groups are able to participate effectively in appropriately structured deliberations, the complaint that deliberative environmental democracy will merely replicate social and economic inequities will lose much of its force. This is a question that requires significantly greater attention, however, because the environmental justice narrative is a critical element of environmental citizenship. It offers a twofold path toward transformation of environmental governance – providing both a *vocabulary* for political opportunity, mobilization, and action, as well as a policy principle that environmental decisions must not disproportionately disadvantage any particular social group (Agyeman and Evans 2006). To the extent that environmental decisions are genuinely democratic, they will prove to be sustainable only if they are also equitable.

A fourth peril facing deliberative environmental democracy is the risk that its effectiveness (and, ultimately, its legitimacy) will be undermined by elites who view deliberation not as a form of public participation but, rather, as a technique of political cooptation. For instance, in a study of the approach of the US Department of Defense (DOD) to public participation in the cleanup activity of contaminated military facilities in Fort Ord, California, Szasz and Meuser (1997) contrasted the concepts of policy design and policy implementation and related them to democratization and cooptation. They studied the implementation of cleanup activity through observation of community Restoration Advisory Board (RAB) meetings and interviews with community representatives. They found that democratization was often cited but the practice of cooptation was clearly applied. Murphree, Wright, and Ebaugh (1996) found, however, that early success at cooptation by elites can be undone. In their study of a waste-siting decision, cooptation eventually failed when local environmental activists (who had not been part of making the original decision) lost confidence in the negotiating process and accused participants of "selling out" to corporate interests and compromising the interests of the community. As a result of protests and citizen awareness campaigns, the opposition forces successfully convinced a regulatory agency to intervene. Although cooptation theory helps to explain the short-lived success of corporate cooptation during the early stages of negotiations, it must also account for the dynamics of failure in the long run. As Dryzek (2000) observed, cooptation of dissent by elites predates the advent of deliberative democracy, and the difference democrats who are among those most concerned about the problem show no confidence that deliberation's aggregative complements or alternatives offer a better option for dealing with the problem. In fact, in the new environment of post-normal risk governance, cooptation is not a rational strategy for anyone in the long run – the resulting loss of policy effectiveness serves the interests of no one (Klinke and Renn 2014).

Finally, a criticism that could be made of deliberative environmental democracy is that it can be, in a peculiar way, too successful. The gist of this argument is that a paradox lies at the heart of deliberative democracy practice. This paradox involves a tension within deliberative democratic theory: the fact that deliberative opinion formation ideally aims to reach consensus, yet a consensus (once established) will be likely to degrade the conditions for further rational public discourse (given the limitations of human reasoning with which we are all familiar). Therefore, over time, deliberative democracy, to the extent it prizes consensus, actually risks undermining both its own theoretical justification and the quality of the decisions that it produces. Proponents of this view suggest that there are at least three cognitive and sociopsychological mechanisms by which consensus might hamper the rationality of public discourse. First, after an agreement, participants cease to develop and evaluate new arguments because none appear to be needed. Second, subscribers to a consensus tend to forget the existing arguments for it – and their limiting conditions. Third, there is a natural fear of deviating from the social norm that promotes conformism over critical reasoning (Friberg-Fernros and Schaffer 2014). To the extent that existing research has neglected to study how consensus in decision-making affects future public deliberation, the seriousness of this peril is unknown and deliberative environmental democracy remains insecure both in theory and in practice.

In order to avoid undermining its own effectiveness, consensus must be equivocal to a considerable degree. "Equivocal" is evoked deliberately here, drawing on more than one of its meanings, including being indeterminate, ambiguous, or of uncertain nature, and having a multiplicity of equally appropriate voices or significations (note that the meaning of "equivocal" is itself equivocal). This uncertainty across different meanings is normatively invaluable. To take advantage of an almost unfathomable human diversity to arrive democratically at what can only ever be tentative and contingent governance choices, amid what is and will remain a changing, ultimately unknowable, and indeterminate environment, will always require a healthy degree of equivocality. Democratic decisions must remain open-ended from a procedural point of view and open-textured substantively – allowing for the possibility that their norms can be revisited, their policy designs revised, and their requirements reinterpreted at the stage of implementation. Equivocality, then, is a crucial norm for democratic earth system governance.[2]

1.3 Progress

The available evidence supports the view that the environmental promise of deliberative democracy far outweighs its attendant perils. But further progress needs to be made in our understanding of this marriage of democratic theory and real-world problem solving. After all, democracy, including deliberative democracy, can be fully adequate from a political perspective and nevertheless produce ecologically irrational results (Goodin 1992). The most ecologically sophisticated policies imaginable will prove unsustainable if they fail the test of democratic legitimacy. So deliberative democracy is a necessary, although not sufficient, element of environmental sustainability. The previous discussion suggests clearly why this is so.

Questions regarding inclusion and representation abound in deliberative democracy. The discursive character of deliberative practice suggests that what it is important to include is the narratives of all, rather than the votes of all. The point of inclusiveness is, ultimately, individual *empowerment*. Because there is no discursive-theoretic reason to weight narratives according to how many peoples' lived experiences they describe, few things could be more empowering for the individual than to say that deliberation is fully democratic to the extent that everything worth saying is said. In pursuit of that goal, it will often make sense to violate – contingently and in the context of a larger system of deliberation – many of deliberative democracy's operating rules of thumb. For instance, a diverse range of participants is thought to be vital to produce deliberative results of value. But where politically disadvantaged populations are concerned, the effective development of their narratives may require (at least preliminarily) enclave deliberation that allows participants to develop, assess, and refine their own narratives in a relatively homogenous environment before exposing them to the rigors of the market place of ideas (Karparowitz, Raphael, and Hammond 2009).

Likewise, with regard to the importance of integrating local knowledge into environmental decision-making, the last word has not been said – nor is it ever likely to be. To be deliberatively effective, knowledge (lay or expert) must be not merely local, but fully *embedded*. Recent field research suggests that the development of democratic deliberation depends more on whether participants situate and link their knowledge than whether the knowledge is local or expert in origin. This suggests that, for scholars who wish to better understand which ways of knowing enable environmental deliberation in participatory processes, a useful concept is grounded knowledge – embedded knowledge actively linked by participants with other sources of knowledge (Ashwood et al. 2014) in ways that can help optimize the complementarity between the realms of governmental and nongovernmental environmental action (Chan and Amling 2019). This kind of embeddedness is imperfectly understood – in part because what it requires is, and is likely to always be, context specific to a considerable degree.

As with empowerment and embeddedness, the demands that *equity* places on deliberative environmental democracy also need to be explored more thoroughly. The pursuit of environmental justice introduces both problematic participants and problematic relationships to deliberative environmental democracy (Baber and Bartlett 2005). As already discussed, the use by environmental justice advocates of their own unique storylines can be an important mechanism for shaping policy meanings and for improving deliberative quality. Although these effects are tempered by discursive and material forms of power and the competition among alternative storylines (Dodge 2014), power relationships of this sort often prove to be promisingly unstable (Sovacool and Brisbois 2019). A new challenge in this regard will be to discover deliberative mechanisms for extending deliberative environmental democracy techniques to the analysis of international equity problems for which they were not originally intended (Baber and Bartlett 2009a, 2015), such as the stubborn gridlock surrounding climate politics (West 2012). Another such frontier is the development of deliberative environmental democracy principles and practices that will allow both scholars and citizens to explore problems of intergenerational justice in ways that are both more practical and defensible (Cotton 2013).

The peril posed to deliberative environmental democracy by the risk of elite cooptation suggests that additional thought needs to be given to what it means to call environmental policy effective. If environmental decision-making meets the criteria we have identified (if it is empowering, embedded, and equitable), then it would seem that its effectiveness could only be degraded if it were coopted by self-serving elites. This will strike many environmentalists as deplorably anthropocentric, and in many ways, it is. But that very accusation is growing increasingly untenable. The concept of the "Anthropocene" (Brondizio et al. 2016) suggests that no part of the natural world today is untouched by humans and, therefore, no solution to environmental problems can avoid placing humans near its center. Even this may understate the case. Humanity today is so omnipresent that the very nature of nature has been altered (Wapner 2014; Arias-Maldonado 2019). The distinction between the human and nonhuman components of nature that environmentalists have used to justify both conservationist and preservationist policies is no longer tenable. Today, there is only a distinction between the human and the much-more-than-human environments. So, in the Anthropocene, environmental protection "involves attuning ourselves to the hybrid character of ecosystems and helping to shape them in ways in which the human voice is *deliberately* one among others fashioning soci-ecological arrangements" (Wapner 2014, 46, emphasis added; Dryzek 1995, 2017a). When one considers the advantages to be gained by enhancing the visibility of the individuals and communities affected by this expanded notion of the human/environment interface (Ward et al. 2019), it becomes clear that deliberative democracy's historical commitment to consensus may have been too narrow rather than over-broad.

It is entirely plausible, at least theoretically, that consensus-oriented political practices will eventually fall victim to the same sort of political decay that plagues their aggregative relatives (Fukuyama 2014). Although the symptoms of political decay in these two cases might appear quite similar, the underlying causes would be very different. Huntington's (1965) original conception of political decay was based on the insight that political and socioeconomic modernization leads to the mobilization of new social groups over time whose new demands cannot be accommodated by existing political institutions. In the case of deliberative environmental democracy, however, other factors would be at work. The danger would be that effective environmental policies would eventually have their effectiveness undermined precisely because they were *empowering*, *embedded*, and *equitable*. About this danger, at least two observations are possible. First, Huntington's analysis suggests that our concerns about political decay should not lead us to abandon deliberative environmental democracy because none of its competitors are capable of producing institutional arrangements that are more lasting. Second, to the extent that deliberative environmental democracy does produce decisions that are genuinely consensual, the problem of political decay has been significantly simplified. If the source of political decay is not to be found in our political stars, but in ourselves, then the remedy for decay is within us as well. What may be required is a more *equivocal* understanding of consensus itself (Baber and Bartlett 2015, 2020; Dryzek and Pickering 2017).

1.4 Back to the Future (Already in Progress)

Deliberative democratic practices are well-suited to many of the challenges earth system governance will face in the future under the conditions associated with the concept of the Anthropocene, and, in particular, that part of the future that is global (Dryzek and Pickering 2019). This capacity is especially important given what we know about the core characteristics of democracy in the Anthropocene (Mert 2019). The inescapable *equivocality* of democratic environmental governance means that discussions are never closed; they are merely transformed as old problems and concerns give way to new. This means, of course, that the *experimental* quality that effective environmental governance possesses is not a transient quality but, rather, a permanent feature of the landscape of democratic decision-making. For these processes to take place without distortion and without posing systemic disadvantage on minority parties, equal access to decision-making and *equitable* allocation of fundamental capabilities are essential prerequisites. These are prerequisites that can only be ensured by institutional arrangements that provide for the *empowerment* of those who are ill-favored by the political and economic status-quo and the *embeddedness* of environmental decision-making in the local communities of fate, where people actually determine their shared life experiences. How are these five democratic normative criteria related to the basic questions (or problems) that environmental governance poses? For a catalog of those questions, we turn to the Earth System Governance Project.

1.5 Institutionalizing Deliberative Environmental Democracy

In its first Science Plan (Biermann et al. 2009), the Earth System Governance Project identified five fundamental research problems related to effective environmental governance: *agency* (particularly agency beyond that of state actors); the *architecture* of governance (from local to global levels); *accountability* (and the various institutions that promote it); *access and allocation* (of resources and of environmental amenities and harms); and *adaptiveness* (governance systems generally).[3] In an age that some scientists have called an entirely new historical epoch (the Anthropocene), this effort to describe the governance of an "earth system" offered a new paradigm for thinking about how humanity can take conscious and intentional (one might say, deliberative) responsibility for its very survival (Biermann 2014, 2016). A preliminary sketch of some of the key connections will introduce the in-depth discussions in the following chapters of the relationship between these analytical problems and the five normative democratic criteria of *empowered*, *embedded*, *experimental*, *equivocal*, and *equitable*.

1.5.1 Empowered

It is not uncommon for critics of various theories of justice to fault them as being apologies for the status quo – insofar as they construct justice from reform of existing practice and foreclose the possibility that there may be problems of injustice embedded in the very structure of capitalist social relations, private property, or the market economy (Wolff 1977; Baskin 2019). One could, for example, argue that theories suggesting that accountability mechanisms can be made fairer, more open, and more democratic if legislative oversight is supplemented (or, in some instances, even replaced) by public participation in administrative rule-making merely paper over the gross injustices of the very mechanisms they seek to reform. Likewise, experimental approaches to the governance problem of adaptiveness can be faulted for being insufficiently revolutionary because they are always based on the assumption that existing governance solutions need only incremental improvement rather than wholesale replacement. Moreover, to advocate solutions to the problems of governance architecture that are embedded in their sociocultural milieus is to implicitly accept those institutions and traditions as givens. Of course, pairing an analysis of governance solutions to problems of allocation with an explicit linkage to the issue of access opens the analysis to the criticism of presuming that the access being discussed will lead inevitably to cooptation.

At this end of this critical litany, however, one arrives at something of a paradox. While it is not impossible for theories of justice ever to become apologies for the status quo, that is certainly a difficult criticism to maintain against the environmental justice movement. Environmental justice is a far broader (and potentially subversive) narrative than environmentalism generally. How can it be, then, that appending the potentially coopting concept of justice to an otherwise mainstream political discourse gives it the revolutionary potential that the environmental justice movement exhibits? The answer, elaborated in Chapter 3, is the normative standard of *empowerment* in its relationship to solutions to the democratic governance problem of *agency*.

At an earlier period in human history, the issue of *agency* in earth system governance could be far more easily addressed. There was a time when the earth's potential agents of governance were thought to consist entirely of that exclusive club commonly referred to as nation-states. Today, however, agents in earth system governance range from "governments to science networks, environmentalists, industry associations, faith-based organizations, farmer unions, and intergovernmental organizations, to name a few" (Biermann 2014, 47). Once the concept of the Anthropocene was invoked to describe a reality in which humanity's impact on the environment had become so pervasive that it no longer made sense to distinguish between the human and the natural, the quaint notion that institutions of national government can, by themselves, control that intimate and integral relationship became obviously untenable. The broader subject of environmental governance, therefore, has come into focus as a set of practices in which governments rely on a vast and growing network of actors stretching far beyond their own institutional boundaries – often producing effects that can usefully be thought of as *de facto* environmental governance (Gupta and Möller 2019). Environmental governance, from local to global levels, increasingly relies on private governance arrangements. Private actors, specifically corporations and civil society organizations, increasingly design, implement, and monitor rules and standards that guide and prescribe behavior in a range of policy areas, including sustainability, banking, and international security, to name just a few. As result, the political and moral responsibility for environmental governance has become as universal as human rights – or, as universal as advocates of rights urge that they should be. The revolutionary potential of this insight is incalculable.

If, indeed, there is no corner of the natural world that is beyond human influence, then no corner of the world lies beyond the human responsibility implied by our political and moral agency. If human agency requires that an ample minimum of capabilities across a wide range of human engagements with the world is (for reasons of political right, simple justice, or normative obligation) a fundamental entitlement, then the answer to the paradox of justice as a revolutionary modifier to the environmentalist narrative becomes clear. If no element of nature (anywhere) lies outside the responsibility of some humans, and if humans become *empowered* (with adequate knowledge, autonomy, and capability) by the ascendance of a regime of environmental justice, radical critique will have become as mainstream an element of environmental governance as impact assessment.

1.5.2 Embedded

The architecture of environmental governance must be firmly embedded in its social and cultural milieu if it is to be effective in both political and ecological terms (Chapter 4). Embeddedness is far from irrelevant to the other basic problems of environmental governance. The necessity for accountability process and institutions to be embedded in their particular sociocultural contexts was clearly in the minds of the American founders when they secured to the various states the right to organize their participation in national elections (within fairly permissive bounds). Likewise, experimental approaches to ensuring the adaptiveness of governance institutions are assumed to be more common and more effective in states and provinces of federal systems of governance – lauded (if, perhaps, dubiously) in the American experience as "laboratories of democracy" (Tarr 2001). At a bare minimum, however, the embeddedness of governance architecture opens opportunities otherwise unavailable for empowerment through agency (Ward et al. 2019). It does this, if in no other way than by raising the level of information available to potential environmental actors and bringing the activities of environmental governance more within their immediate reach. This has the potential to allow for the problematization of inequitable allocations of environmental benefits and burdens. But the primary focus of embeddedness as a normative standard of evaluation is likely to remain, for practical reasons at least, upon governance architecture. The problem of climate governance architecture is a concrete example that shows why this is so.

A growing body of academic literature is devoted to the evaluation of rival governance architectures and policy mechanisms designed to mitigate the risks associated with global climate change. The United Nations Framework Convention on Climate Change (UNFCCC) of 1992, the Kyoto Protocol to the UNFCCC of 1997, the Copenhagen Accord of 2009, the Paris Agreement of 2015, and several other less-binding declarations have all been subjected to intense analysis in this literature. Typically, these analyses of climate governance have focused on the environmental effectiveness, economic efficiency, and global distributive consequences of alternative climate architectures and policy mechanisms. A question often overlooked in this literature has been the performance of these climate architectures (and the policies they systematize) in terms of normative ideals whose meaning and significance cannot be fully captured in terms of a goal limited to the economic-least-cost improvement of environmental quality with minimal worsening of existing global inequalities. Two such ideals are those of political legitimacy and procedural justice. One particularly important component of the emerging climate architecture, greenhouse gas emissions trading, raises significant questions of political legitimacy and procedural justice. The well-understood cost efficiency and environmental quality benefits of emissions trading schemes come at the price of imposing low levels of participation, accountability, and transparency on climate decision-making (damaging legitimacy) and producing results that, by ignoring the social complexity of carbon emissions, replicate the inequities of existing national and local economic structures (Page 2012).

This critique reminds us of something that is vitally important to our understanding of the architecture of climate governance. Often overlooked, the institutional continuum of climate governance has two ends. The focus on treaties and international agreements is the global end. But climate change governance necessarily involves a wide range of both global and local issues related to questions of environmental security. Climate change governance poses seemingly insurmountable challenges for political, economic, social, and administrative systems at all levels of governance. Before simply condemning these existing systems for their inflexibility, we should remind ourselves that they evolved to handle other sorts of problems. Climate change thus poses profound challenges to organizations of every type, requiring a wide variety of organizational responses. The drastic depth of cuts in emissions of greenhouse gasses proposed by many governments and nongovernmental organizations (NGOs) is likely to require radical shifts in sociopolitical structures, technological and economic systems, organizational forms, and modes of organizing. As a result, climate change is more than just an environmental problem requiring technical and managerial solutions. It constitutes a political space in which a variety of organizations – local and national state agencies, private firms of all size, industry associations, NGOs, and multilateral organizations – engage in contestation as well as collaboration over evolving regimes of climate governance. There is, therefore, an urgent need to better comprehend the transformative impact of climate change on the human landscape and its policy architecture at the level where people (as both polluters and protectors of the environment) live their lives (Sarkar 2011; Chan, Ellinger, and Widerberg 2018). To achieve this, we must overcome our habit of thinking only globally. We must embed in the places that people value and where they live every day both ourselves as policy architects and the architectures we design (Meyer 2015; Schlosberg and Craven 2019).

1.5.3 Experimental

The criteria of experimentality is closely related to that of equivocality. If we believe that all voices should be heard and that all decisions should be regarded as tentative, then it is clearly reasonable to adopt an experimental attitude in efforts to institutionalize deliberative environmental democracy. This attitude is potentially useful in addressing the several earth system problems of governance. For example, if the evidence-driven character of experimental approaches to governance ever were to become the norm, efforts to hold government officials accountable might well be enhanced by the resulting availability of information regarding agency performance. Moreover, finding ever more equitable allocations of environmental resources and risks, as well as more effective architectures of environmental governance, would certainly be made easier if a large number of possible distributions could be assessed in a series of interstate or cross-national comparative trials. The advent of citizen science in support of environmental advocacy is just one data point suggesting the potential advantages of an experimental approach to environmental governance in terms of expanding opportunities for agency. But the densest web of relationships between the norm of experimentality and the challenges of institutionalization involve the problem of adaptiveness.

Unlike the relationship of apparent opposition between equivocality and accountability, the connection between experimentality and adaptiveness is more likely to provide too much of a good thing. The challenge of achieving some level of adaptiveness in global governance, particularly in environmental governance, is daunting indeed. Much of the analysis of this challenge has focused on the level of global governance where entire international regime systems reside. For example, a listing of the regimes that would have to be included in any assessment of the global challenge of climate change would inevitably include global governance of water systems, food security, health programs, and efforts to alleviate poverty.

Climate impacts on economic governance and even international security would also have to be considered (Biermann 2014). These challenges, along with many others, consume the days and complicate the lives of countless diplomats and elected officials around the world and threaten to overwhelm their already stretched cognitive capacity to achieve effective climate governance (Milkoreit 2017). But is it from this quarter that adaptiveness in global environmental governance can really be expected? Will the world's roughly two hundred national governments be able to overcome the analytical complexity that such problems entail and forge master plans that are of sufficient scope and robustness to deal adequately with the myriad implications of environmental degradation – in other words, are these problems that nations can "learn their way out of" (Gerlak et al. 2018)? Alternatively, will they allow the creation of a global government capable of doing so? Or is the solution to what ails the earth even a matter of global learning in the first place (Gerlak et al. 2019)?

To pose these questions is to fairly invite confusion (if not derision). If, however, the challenge of adaptive governance bids fair to overwhelm global institutions, perhaps the solution is closer at hand – to be found in the practice of co-production of governance knowledge (van der Hel 2016). As an example, collaborative and decentralized systems for promoting the long-term sustainability of common property resources (CPRs), in which "the appropriators themselves make all major decisions about the use of the CPR" (Ostrom 1990, 64) are not unusual, nor are they poorly understood as a theoretical matter (Baber and Bartlett 2005; Baber 2010). In fact, it is widely recognized that they offer distinct advantages over more centralized approaches that emphasize the development of uniform rules.

First, those who appropriate local CPRs over a long period of time have usually developed a relatively accurate understanding of how their particular biosphere operates because the success of their endeavors relies on it. They are also likely to have knowledge of the other locals and the norms of behavior that they would consider appropriate. Using these disaggregated, often tacit, forms of knowledge, they are more likely to craft rules that are better adapted to local CPR management than any general system of rules. Second, locals are able to devise rules that will increase the probability of trustworthy and reciprocal behavior, thus reducing the need for enforcement efforts. Because local appropriators of a CPR have to bear the costs of monitoring compliance, they are more likely to craft rules that make infractions obvious and easy to avoid. Third, and finally, a system of local and collaborative CPR rules is more likely to be regarded as legitimate (producing greater rule conformance) and less likely to prove ineffective over a wide geographic region because of the use of parallel and autonomous systems of rule-making, interpretation, and enforcement.

In other words, a structure of local and collaborative policies in pursuit of a well-understood and widely accepted general objective is likely to work better than solutions – no matter how technically sophisticated – brought to a problem from afar (Ostrom 2005, especially 279–282). So where indigenous systems for environmental management exist and work well in their particular context, the job of national and international environmental actors is simple: Resist the temptation to uncritically rely on the "authority" of rhetorical strategies employed by internationally based scientific institutions (van der Hel and Biermann 2017), learn from experiments conducted by local experts, and don't fix what's not broken (Patterson and Huitema 2019). The effective implementation of environmental governance norms, even those found in international agreements, will likely rely on substantial reinterpretation at the local level (Elmer, Lutz, and Schuren 2016). A more thorough exploration of these systems, and related topics, is forthcoming in Chapter 5.

1.5.4 Equivocal

If equivocality is, on balance, a positive influence on deliberative environmental democracy, what are its implications for the basic questions of governance that the Earth System Governance Project identified? If the central challenge of agency in the Anthropocene is to create a space for and legitimize the participation of nonstate actors (agents) in environmental governance, a normative attitude of equivocality would seem to be quite reasonable. The essentially open-textured quality of political discourse that an equivocal (equi-vocal) attitude suggests does not simply allow for many voices to be heard – it mandates it. Likewise, the architecture of governance stands to benefit from the pragmatism inherent in a norm that eschews absolutes and formulaic solutions in favor of bespoke designs, tailormade for environmental problems that vary in character by location and time (Reed and Abernethy 2018). Concerns over the allocation of environmental resources, risks, and rewards might also be ameliorated to a significant degree if allocations were approached with an equivocal attitude. Issues of distributive justice are more easily attended to when distributions are thought of as tentative from the outset and the considerations supporting them are recognized as contingent (Coolsaet 2015b). The need to have governance systems that can adapt to changing external circumstances and shifting political demands cannot help but be enhanced where those systems have been developed with an awareness that alternate arrangements are within the realm of possibility and might eventually prove to be preferable. But this will require analytical models to cover more adequately a wider range of real-world adaptive responses to environmental change than they currently do (Holman et al. 2019).

If there is a fundamental problem of governance that could be thought to put equivocality in conflict with effectiveness, the need for accountability would seem to be that problem. After all, a key failing of modern liberalism (Lowi 1969) is the loss of accountability resulting from liberalism's willingness to abandon strict legislative oversight in the process of trying to serve all vocal interests equally. After all, the primary mechanism for holding administrative agencies accountable in democratic states has been the practice of legislative oversight. But the circumstances of the Anthropocene present this model with a serious paradox. Humankind's ability to disturb ecosystems in fundamental ways creates the need for effective governance responses, which must unavoidably rely on strong administrative capacities. At the same time, the forces of globalization that combine to create this ecological challenge (the internationalization of capital and weakening of the Westphalian nation-state) also conspire to make legislative oversight of administrative action difficult, if not impossible, by multiplying accountability challenges across multiple governance levels and processes (Scobie 2018).

In Chapter 6, we confront this problem by analyzing some of the emerging administrative practices of the European Union, practices that constitute a model of democratic accountability not relying on legislative oversight. Using existing administrative competencies, a deliberative model of transnational democratic accountability can build on the functions that intergovernmental organizations already perform tolerably well without relying on new legislative inputs or continuous monitoring by elected officials. Two features of democratic deliberation – its tendency to reduce moral disputes and to promote consensus – can reduce the costs of organization maintenance in stakeholder communities that offer nonlegislative alternatives for administrative oversight. By narrowing the grounds of disagreement among participants and reducing the range of possible policy outcomes with which any final decision procedure must deal, these two tendencies amount to a tacit agreement that deliberative results must be equivocal to a certain degree because participants in deliberation must always be willing to say less than they actually mean.

1.5.5 Equitable

Finally, among the general standards of normative evaluation one can apply to problems of governance, equity may well be the most broadly deployable. Almost anything involved in governing, no matter how technical in nature it may seem, can be done either more or less equitably (Biermann and Möller 2019). For example, as mechanisms of accountability, elections can be equitable insofar as their rules respect the maxim of one-person-one-vote or inequitable insofar as they do not. The need for adaptiveness in governance can be answered with experimental policy reforms (e.g., replacing entitlement programs with block grants) that pit clientele group against one another in an endless "hunger game" that weakens the already weak. Changes in rule-making processes intended to answer questions regarding agency can either reinforce the positions of the privileged and powerful or make more room at the table for historically un- or under-represented persons. Pieces of governance architecture – environmental impact assessment, for example – can be designed to either narrow or broaden the scope of decision-making, with entirely predictable consequences for equitable concerns. But the most obvious cluster of governance problems with implications for the normative standard of equity is that related to questions of allocation (and allocation's most basic feature, access). Indeed, the equity-related features of other governance problems we have mentioned can most usefully be thought of as intrusions of allocation into those other problem domains.

Problems of allocation (of environmental resources and risks) and access (to environmental decision-making) pose a serious challenge for environmental governance. Moreover, problems of this sort have a dual character. They are sources of human insecurity as well as aspects of the question of justice – corresponding as they do to the procedural and distributive dimensions of that concept. Critically analyzing patterns of access and allocation and how they relate to each other will illuminate and, ultimately, institutionalize the duality implicit in the idea of environmental justice. But conventional legislative, judicial, and executive tools of the liberal democratic state have so far proved inadequate to the task of identifying, much less achieving, environmental justice – and they remain almost wholly inapplicable to the many issues of justice and security that extend beyond the state. Indeed, even the basic research of the natural sciences, which many have hoped will ultimately banish equitable concerns from environmental governance, has transformative potential that is deeply political (van der Hel 2018). As often as not, it magnifies normative challenges to governance rather than reducing them.

Central as it is to present concerns, however, environmental justice and environmentalism (or environmental protection) are far from coterminous. In fact, the environmental justice discourse is actually "a set of overlapping discourses, not to be confused with the environmental justice movement, nor the ill-bounded collection of networks and organizations that comprise it" (Baber and Bartlett 2015, 71). It faces daunting burdens when confronting the challenges of environmental governance at the global level (Orsini 2016). In comparison with other discourses of environmental governance, environmental justice "integrates both social and ecological concerns more readily," while paying particular attention to "questions of distributive justice, community empowerment, and democratic accountability." Moreover, environmental justice is a set of discourses that asserts that "human societies and the natural environment are intricately linked and that the health of one depends on the health of the other" (Taylor 1999, 57). Beyond these practical and philosophical differences between mainstream environmentalism and environmental justice discourses, however, there are significant political differences that mark out environmental justice as a realm of both peril and promise.

Much environmental justice activism is sustained (and sometimes even led) by economically disadvantaged women of color. These individuals are often motivated (at least in part) by underlying religious perspectives and convictions. This recurring pattern suggests that environmental justice discourses have the potential to bring together "the richly diverse discourses of ecofeminism, environmental racism, socialist-inspired critical ecology, and the more 'spiritual' strains of deep ecology" (Baber and Bartlett 2009a, 148), offering a new and more comprehensive challenge to liberal environmentalism and its tendencies toward elitism and cooptation. This quality of environmental justice suggests that it may be a discourse that, in comparison with other approaches to environmentalism, would be more compatible with the capabilities approach to the problem of equity (mentioned in an earlier subsection), in that it more easily attends to a wide variety of substantive freedoms and the conditions necessary to secure them. But, if it succeeds in capturing a richer and more detailed picture of the environmental problematique, does environmental justice have the capacity to deal effectively with the problems that it will have rendered even more complex than before? This question is addressed in greater detail in Chapter 7.

2

Toward Consensual Earth System Governance

> The problem is that no ethical system has ever achieved consensus.
> Ethical systems are completely unlike mathematics or science. This is a
> source of concern.
>
> *Daniel Dennett*

The phrase "global governance" developed a remarkable popularity in the twenty-first century. Whereas an internet search in 2004 produced fewer than 3,500 references to global governance (Biermann and Pattberg 2012), by December 2014 the count had approached 36.5 million references. If quantity is any indicator, global governance is an idea whose time has come. What is far less universal is the idea that global governance (in contrast to mathematics or science) can reasonably aspire to achieve a meeting of the minds – in short, a governing consensus. The reluctance to talk in terms of a global governing consensus most usually derives from two assumptions, that governance requires government institutions and that polarization of the "unfathomable human diversity" we see around us is an insurmountable obstacle to a single, global government (Orwin 2014). These assumptions imply that global governance can never have a consensual character.

Against this background of a culturally diverse and politically divided global society, humankind's search for the self-governance required to protect the environmental preconditions of its own existence might seem especially problematic. Here might be a problem that is among those least likely to prove an exception to the received wisdom about polarization and global consensus. Indeed, the complexity of the environmental problematique (when added to the complexity of human culture) may make governing interaction with the earth's natural systems the most daunting challenge humans will ever face. For these reasons, determining whether it is possible to develop an approach to earth system governance that is both consensual and effective will turn on the central questions, methods, and processes of global research on governance, rather than on breakthroughs in the natural sciences. At a minimum, earth system governance must confront five core analytical problems identified in the first Science Plan of the Earth System Governance Project (Biermann et al. 2009):

One, the *architecture* of earth system governance includes questions relating to the emergence, design, and effectiveness of governance systems as well as the overall integration of global, regional, national, and local governance.

Two, understanding effective earth system governance requires an understanding of the *agents* that drive earth system governance and the role that each must play. The particular research gap here is the influence and responsibilities of actors apart from national governments (such as businesses, social action networks, and nonprofit organizations), the ways in which authority is granted to these agents, and how they exercise that authority.

Three, earth system governance must respond to the inherent uncertainties in human and natural systems. It must combine the stability necessary to ensure long-term governance solutions with the flexibility needed to react quickly to new findings and developments. In other words, humans must better understand and further develop the *adaptiveness* of earth systems and their governance.

Four, the greater regulatory competence and authority that is conferred on larger institutions and systems of governance – especially at the global level – the more we will be confronted with questions of how to ensure the *accountability* and legitimacy of that governance.

Five, earth system governance is (like any political activity) crucially about the distribution of material and nonmaterial values. It is, in essence, a conflict about the *access* to goods and about their *allocation*. It is about justice, fairness, and equity (Earth System Governance Project 2009).

These challenges of governance`e are not, of course, challenges of a scientific or technical nature. The advent of the Anthropocene – grounded though it may be in the scientific progress that has invested humanity with the responsibility for its own environment (Castree 2019) – seems not to have given us an equivalent ability to resolve the differences that we discover among ourselves. Although environmental governance must be broadly democratic if it is to be effective (Baber and Bartlett 2005), the course of our development seems to have provided us no clear path leading to principles that will command the assent of humanity in the way those of mathematics or science do.

A source of concern, indeed.

2.1 Conceptualizing the Problem

> A consensus means that everyone agrees to say collectively what no one believes individually.
>
> *Abba Eban*

The search for deliberatively democratic consensus has generally focused either on choices between competing policy models (like direct regulation of carbon emissions versus market-based regulatory strategies such as tradable permits) or on the development of local or regional implementation agreements within the context of an existing regulatory regime. But a process of "juristic deliberation" could be used to identify widely supported normative principles through the adjudication by citizen juries of hypothetical cases involving disputes over environmental issues (Baber and Bartlett 2009a, 2015). It is relatively easy to construct such concrete but hypothetical disputes. In the area of water resources, for example, one can easily describe contending parties to a dispute that pits the doctrines of *prior appropriation* (according to which rights to water are established by a "first in time, first in right" rule) against claims of *equitable utilization* and state necessity (based on a "public trust" doctrine under which resources like water are held in trust for general use). This process of generating hypothetical scenarios could be carried out across a wide range of factual circumstances without directly engaging the perceived interests of the participants in a group deliberation. Juristic deliberation using hypothetical dispute scenarios to identify basic normative principles is represented by the entries in the first row of Table 2.1.

Deliberative democratic techniques are more commonly used at stage of the policy process where a choice is made among competing policy models. Within the field of deliberative democratic practice there is a planning technique that is generally well-suited to the task of selecting from among competing policy paradigms, in the United States usually referred to as deliberative polling (Fishkin 1995) and in Europe as the policy or citizen jury (Huitema, van De Kerkhof, and Pesch 2007). This technique involves convening deliberative assemblies of from one to several hundred individuals who are presented with real-world information

Table 2.1 *A deliberative policy matrix*

Policy problem	Deliberative technique	Deliberative material	Deliberative product	Regulative standard
Conflicting basic principles	Juristic deliberation	Hypothetical legal cases	Normative principles/ legal rules	Normative consensus
Contending policy proposals	Deliberative polling	Alternative policy paradigms	Policy goals and objectives	Political consensus
Competing courses of action	Stakeholder partnerships	Contending local discourses	Plans for policy implementation	Social consensus

Adapted from (Baber and Bartlett 2015, 14)

regarding an existing public policy issue and the leading alternative approaches. These assemblies are then divided into juries of twelve to fifteen persons. Each jury deliberates the choices with which it has been presented. In some cases, the jury is asked to come to the most inclusive consensus that it can. In other cases, no final conclusion is asked of the jury. Rather, the participants are surveyed after their deliberations to determine their "considered opinions" and the degree to which those differ from their initial preferences. As an example, biodiversity policy in the United States has long been dominated by the Endangered Species Act (ESA), which imposes strict (some would say draconian) restrictions on the "taking" of living beings once their species has been determined to be endangered. Another paradigm is the biodiversity policy of Italy, which emphasizes a comprehensive planning approach in which both the direct and the indirect effects of government decisions across a wide range of policy areas are to be evaluated for their impacts on plants and animals (Baber 2011). It would be simple enough to summarize these contending policy paradigms, present participants with arguments pro and con, and elicit their post-deliberative opinions. The practice of deliberative polling at the stage of the choice between contending policy paradigms in order to identify basic policy objectives is represented in the second row of Table 2.1.

Finally, deliberative democracy is already a familiar feature of environmental and natural resources management at the level of action plans and policy implementation in the form of stakeholder partnerships (Sabatier et al. 2005). Regional and local stakeholder groups of this sort have already engaged the interests of deliberative democratic theorists (Baber and Bartlett 2005). These structures of governance can best be understood as arrangements for organizing and reconciling competing local discourses about the implications of general legal requirements when applied to local questions. The objective is to develop implementation plans at the subnational level that will achieve national (or international) objectives through the coproduction of regulatory management. One example of this approach has been described as "collaborative learning" (Cheng and Fiero 2005). Collaborative learning is a recent innovation in public participation that differs from the traditional focus on issues and interests. It is designed specifically to address the complexity and rancorous conflict that often characterizes the management of public lands. Collaborative learning is characterized by a systems approach to understanding natural resource issues, the promotion (instead of avoidance) of dialogue about differences among stakeholders, and a focus on feasible improvements in concrete circumstances rather than idea outcomes over the longer term. Collaborative learning employs landscape-based working groups whose membership contains individuals who represent key stakeholder groups. The most common example of such groups is the watershed partnership (Clark 1997). These groups of volunteers possess no formal authority and are open to anyone wishing to participate. In practice, they generally attract large landowners and corporations whose behavior will affect watershed outcomes, environmentalists who can take up or forgo their right to sue under a variety of statutory schemes, and government officials who want to chart a safe course in between. This process of using stakeholder partnerships to sort through contending discourse among local contributors to policy implementation is represented in the third row of Table 2.1.

The first four columns of Table 2.1 summarize the three levels at which policy problems occur, the deliberative democratic techniques appropriate to those problems, the deliberative material (or substantive content) used in those practices, and the deliberative output to be expected. The fifth column suggests the existence of regulative standards for each of these levels of democratic deliberation. It is here, at the point where the results of deliberative democratic practice are judged, that the challenge of achieving consensus is most directly posed. What does, indeed what can, consensus mean at each of these levels of policy practice?

Thinking about the challenge of consensus at the level of normative principle is, perhaps, the most daunting challenge faced by deliberative democratic theorists. Advocates of the view that consensus at any stage of the policy process is nearly impossible might be at their most persuasive when debate turns to the issue of fundamental governing norms. It is difficult to argue with the proposition that conceptual creatures like "the American Consensus" are short-lived at best and chimerical at worst (Higham 1959). The discourses of consensus at this level often seem to involve either the language of symbolic politics, which allows us to express our mutual fear and loathing without doing any real harm, or the language of jingoistic patriotism, which allows us to express our longing for solidarity without doing any real good. Simultaneously, we also conspire to build a consensus on comforting fairy tales such as "the market" or "the middle class" that allow us to ignore reality – even to our own peril. All this pessimism about consensus may be well-founded without being dispositive of (or even relevant to) the question of whether a useful normative consensus in the practice of global governance is actually possible.

In coming to grips with the question of how plausible it is to expect governance processes to produce consensus, it may be helpful to begin with a brief discussion of the work consensus needs to do. The point of departure for this discussion is the fifth column in Table 2.1. Beginning with the most general level of policy discourse, to say that deliberative democratic practice at the level of normative discourse should be held to a standard of normative consensus is entirely unhelpful if that standard is not fleshed out. As already suggested, the languages of symbolic politics, national patriotism, and self-delusion are probably destined to either exacerbate dissensus or paper it over. But empirical research has revealed that when normative challenges are posed to citizens in the form of concrete (but hypothetical) disputes, they are quite capable of arriving at consensual conclusions that suggest an agreement on fundamental normative principles (Baber and Bartlett 2015). Formulation of the "normative principle" at work in experimental deliberations is far from the final word that would need to be spoken on the subject. But in the United States, for example, it would be more than sufficient to satisfy the requirement that a legislature articulate an "intelligible standard" when it delegates its authority to formulate binding rules to public bureaucracies (Tribe 1988, especially section 5-17). The intelligible standard requirement is not especially demanding. It performs the essential work of providing bureaucrats with justification for their actions and judges with practical guidance that legitimates their eventual review of those actions. When this functional description of an intelligible normative standard is married to a specific deliberative democratic technique, a more genuinely democratic process of administrative rule-making, in polities that is at least nominally democratic to begin with, becomes possible. Moreover, the application of this pairing to global governance offers one option for addressing the legislative deficiencies of global politics (Slaughter 2004) with a democratically legitimated substitute grounded in administrative action.

A standard of consensus also needs to be understood at the level of choice between competing policy paradigms (ignoring those circumstances – which, though uncommon, do arise – wherein the available policy paradigms in a given issue arena do not present a forced choice). When moral exhortation, education, incentives, and enforceable regulation can reasonably be combined, the answer "all of the above" would appear to be a readily available option for building a political consensus policy model. These are rarely going to be the shoals on which democratic governance founders. A more common pattern is that the choice of one basic policy model (for example, tradable pollution permits) rules out its competitor (direct command-and-control regulation). Let us assume that this choice is faced by a polity that enjoys the kind of fundamentally free and fair political process that today can only rarely be found in the real world – that is, coercion outside of the structure of the rule of law is absent, existing decision-making processes are open to all on equal terms, and (most improbably) inequalities of resources do not fundamentally disadvantage particular parties who seek to influence the course of events. To expect unanimous support for either tradable permits or direct regulation under those conditions is foolish. It is also not what democratic consensus is about. For consensus in a democracy to perform its necessary functions at the stage of policy system design, it need only produce a circumstance in which both the majority and minority participants agree that the time for decision has arrived, that a clearly preferred alternative has been identified, and that it can be pursued without foreclosing the possibility that (as a result of continued deliberation) the minority party may either reverse the decision or justify exceptions to it at the level of implementation (Baber and Bartlett 2005). In the example we have been using, a consensus regarding policy design would exist when tradable permits are the clear choice of most deliberators, substantially all deliberators agree that further deliberation is unlikely to change matters soon, and the opportunity will exist to revisit the decision or to impose direct regulation in circumstances where a permit system proves ineffective. The key to this functional understanding of policy design consensus is that it allows moving to the implementation stage with the assurance that a genuinely more consensual policy model is unavailable (and, therefore, without a loss of participants that would undermine the legitimacy of the policy process).

Finally, deliberative decision-making at the level of policy implementation should be governed by a regulative standard of social consensus. As a general matter, this simply means that those involved in applying the existing policy model to concrete circumstances and problems are able to do so in a way that is sufficiently satisfying to them that they do not opt out of the implementation process. This is likely to involve considerations similar to those for political consensus. Implementation decisions need to reflect the widest possible agreement within the deliberating group, provide concrete steps that can be taken to address immediate regulatory requirements, and keep open opportunities for future adjustment, deviation from, or even reversal of the implementation plan being pursued. It should be evident by this point that a deliberatively democratic policy process holds the concept of consensus to only as high a standard as each stage of that process requires, from a functional perspective. A search for broad social consensus at the level of normative principle can easily descend into symbolic politics and empty gesturing. Fortunately, it is rarely required and should be just as rarely desired. A political consensus unavoidably involves considerable deferral and bracketing of important issues, and is necessary only to operationalize the identifiable normative consensus with sufficient specificity to allow those concerned to move to the implementation stage. Once engaged in implementation, participants in a deliberatively democratic policy process are rewarded for patience and persistence; the kind of social consensus that actually solves real-world problems is an emergent property of community action and is, therefore, in a perpetual state of becoming.

2.2 Transparency in Earth System Governance

> Uniform ideas originating among entire peoples unknown to each other must have a common ground of truth.
>
> *Giambattista Vico*

Analysis of the concept of transparency can provide a better understanding of the role of consensus in democratic environmental governance. Transparency does not rely on uniformity among entire peoples unknown to each other to play its role in environmental governance. This is not to say that the concept of transparency in governance necessarily involving some kind of consensus is uncontested ground – as the heated dispute over the 2010 WikiLeaks controversy amply demonstrated. Calls for greater transparency in governance have become a standard element in areas as diverse as efforts such as the "design of 'robust' international monitoring, reporting, and verification systems for global climate mitigation; to calls for transparency to combat opaque business practices implicated in the global financial crisis" (Gupta and Mason 2014). The concept of transparency in environmental governance has a long history. Its origins can be traced to the "right-to-know movements in the 1960s and 1970s, particularly in the United States and other advanced industrialized democracies" (Mol 2014, 39) and even earlier to the US Administrative Procedures Act of 1946. But the transparency bandwagon has travelled more widely – stopping in countries rich and poor, democratic and authoritarian (Florini 2007). This broadly emerging consensus has been driven in part by trends toward democratization and marketization but also by processes of transnational learning that have led to both a growing domestic receptivity to transparency-based governance (Florini and Jairaj 2014) and to public disclosure obligations imposed by the 1998 Aarhus Convention on Access to Information, Public Participation in Decision-Making and Access to Justice in Environmental Matters (Mason 2014).

Before considering manifestations across a range of environmental governance issues, it is worth pausing briefly to consider the general outlines and core assumptions of this "transparency consensus." At neither the national nor international level do transparency's advocates claim that it is a panacea. Never can they be heard claiming that public disclosure alone, by either government or industry, will actually solve environmental problems. They do, however, have compelling arguments to make on transparency's behalf (Ciplet et al. 2018). As a starting point, access to information is an indispensable prerequisite for the development and deployment of environmental rights generally (Hayward 2005). Moreover, a normative argument can be made that people who are subject to risk as a consequence of environmental decisions taken by others have a fundamental right to know about their circumstances (Beierle 2004). Beyond this fundamental moral commitment, there are a number of procedural advantages assumed to result from transparency (Gupta, Boas, and Oosterveer 2020). For instance, strong transparency policies are likely to make public participation in decision-making processes more effective by fostering a process of public learning through disclosure (Auld and Gulbrandsen 2014; Mason 2020). Moreover, transparency policies are potentially useful in holding environmental decision-makers accountable – a particularly challenging problem in the global governance context, where detachment of accountability mechanisms from electoral or representative accountability systems (Keohane 2006) makes accountability of global environmental governance and transnational private governance all the more elusive (Biermann and Gupta 2011). These procedural advantages, when realized, could be expected to result in empowerment of the recipients of disclosure – redressing in some measure the information gap between elite groups and average citizens (Mason 2020). Transparency policies have as one of their important aims the adoption of public policies that reduce ecological damage, mitigate risk, and lead to overall environmental improvements (Fung, Graham, and Weil 2007). Moreover, transparency policies are expected to contribute to efforts to achieve policy coordination and integration (Bartlett 1990; Bührs 2009). These fundamental values – effective public participation, the right to know, public accountability, citizen empowerment, and effective environmental protection – constitute the normative consensus underlying what can be described as "governance-by-disclosure" (Gupta and Mason 2014). Not even the critics of this form of governance dispute its underlying normative objectives, which amply demonstrates the consensual nature of this normative perspective. Transparency critiques invariably focus on the disclosure policy models that are adopted and the implementation actions taken in their pursuit – as can be seen through the lens provided by the five Earth System Governance analytical problems: architecture, agency, adaptiveness, accountability, and allocation/access.

2.2.1 The Architecture of Transparency

In the context of earth system governance, the concept of "architecture" draws our attention to widely shared and interlocking webs of institutionalized principles and practices in a given area of environmental policy. Analysis of phenomena for which the term "governance" is preferable to "government" directs attention to the interactions among formally constituted and fully public organizations and nongovernmental organizations and more loosely identified elements of civil society. From early research on the formation and structure of international regimes (Krasner 1983; Young 1989, 1998) to more recent analysis of how different international norms and verification procedures, compliance management systems, and external factors influence regime effectiveness (Stokke 2012), these emergent networks of global political order have become prominent in thinking about international relations.

In applying the concept of architecture to the question of transparency, a useful example is "the form of governance by disclosure through prior informed consent" (Jansen and Dubois 2014, 107), represented in the Rotterdam Convention on the Prior Informed Consent Procedure for Certain Hazardous Chemicals and Pesticides in International Trade. The Rotterdam Convention is a multilateral treaty with 161 parties. Its general objective is to promote shared responsibilities in relation to importation of hazardous chemicals. The convention promotes open exchange of information by requiring exporters of hazardous chemicals to use proper labeling, include directions on safe handling, and inform purchasers of any known restrictions or bans. Party nations can decide whether to allow or ban the importation of chemicals listed in Annex III of the treaty. Exporting countries are obliged to ensure that producers within their jurisdiction comply with the terms of the Rotterdam Convention.

This relatively simple disclosure architecture is the institutional expression of a fundamental normative consensus (Baber and Bartlett 2015) that nations have an inherent right to control the flow of hazardous chemicals into their territory. It also an implicit rejection of the far stronger demand for an outright ban on the use of hazardous pesticides that might better serve the needs of developing nations that often lack both analytical and enforcement capacities (Jansen 2008). The policy model embodied by the specific provisions of the convention reflects a "techno-statist" political consensus about an approach to governance, one that emphasizes networks of science specialists delivering pesticide risk information as a public good, which governments can then use to regulate their exposure to the uncertainties of a complex and technologically sophisticated global market. It rejects both the "neoliberal" alternative of leaving chemical end users and providers to negotiate their own arrangements in a *caveat emptor* environment and the "deliberative democratic" option of problematizing the tacit normative framings of markets and prescribing a participatory risk management system grounded in a democratized form of science and technology (Kraft, Stephan, and Abel 2011; Tyfield 2012; Berg and Lidskog 2018). Indeed, the Rotterdam Convention institutionalizes a "meta-consensus": that the social consensus required for the implementation of its particular expression of governance-by-disclosure should be crafted below the level of international governance through the political processes of the various signatory states. The core aim of the Rotterdam Convention is to help states exert their sovereign power to regulate the flow of listed substances into their territories. The broader (and more challenging) issues of accountability, legitimation, and democracy are of a distinctly secondary concern (Biermann and Gupta 2011; Mitchell 2011).

The architecture of the Rotterdam Convention is the result of several decades of experimentation, which has led to a "more-or-less functioning, though modest, governance-by-disclosure regime" with respect to pesticides and other hazardous chemicals. This prior informed consent system seems to produce the public good that its designers sought – more "information regarding regulatory decisions on banning and restricting the use of pesticides" as well as "scientific evidence of harm" resulting from their misuse (Jansen and Dubois 2014, 124). When it comes to the question of empowering substantively better and procedurally more democratic environmental decision-making, the record is decidedly more mixed. Regime effectiveness at the level of implementation is limited by a deficit in "analytical and decision-making abilities of some nations." To the extent that these broader objectives require "shifts in unequal power relations" – either among nations or within them – little appears to have been accomplished (Jansen and Dubois 2014,125). It may well be that this possible outcome was surrendered when a techno-statist norm was adopted instead of a deliberative democratic approach that might have challenged the implicit commitments underlying the ideas of value-neutral science and national sovereignty (Baber and Bartlett 2015).

2.2.2 The Agents of Transparency

As a field of scholarly inquiry, earth system governance highlights the difficulty of identifying which groups and individuals (agents) actually produce governance outcomes – real-world changes in human behavior. It is, by now, a commonplace observation that processes of global environmental change challenge the capacity of nation-states to respond to and mitigate the impact of those changes. Of course, this capacity varies across various regional, national, and subnational governments (Baber and Bartlett 2009a). The effectiveness with which governments are able to deploy their existing capacities depends to a significant degree on the balance of cooperation and resistance that they encounter in their dealings with nongovernmental actors.

One governance-by-disclosure approach designed to address these difficulties with governmental responses to environmental challenges is the creation of nonstate certification programs. Nonstate certification shares with other transparency policies the attractive quality of allowing the end users of goods and services to make their own market decisions after having been provided with the "public good" of information that would otherwise be difficult (or impossible) for them to acquire. The normative consensus embodied in this approach is the hope that certification will serve as a tool for nongovernmental organizations, investors, governments, and consumers to identify and support (via their market selection of labeled products) high performing businesses. In this way, all of these groups and individuals can be agents in the creation of an upward pressure that does not involve coercive regulation on entire sectors of an economy (Auld and Gulbrandsen 2014; Gulbrandsen 2018).

The political consensus supporting nonstate certification as an approach to governance-by-disclosure exhibits an interesting form of bifurcation. One policy model is for participants in a production market to create a membership organization to design and implement a certification system (consisting of both certification standards and procedures). An example of this approach is the Forest Stewardship Council, which is a result of the widely shared disappointment with the failure of the 1992 Earth Summit to achieve any significant progress on the topic of deforestation. Frustrated with the inability of international politics to produce results, various NGOs turned their attention to industry itself to provide more results-oriented nongovernmental solutions (Welford and Starkey 2001). With membership to its environmental, social, and economic chambers open to both organizations and individuals, the Forest Stewardship Council seeks to maintain a highly participatory and "transparent" approach to transparency (Kirton and Trebilcock 2004).

A second policy model falling under the general heading of nonstate certification is represented by the Marine Stewardship Council. At its inception, the Marine Stewardship Council was a joint undertaking of the World Wide Fund for Nature and Unilever (Fowler and Heap 2000). Now independent of its founding organizations, the Marine Stewardship Council has developed a set of standards for sustainable fishing in consultation with approximately 300 organizations and individuals worldwide. But the Marine Stewardship Council has not followed the Forest Stewardship Council's model of membership organization in its search for political legitimacy. Instead, it relies on the consistency of its standards with the "Guidelines for the Eco-labeling of Fish and Fishery Products from Marine Wild Capture Fisheries" adopted by the UN Food and Agriculture Organization in 2005 and on an "assessment" program conducted by professional staff and overseen by the Marine Stewardship Council Board of Directors that is open to the submission of information by interested parties. The Marine Stewardship Council approach to transparency, therefore, appears more instrumental and science-driven than that of the Forest Stewardship Council (Auld and Gulbrandsen 2014).

This apparent "diversity" within the political consensus supporting nonstate certification transparency can, perhaps, be explained (and even justified) by the fact that this particular instance of political divergence does not necessarily suggest any lack of social consensus at the level of policy implementation. This is possible because of the operating assumptions about how eco-labeling actually works in practice. Unlike product labels mandated by various national product safety standards, eco-labels provide the individual consumer with relatively little information. In the absence of a very significant (and costly) outreach and marketing effort, most consumers cannot reasonably be expected to critically assess either labeling standards or the organizations that develop and implement them. Research suggests that the operative influence of nonstate certification is actually a function of public interest NGO targeting of major buyers, who respond by demanding certified products from firms in their supply chains (Gulbrandsen 2006). If this is correct, then the public preference for sustainable products is effectively mediated by NGOs that are better suited to assess certification standards (and their authors) than are individual consumers. As a result, the provenance, organization, and governance of certifying organizations may matter far less than one would ordinarily assume. It may be that governance-by-disclosure can, in fact, tolerate something less than complete transparency. As long as transparency of procedures and outcomes is sufficient, policy models featuring either robust or relatively leaner patterns of stakeholder monitoring can be sustained (Auld and Gulbrandsen 2014, 289–290).

2.2.3 Transparency and Adaptiveness

Adaptiveness, in the context of earth system governance, is something of a catch-all for a set of distinct but related concepts – including "vulnerability, resilience, adaptation, robustness, adaptive capacity, social learning," and so on (Earth System Governance Project 2009, 45). Each of these concepts captures something important about changes made by social groups in response to, or anticipation of, changes in the natural environment. Adaptiveness includes at least three kinds of social-ecological responses to environmental change: narrowing the gap between current responses to change and imagined best responses; tracking changes in what counts as a best response (when that shifts as a result of environmental change); and transforming institutions when a best response requires a change from one governance regime to another (Earth System Governance Project 2009). In effect, the concept of adaptiveness suggests a constant need for information about the policy target, how it is moving through the shared governance space, and when it might be approaching an understood boundary of that space.

Insofar as governance-by-disclosure always involves the flow of information among actors in governance processes, any techniques falling under that heading might be assumed to involve adaptiveness as we have described it. Focusing on risk governance usefully illustrates the relationship between transparency and adaptiveness in a governance arena where narrowing, tracking, and transforming seem to take place simultaneously and (according to the varying accounts of particular agents) point us in conflicting directions. This can be seen most clearly in the case of risk governance associated with the transboundary transfer of genetically modified organisms (GMOs).

The Cartagena Protocol on Biosafety is an expression of one of the most widely subscribed principles in earth system governance – the precautionary principle. In brief, this principle declares that where there are threats of serious or irreversible damage, lack of full scientific certainty shall not be used as a reason for postponing cost-effective measures to prevent environmental degradation. The Cartagena Protocol, which currently has 172 parties worldwide, applies the precautionary principle to international trade in GMOs. The form this application takes is a requirement for "advance informed agreement" for the importation of GMOs. This requirement (an offspring of the longer established notion of prior informed consent) is a virtually uncontested corollary of the basic principle of national sovereignty as it applies to environmental governance (Gupta 2000). As with all informed agreement regimes, a broad normative consensus on the value of transparency is fundamental.

The Cartagena Protocol also represents a political consensus of exactly the sort that one might expect from a prior informed consent arrangement. It promotes biosafety by establishing rules and procedures for the safe transfer, handling, and use of GMOs, with specific focus on transboundary movements of GMOs. It features one set of procedures for GMOs that are to be intentionally introduced into the environment (the advance informed agreement procedure) and another procedure for GMOs that are intended to be used directly as food or feed or for processing. Parties to the Cartagena Protocol must ensure that GMOs are handled, packaged, and transported under conditions of safety. The shipment of GMOs involving transboundary movement must be accompanied by appropriate documentation specifying, among other things, the identity of any GMOs and the contact point for further information. These procedures and requirements are designed to provide importing parties with the necessary information needed for making informed decisions about whether or not to accept GMO imports and for handling them in a safe manner. The importing party is required to make its decisions in accordance with scientifically sound risk assessments. The Cartagena Protocol also sets out principles and methodologies for conducting a risk assessment. In case of insufficient relevant scientific information, the importing party may rely on the precautionary principle in making its decisions on importation. Where the Protocol reveals its essential nature, however, is in the character of the social consensus exhibited in its implementation.

The implementation of the Cartagena Protocol is an outstanding example of the aphorism that policy is procedure. The central issue of implementation is the application of the Protocol's disclosure requirement to agricultural commodities – a task that is daunting in both scope and complexity. Many of the most heavily traded food commodities have GMO varieties, and GMO varieties of other commodities are under development (James 2012). Moreover, politically critical countries wear more than one hat in the GMO arena – alternately playing the roles of GMO exporter and importer (Falck Zepeda 2006). To make matters even more difficult, the crucial axis of GMO politics pits economic powerhouses against one another – with the United States leading an export-oriented coalition and the

European Union at the center of a somewhat more diverse import-oriented group of nations (Gupta 2014). The quality of the discourse in which this array of forces has engaged has not been significantly improved by the efforts of scientists. GMO proponents appear to have profited little from meta-data research showing that an increasing number of primary research studies fail to show any health risk associated with GMO use (Domingo and Bordonaba 2011; Snell et al. 2012). GMO opponents are unfazed by criticisms that they are ignoring the problems of demanding that their adversaries prove a negative.

This description of the universe of discourse within which Protocol implementation is taking place might seem to be the very antithesis of the idea of social consensus. But that impression ignores the underlying commonality of the views being advanced on the subject of GMO crops. Both the opponents and proponents of GMO technology are convinced that a sufficient quantity of science-based information will eventually acquit their views. Against that backdrop, a regime of minimal disclosure (labeling which declares that GMOs *may* be contained in a bulk shipment) together with a *caveat emptor* standard for decision-making may be the uniquely appropriate one for the circumstances. GMO import decisions differ from other risk-based decisions in that they are actually decisions about the risk of risk. Given the logic of a "no measurable risk" conclusion, from research that can never meet the standard of "no possible risk," decision-makers are deprived of probabilistic reasoning. So the transparency policy involved in an "advance informed agreement" system leaves disclosure recipients no better off than they were prior to disclosure because they have always known that commodity shipments might contain GMOs. Of course, the converse is true – disclosure of a risk of risk leaves GMO exporters no worse off because no genuinely new information has been exchanged.

Outcomes of this sort are often produced where a "least common denominator" agreement is regarded as better than no agreement at all. But where a problem like the risk of risk is at issue, an agreement that imposes little but initiates much may actually constitute a "best practice" rather than a poor compromise – and especially so from the perspective of institutional adaptiveness. Much of the effort to implement the Cartagena Protocol has shifted from the disclosure mandate to the improvement and standardization of sampling, testing, and verification infrastructures. This, of course, runs the risk of privileging some forms of expertise over others (Gupta 2004). It also provides an opportunity to address what is probably the most telling criticism of the Protocol – precisely that it helps least those countries that need help the most (Gupta 2014). As seen in other contexts, governance-by-disclosure can place unsupportable burdens on developing countries that lack both the analytical and institutional capacity to effectively interpret and utilize disclosed information.

In the case of GMOs, however, a mirror image of that inequity can be discerned. Many developing countries that could benefit from GMO technology will not take it up as long as they believe that there remain significant areas of concern about GMO safety and that they would not be able to export their food commodities to the EU market (Key, Ma, and Drake 2008). In light of these considerations, the Protocol should not be condemned for the apparently undemanding quality of its social consensus with respect to what it mandates. It should, rather, be appreciated for the adaptive potential it provides by addressing the inescapably political challenge of ensuring biosafety through the development of institutions and practices of sampling, testing, and verification that can be recognized to be reliable, accurate, and trustworthy means for discovering the true risks of GMO risk (Gupta 2010). If GMO policy is ever to go beyond narrowing the gap between the status quo and best practices, much less track the ongoing changes in what best practices really are, it is likely to be because the kind of basic empirical work that the Cartagena Protocol sustains eventually will allow transformation of perceptions of the boundaries of GMO discourse.

2.2.4 Transparency and Accountability

The very concept of "governance" involves a central question of accountability. At its most basic level, environmental governance refers to the multifaceted and multilayered nature of "governing" humans with respect to the borderless and state-indiscriminate natural environment. How one does that in ways that hold agents accountable (in any traditional sense) is a persistent challenge – especially for those who argue that environmental governance must be fundamentally democratic in order to be effective. Accountability is rendered even more attenuated with respect to transparency policy because governance-by-disclosure so often depends in critical ways on nonstate actors, an excellent example of which is provided by the Global Reporting Initiative (GRI).

Sustainability reporting is a recent concept that encourages businesses and institutions to report on their environmental performance (Herzig 2006). Given its entirely voluntary character, it is unsurprising that a high level of normative consensus exists in support of this form of transparency. By its very definition, sustainability reporting is self-regarding. It is a way for businesses to assess their own environmental accomplishments and failings, reflect on this performance, and subsequently transfer this information into the public domain. This broad conceptual enterprise has been described as "reflexive environmental law" by some academics. Reflexive environmental law is an approach in which industry is encouraged to "self-reflect" and "self-criticize" the environmental externalities that result as a product of their activity, and presumably to act on these negative social

2.2 Transparency in Earth System Governance

impacts in a way that dually safeguards growth and protects the environment (Orts 1995). Not unrelated to this reflexive quality of GRI's self-criticism process is the fact that other environmental actors who wish to use GRI disclosures for their own purposes are often frustrated by a certain degree of user-unfriendliness. That problem becomes clearer by examining the policy model at work in the GRI.

GRI is entirely a private sector effort, the purpose of which is to harmonize reporting standards for all organizations, of whatever size and geographical origin, on a range of issues with the aim of elevating the status of environmental reporting to that of, for example, financial auditing (Willis 2003). Environmental transparency is one of the main areas of business within the scope of the GRI. The GRI encourages participants to report on their environmental performance using specific criteria. The standardized reporting guidelines concerning the environment are contained in the GRI Indicator Protocol Set. This indicator set includes criteria on energy, biodiversity, and emissions – with the thirty specific environmental indicators ranging from "materials used by weight" to "total environmental expenditures by type of investment." In theory at least, disclosure of this kind of data and its collection in an organized database does more than allow business to engage in self-criticism. It should also empower environmental actors outside the corporate sector by redressing the information imbalance from which they often suffer. The prospect of providing a more level playing field for the three-sided contest among businesses, governments, and civil society sustains a powerful political consensus in support of such voluntary disclosure regimes. But the devil, as is so often the case, is to be found in the details of implementation.

Implementation of the GRI is, almost by definition, an expression of social consensus. In this instance, however, the consensus (though genuine enough) occurs in too small a "society" for it to serve all the purposes that it might. The effectiveness of GRI's social consensus is limited by a number of factors. First, the disclosure language of GRI fails to adequately specify what counts as transparency and what purposes it is meant to serve. A second weakness, not unrelated to the first, is that corporations can comply with GRI's basic transparency requirement while having disclosed their information in forms that make it not easily comparable to that of others. Finally, the information infrastructure surrounding GRI remains relatively weak. In contrast to other disclosure schemes, civil society actors have not gathered around GRI in sufficient numbers to translate its data into more valuable, accessible, comprehensible, comparable, and actionable forms (Dingwerth and Eichinger 2010).

Advocates of GRI are not unaware of these concerns, nor have they been entirely unresponsive. But the most significant response to these limitations of GRI has been by other business organizations. In particular, GRI (as well as other disclosure systems) supports a thriving market in the management and delivery of that data. Some companies collect and aggregate data, rendering it in a comparable and consistent format to their clients. Other firms go further, offering interpretations of the data and investment recommendations based on them (Dingwerth and Eichinger 2014). As a basic tool for large individual and institutional investors, a service of this kind may be invaluable. If this were as far as GRI went, one could plausibly argue that it is held accountable for its performance by precisely the same investment market that its disclosure regime seeks to influence. But neither GRI's own rhetoric nor hopes for governance-by-disclosure allow stopping there. Extended analysis of disclosure systems of this character makes two central challenges apparent.

First, the introduction of a class of environmental actors who serve as intermediaries between information disclosers and end users creates a new level of complexity – and, with it, a new accountability challenge. The history of governance-by-disclosure may be judged to have been positive (on balance), but that is no guarantee that it will always be so. Information intermediaries play a role in the development of transparency-based governance that is somewhat similar to that of lawyers in the development of hard law regimes. Lawyers serve as a sort of translation matrix for those seeking to acquit the political values associated with the rule of law, helping members of divergent knowledge communities to communicate with each other (Habermas 1996). In that context, lawyers are subordinates in a clear principal/agent relationship. The contours of that relationship are well defined and lawyers' relationship of accountability to their clients is enforceable by law. Information intermediaries in governance-by-disclosure systems occupy a more ambiguous position. They will commonly have valuable contractual relationships between both disclosers of information and end users of their restatements of that information. As demanding as it may be to navigate that interstitial territory, success in doing so is no guarantee at all that the result will either serve the public interest or protect the environment. So the first question we face in the era of transparency's lost innocence (Mol 2014) is, who will watch the watchers?

Second, the advent of the information intermediary as a business concern poses another question worth pondering. Information disclosed by the GRI has come to represent a tradable good that profit-seeking intermediaries seem to value (Dingwerth and Eichinger 2014). Yet not-for-profit intermediaries have seemed to shy away from this particular source of information. In light of this asymmetry, one must ask whether transparency regimes of this sort contribute to the marketization of transparency (Gupta and Mason 2014). If not, we can reasonably wonder whether the ideal of governance-by-disclosure advocates, to level the political playing field and to empower the historically disadvantaged, will prove viable in the long run or whether transparency policies will eventually end up replicating the inequities that motivate the environmental justice movement.

2.2.5 Transparency, Access, and Allocation

A critique of transparency policy for risking the replication of socioeconomic inequities reminds us of something that contemporary discourses of governance can lead us to forget. Governance is inescapably political – and politics involves questions about who gets what, when, and how (Lasswell 1936). In the context of earth system governance, this key question has been conceptualized as the problem of allocation and access. This analytical problem is likely to be ever present in global environmental governance, because "the most vulnerable to earth system transformation will be those who live in the marginalized lands and coastal zones of the developing world" (Earth System Governance Project 2009, 59). In exploring the politics of equity in earth system governance and its relationship to transparency, it will be useful to concentrate on a governance-by-disclosure approach that is centrally concerned with access to and sharing of environmental goods.

The Convention on Biological Diversity (CBD) identifies transparency as a key element in the international governance of genetic resources. Central to the governance of genetic resources under the CBD is the concept of access and benefit sharing. Access and benefit sharing constitute recognition by the CBD of the inherent right of nations to utilize their genetic resources under environmental laws of their own choosing. To acquit this right, genetic resource users are required to secure permission from the states whose territories provide those resources. The Convention on Biological Diversity also established fair and equitable benefit sharing as the standard for evaluating schemes that compensate genetic resource providers for permission to exploit resources found within their borders (Orsini, Oberthür, and Pożarowska 2014). For this equitable standard to be met, it is necessary that both the conditions under which access to genetic resources is granted and the benefits accruing from their eventual use should be as transparent as possible. That necessity was answered by adoption, under the CBD, of the Nagoya Protocol on Access to Genetic Resources and the Fair and Equitable Sharing of Benefits Arising from their Utilization in 2010.

In addition to affirming the right of nation-states to benefit equitably from the utilization of their genetic resources through transparent agreements, the Nagoya Protocol also recognizes the role in access and benefit sharing of traditional knowledge related to genetic resources that is possessed by indigenous and local communities. It is frequently the case that genetic resources utilization results from the accumulated traditions, practices, and knowhow of indigenous and local communities and that these communities often continue to rely on those resources in their day-to-day existence. The special interest of such communities in the utilization of genetic resources is clearly distinguishable from the market-oriented interest of the national governments within whose territories those communities lie. So, in addition to achieving an equitable balance in the allocation of benefits from genetic resources utilization between providers and users, the normative consensus supporting the Protocol also provides a forum for the assertion of access rights to genetic resources on the part of those who were responsible originally for their development and stewardship (Marion Suiseeya 2014). In effect, the Nagoya Protocol extends the concept of transparency to include the "disclosure" of traditional forms of knowledge that the complex architecture of biodiversity governance (Oberthür and Pożarowska 2013) all too often overlooks.

The transparency requirements of the Protocol must be implemented at two distinct levels – in the negotiation of utilization agreements on mutually agreed terms between users and providers and in the allocation of genetic resources benefits. The CBD explicitly extends the sovereign rights of states over the genetic base of life and couples it with the commitment of contracting parties to facilitate access to genetic resources for environmentally sound uses and not to impose restrictions that run counter to the Convention's objectives. Moreover, the Convention obliges all contracting parties to take appropriate measures to share in a fair and equitable way the results of research and development and the benefits arising from the commercial and other utilization of genetic resources with the contracting party providing these resources. Sharing the benefits arising out of the utilization of genetic resources constitutes one of the three major objectives of the CBD (the others being conservation and sustainable use of biological diversity). The Nagoya Protocol significantly expands and fleshes out this general framework on access and benefit sharing using a well-established governance-by-disclosure technique. Article 6.1 of the Nagoya Protocol (on "Access to Genetic Resources") places the right of parties to require prior informed consent in the context of the exercise of sovereign rights over genetic resources. Furthermore, Articles 6.2 and 6.3 (f) of the Protocol oblige Parties to ensure that prior informed consent or approval and involvement of indigenous and local communities be obtained for access to genetic resources where these communities have the established right to grant access to such resources (Buck and Hamilton 2011). This political consensus on access, benefit sharing, and prior informed consent as the appropriate transparency policy model for genetic resources access is the core achievement represented by the Protocol.

The Nagoya Protocol came into being against the backdrop of a general lack of transparency in genetic resources access. Often, the terms of access agreements were denied to the public by a norm of industrial confidentiality (Orsini, Oberthür, and Pożarowska 2014). Moreover, a general reluctance to disclose information was exacerbated by resistance to the very idea of selling public natural resources to private companies – an attitude often most pronounced among indigenous and local communities (Miller 2006). The frequent characterization by developing countries, indigenous and local communities, and NGOs of nearly any use of genetic resources that did not respect the principles of prior informed consent and mutually agreed terms as "biopiracy" was a dominant force for transparency by the time the Nagoya Protocol came into force (Bled 2010). The Protocol's uptake of transparency as a tool of governance was, therefore, "directly linked to the marketization of genetic resources on the one side and to concerns over biopiracy on the other" (Orsini, Oberthür, and Pożarowska 2014, 163). This accounts for the "decentralized, contract-based marketization approach" (166) on which this governance system is based. With the requirement of mutually agreed terms as a precondition for the granting of prior informed consent, access agreements become dense contractual arrangements containing detailed terms and conditions that are imposed on both provider and user (Pisupati 2007). This preexisting social consensus regarding the commercialization of genetic resources both structured the Protocol and was, in turn, refined by it. But this social consensus may have unfortunate implications.

The liberal market logic of the system could be regarded as a major achievement in international biodiversity policy-making and more broadly in global environmental governance. Optimistically, its implementation may lead to collaboration and partnerships in research that could provide for fruitful multi-party dialogue, because most access activities are undertaken by researchers (often with non-commercial intent) and because their activities will primarily focus on the research and development part of the innovation chain. A collaborative approach to implementation could further be facilitated by a major emphasis on the exchange of best practices between parties and stakeholders in the prior informed consent process – eventually resulting in the development of research and industry standards on access and benefit-sharing (Buck and Hamilton 2011). But there is a long-existing imbalance between transparency for access and transparency for benefit-sharing. The Nagoya Protocol enhances transparency of access conditions, but it does nothing to redress comparative disadvantages with respect to access and benefit sharing (Orsini, Oberthür, and Pożarowska 2014).

Access and benefit sharing negotiations and experience with the issue since 2010 demonstrate the challenges and complexities of the pursuit of justice for indigenous and local communities. The lack of progress in this area demonstrates the limited nature, scope, and engagement in the justice discourse at Nagoya and suggests the existence of a justice meta-norm that is indifferent (or even hostile) to the pursuit of indigenous and local community justice. Not only was indigenous and local community justice pursued primarily by a handful of actors in a small subset of events, but their engagement centered on deliberating how to deliver a preestablished notion of justice rather than tackling the questions of what and whose justice should be demanded. Although plural and multivalent understandings of justice were represented, in the access and benefit sharing negotiations there was a convergence toward a preexisting set of justice practices underpinned by market-liberal justice norms and ideas (Marion Suiseeya 2014). This absence of contestation over meaning is troubling because achieving indigenous and local community justice ultimately demands shifts in the normative fabric and orientation of global environmental governance – shifts that are only possibly through debates over the substance of justice, which the social consensus underlying the Nagoya Protocol appears to inhibit. Explicit attention to the relationship between transparency and broader concerns for equity and legitimacy is essential if environmental policy instruments are ultimately to serve the cause of justice when and where real people encounter those policies (Isyaku, Arhin, and Asiyanbi 2017).

2.3 A Way Forward

> We must indeed all hang together, or, most assuredly, we shall all hang separately.
>
> *Benjamin Franklin*

Having examined the implications of transparency policies for five core problems of earth system governance, what conclusions are warranted? If we can say nothing else, it is clear that the relationship between environmental transparency and public accountability is neither linear nor politically neutral (Rajão and Georgiadou 2014). Most obvious, perhaps, is that the concept of consensus must be understood in a more complex and contingent way than it often is (Baber and Bartlett 2015, 2020). In the context of environmental governance, consensus is that level of agreement among all parties to the decision process that allows them to "hang together" as they move from one stage of that process to the next. Consensus in governance is not, and never could be usefully thought of as, synonymous with simple unanimity. The major elements of consensus – the normative, the political, and the social – all relate to different kinds of agreement, each with its own regulative standard. These elements vary in relative importance as participants in a shared decision process move between the poles of general and abstract discourse and the specific and concrete actions of everyday life. Consensus does not need to have a reach that is either wide or deep in order to merit our approbation as a source of democratic legitimacy.

A second conclusion is that the character of each distinct analytical problem of governance places its own demands and limitations on the transparency consensus. For instance, a prior informed consent approach can provide satisfactory architectural solutions for governance-by-disclosure (it can be stable, useful, and consensual) while failing to resolve (or even exacerbating) problems of access and allocation. Environmental transparency requirements can produce very low levels of compliance when applied to agencies that, for a variety of possible reasons, lack technical capacity, resources, or political support (Bizzo and Michener 2017). This is an especially important insight in light of broad reliance on federal structures of governance. In this context, the effectiveness of transparency regimes has been found to depend to a significant degree on the level of administrative capacity at subnational levels of governance (Sun et al. 2019).

Third, transparency policies can provide an institutional and procedural context for environmental agency that is widely supported in spite of the fact that it does little to advance environmental governance outcomes that actually improve the environment or governance in any substantial way. For example, a common pattern is for transparency policies to become subsumed by a neo-liberal paradigm in which a "measurementality" aligns transparency with concepts of effectiveness and efficiency to produce a managerial and scientific approach that sacrifices normative commitments to the production of raw materials for subsequent institutional exchanges without rendering the science–policy interface any more use-friendly to non-elites (Turnhout, Neves, and de Lijster 2014). Enhancing the visibility of the individuals and communities involved in the assessment of green infrastructure engineering has been found to be crucial to achieving full social inclusiveness in urban resilience planning (Ward et al. 2019). That being so, we may face a situation in which the presence of transparency policies is no guarantee of more just, democratic, and sustainable outcomes but the absence of transparency is a near-guarantee of unjust, elitist, and unsustainable policy. This "necessary but not sufficient" characterization of democracy would also be consistent with the observation that in the presence of authoritarian political structures, improved governance structures (per se) do not translate into stronger accountability (Tan 2014).

To have produced a patchwork quilt of observations might seem to be a disappointing result, but that is only a problem if we expect that our accounts of governance phenomena must have the character of nomothetical explanations grounded in general theory. A more appropriate set of expectations results if we accept the fact that governance (especially at the global level) can most appropriately be represented by models that both describe and explain. Commonly referred to by philosophers of science as pattern explanations (Kaplan 1964), these models explain both a theme and a relationship simultaneously by specifying their place in an empirical pattern. If further explanation of other phases or aspects of the same theme is desired, one traces out more relations between the theme and other things (Diesing 1971, 157–160). A pertinent example is the necessity to situate transparency policies, such as national environmental reporting systems, within the broader context of internationally recognized accountability frameworks and their wider relationships to environmental management and other policy domains (Petrie 2018). Having recognized that having a better understanding of earth system governance requires pattern explanations of this sort, the scattering of insights produced by looking at the relationship among the core analytical problems of polarization, governance, and a collection of variations on the theme of transparency should be far more satisfying. Like pieces in a complex puzzle, they represent touch points for further development of the explanatory pattern. The shapes that they have begun to reveal may as yet be impossible to specify fully. But their colors are sufficiently rich and harmonious to suggest that additional work on the puzzle is likely to be highly rewarding.

3

Empowered Democratic Agency in the Anthropocene

Reconciling People to Nature and Each Other

Were the world a simpler place, an earlier place, the issue of agency in earth system governance could be far more easily addressed. There was a time when the range of the earth's agents of governance was thought to consist entirely of that exclusive club commonly referred to as countries or nation-states – entities possessing a permanent population, defined territory, singular government, and the capacity to enter into relations with other such entities (Shaw 2003). It is that last characteristic, the relations between nations, that combined with the various national legal orders was thought to constitute the entirety of global governance.

Early cracks in this structure appeared at the national level, most notably in the form of private regulation – industry-based standards intended to serve the regulatory functions of governance without resorting to actual government (Freeman 1999).[1] Today, agents in earth system governance range from "governments to science networks, environmentalists, industry associations, faith-based organizations, farmer unions, and intergovernmental organizations, to name a few" (Biermann 2014, 47; Van der Heijden, Bulkeley, and Certomà 2019). It is important to note, however, that agents of governance are not merely political actors. They are, rather, authoritative actors. They have both the legitimacy and capacity to act (Dellas, Pattberg, and Betsill 2011). The question of agency is critical to any strategy of global political transformation one might imagine (Boswell and Chose-Dunn 2000; Linnér and Wibeck 2019). In order to more fully appreciate the challenge to democracy posed by this new formulation of agency, it is necessary to trace agency back to its roots – before the age by which humanity so interpenetrated the natural world that no corner of the biosphere remained untouched by human influence – before, that is, the dawn of the Anthropocene.

3.1 Agency before the Anthropocene: Slaves, Servants, and Selves

As a legal concept, the notion of agency is ancient in the extreme. In both the civil and common law traditions, agency has long been an important element in the process of assessing the responsibility of individuals for their actions. A civil law theorist described agency as a circumstance in which a person has brought it about "that certain declarations by another individual, his 'agent,' have the same effect as similar declarations by himself, the principal" (Kelsen 2006 [1949], 83). This apparently simple agent–principal relationship achieves a broader social significance in that it allows a corporation to have the "will" it must have "in order to be a juristic person" (107). Likewise, the doctrine of principal and agent has long been recognized as part of law, under which "men daily have to pay large sums for other peoples' acts, in which they had no part and for which they are in no sense to blame" (Holmes 1991 [1881], 16–17). The doctrine of agency liability dates to the earliest days of English common law, wherein the master was held to "answer for the neglect of his servant" (Blackstone 1979 [1765-9], bk. 1, ch 14, 418).

We are comfortable with this sort of vicarious liability because, among other things, we recognize it to be the constitutive and energizing force behind the modern corporation and all of the modern blessings that legal form bestows. It might be regarded, therefore, as the foundation of all of the material advantages of modernity. But agency has an even deeper and darker history. As Holmes reminds us, "the history of the whole modern doctrine of master and servant, and principal and agent" was developed "on special grounds in a special case, when servants were slaves" (Holmes 1991 [1881]). Plato tells us that when a slave injures anything or anyone, "the master of the slave who has done the harm shall either make full satisfaction, or give up the slave who has done the injury" (Plato 1952, 783). Not only could the slave/agent be offered up in satisfaction of claims against his master/principal, he could have no possessions of his own, "on the practical ground of his owner's power over him" (Holmes 1991 [1881], 228), which made whatever he might possess the property of his master.

As Kelsen (2006 [1949], 107) reminds us, any form of representation, including that of an agent and his principal, is "a relationship between human beings" (107). Here, with respect to how people should be treated, we find a certain difference of opinion – even in ancient times. In the time of the Torah, a slave owner who hit his slave in the eye, causing the eye to be lost, was required to free the slave in compensation (Exodus 21:26). If a slave could free himself, the residents of a community to which he escaped were required to give him refuge and to allow him to live wherever he chose without oppression (Deuteronomy 23:15–16). By the time of the Christian New Testament, new and less favorable views had emerged. There, slaves were enjoined to submit themselves to their masters, "not only to those who are good and considerate, but also to those who are harsh" (1 Peter 2:18). The slave was told to submit "as if you were serving the Lord, not men, because . . . the Lord will reward everyone for whatever good he does, whether he is free or slave" (Ephesians 6:5). This submissive quality of enslavement is, undoubtedly, what led Plato to argue that the suffering of injustice is "not the part of a man, but of a slave, who indeed had better die than live" (1952, 271). Even more directly relevant to our present concerns, Plato extended this view to that most ancient of agents, the lawyer, who Plato characterized as a servant "continually disputing about a fellow-servant before his master, who is seated, and has the cause in his hands." This way of life imposes on the lawyer a condition "which has been that of a slave from his youth upwards" and which "has deprived him of growth and uprightness and independence" (1952, 528). Therefore, the lawyer (and all other agents) would be thoroughly ill-suited to the practice of politics – which is uniquely the province of the citizen, not the slave.

Beginning a search for the roots of agency by briefly examining its deep history as a legal concept appears to lead to the conclusion that the agent is, quite literally, damaged goods. Agents are latter-day slaves, whose existence and actions are justified by the ends of their masters and whose responsibilities in life run only to that source of ordering will. Not only is this a state that no self-respecting person would want to submit to, but it is a condition that destroys the very capacity for self-respect that allows existence as members of a community of others. The agent is capable of having a relationship (if it could even be called that) only with that "other" who is his principal, so he is incapable of acting as an "other" for members of a polity. Yet this is certainly not the view of agency that dominates the discussion of it as a political concept. In fact, when we come to understood governance as a search for rules to guide action, we begin to see questions of governance manifested in any effort to "coordinate the plans of a variety of agents." In this context, ends are understood to be a broad category, including all of "the intended results of the intervention of an individual or collective agent in the world" (Habermas 1993, 63).

This political conception of agency is more positive than the legal conception in two distinct but related ways. First, the political agent is positive (in comparison with the legal agent) in that he or she is an independent source of intentional action. Indeed, we must move beyond the bare facts of behavior in order to make sense of another person as "a rational agent who harbors beliefs and desires and other mental states that exhibit intentionality or 'aboutness' and whose actions can be explained (or predicted) on the basis of the content of those states" (Dennett 1991, 76). On this view, agency is not a Kantian metaphysical freedom of will but, rather, "a natural function of the evolved human brain" (Flanagan, Sarkissian, and Wong 2008, 7). Attributions of agency are "partially rooted in pattern-seeking cognitive machinery that is uniquely well developed in *Homo Sapiens* and which is dedicated to imposing order on our interactions with the physical world across time" (McGeer 2008, 250–251). When it runs amok, this machinery can cause us to attribute events in the natural world as the intentional acts of supernatural beings (Dennett 2006). But when turned on our fellow humans, the concept of agency (as a function of reasons and rationality) allows us to make the behavior of the other intelligible, to "grasp how they do, and could, see the world, so that we can interact with, or at least understand them" (Gaus 2011, 235). In fact, agency is so basic to our "understanding of the self" that we have a hard time seeing non-agents as persons – often describing people without a sense of their own agency as having "personality disorders" (337). Here we have the second sense in which this political conception of agency is positive. In addition to involving a proactive element, this conception of agency carries a positive affect – an expression of what is normal or right.

The political notion of agency "encompasses all the goals that a person has reason to adopt, which can inter alia include goals other than the advancement of his or her own well-being" (Sen 2009, 287). Human agents are strong evaluators, in the sense that they have not only first-order desires but second-order desires as well. These are, so to speak, desires *to desire* or *not to desire* certain things. These second-order desires, taken together, form attitudes about the worthiness of first-order desires. They constitute our expectations about others and our aspirations about the kind of persons that we want to be ourselves (Taylor 1985). The human cognitive architecture is "densely populated with a large number of evolved, content-specific, domain-specific inference engines (or evolved mechanisms for their acquisition), in addition to whatever more domain – or content – general inferential competencies may exist" (Cosmides and Tooby 2008, 68). Among these, there is a system for interpreting social exchanges and choosing among the patterns of response that are available to agents involved in those exchanges. Social contract theory can be viewed as "an account of the computational procedures by which these interpretations are assigned: what cues are necessary and/or sufficient, which inferential transformations these procedures license, and so on" (68–69). The existence of this interpretive capacity is the feature of the human mind that allows us to maintain "our self-image as agents making 'free' decisions and choices, for which we might properly be held responsible" (Dennett 2003, 34). It is this possibility of being held and of holding others responsible that allows us to bridge the gap between legal and political agency.

How should we understand the distinction between the legal agent (who is little more than a slave, lacking plans, property or responsibility) and the political agent (who acts on his own behalf and stands ready to judge and to be judged by others)? Is the use of the term "agent" in these two conflicting ways merely a regrettable coincidence, leading us to an understandable linguistic confusion? Or are legal and political agency connected in some essential way – two sides of the same coin? The apparent conflict between legal and political agency can be understood as a product of alternate responses to the problem of distinguishing intentional action

3.1 Agency before the Anthropocene: Slaves, Servants, and Selves

from mere behavior arising from historically contingent sets of circumstances. If, as we have argued, human beings are equipped with an inference engine that operates to interpret social events as the results of conscious intentions, that engine needs learned programming that will allow it to recognize the range of individual "others" whose responsibility for a given event might require evaluation. This decision process cannot be hardwired, because the range of possible variations in human social arrangements is simply too great.

For instance, the social and economic circumstances in which legal agency was born (in the form of the master/slave relationship) involved a society wherein male heads of household were the sole locus of responsibility. Slaves were no different from wives or children in this regard. They were, however, far more useful as tools of their masters' intentions. As mentioned earlier, a slave who harmed the person or property of another was not responsible for the damage – his master was responsible. The slave could be given up to the aggrieved party if the cost of compensation seemed to his master to be too high. As societies became more egalitarian, this "disposability" of persons became increasingly untenable. With the expansion of the political franchise and as every individual became a potential bearer of responsibility, "reciprocal recognition by agents of their equal agency" became an integral part of "the practical contexts of social interaction which are the framework for individual self-development" (Gould 1988, 71). Indeed, the superstructure of democratic politics (as it is understood in contemporary Western societies) rests on a concept of reciprocity that has its "ontological basis" in the equal agency of individuals and constructs a complex of equal rights on that same "equal agency of persons" (132, 68). This emancipation of the individual from the radical inequality of legal agency set the concept free to organize new areas of social relations. As previously noted, the principal/agent legal construct was the foundation for the modern corporation, in which the liability of the investors (principals) is limited to the sum of their investment. Moreover, in modern democratic regimes, "representation is actually a form of agency" (Hampton 1994, 39). Through the use of various forms of voting, public officials can be empowered to act as agents of the voters and, more important, they can be removed from power nonviolently. These agents can then be empowered to hire others and to create institutions that also can act as agents of the voters. Seen from this perspective, the advent of modernity – with its individualist ontology and its institutional reliance on markets and political representation to organize social interaction – can be understood as a product of the historical evolution of the concept of agency. This evolutionary trend has a logical destination in the stakeholder approaches that have already been shown to provide cognitive and political advantages (Stevenson 2016) as well as a broadly empowering concept of what agency can (and should) become in the Anthropocene (Coleman et al. 2017).

3.2 Agency in the Anthropocene: Bureaucrats and Billionaires, Academics and Activists

The concept of the Anthropocene is invoked to describe a reality in which humanity's impact on the environment is so pervasive that it no longer makes sense to distinguish between the human and the nonhuman nature. Today, the only division of reality that makes sense is between the merely human and the more-than-just-human. As one might imagine, environmental governance in such circumstances becomes far more challenging than it was when nature could be conceived of as an object "capable of being acted upon" by the only force significantly capable of intentionally manipulating it – the human agent (Dryzek 2006, 165, n. 1). Once the natural world comes to be understood as thoroughly penetrated by human influence, the quaint notion that institutions of government can, by themselves, control that intimate and integral relationship becomes obviously untenable. In light of this complexity and interpenetration of humans and their environment, human agents in the Anthropocene can be characterized as locations of embodied uncertainty (Sword-Daniels et al. 2018). The broader subject of environmental governance, therefore, comes into focus as a set of practices that relies on networks of actors stretching far beyond the institutional boundaries of any government or governments and relating to one another in increasingly indeterminate ways. But it makes sense to begin discussion of the agents of global environmental governance within the increasingly porous limits of what is actually governmental.

3.2.1 Of Bureaucrats

When we say that a governmental agency is governmental, we mean something different at the global level than we would if we were referring to an organization within the nation-state wherein all levels and branches of government have the capacity to promote, enable, and partner in adaptive governance (Kashwan 2016; Kronsell and Mukhtar-Landgren 2018; May 2019). International bureaucracies are the creation of governments, but they are not actually situated within any government (though they are often affiliated with international organizations that are subject to varying levels of oversight by national governments). These creations of national governments have the same hierarchical structures, career civil servants, formal rule systems, and defined policy mandates that national bureaucracies have. They are not, however, subject to the direct control of any national government (Biermann and Siebenhüner 2009). A noticeable characteristic of global environmental governance in the Anthropocene has been the proliferation of these international bureaucracies (Burke and Fishel 2019). Why would sovereign states authorize the creation of these governmental agencies outside the structure of their own governments and why would they allow them the significant level of autonomy that they enjoy?

At one level, the answer to this question is relatively simple. The existence of international bureaucracies provides an expedient means for national governments to address their shared environmental concerns, and the level of autonomy that these agencies enjoy is a revocable tradeoff for their potential, and often actual, effectiveness (Reinalda and Verbeck 2004). A more challenging question is whether this assumption is accurate – that is, whether the tradeoff involved in the creation of international bureaucracies is actually a good one. A body of careful and sophisticated research addresses that question (Bauer, Andresen, and Biermann 2012). The Global Governance Project employed extensive field research, including interviews with approximately one hundred international civil servants and external governance experts, to evaluate the environmental departments and divisions of the World Bank, the Organisation for Economic Co-operation and Development, as well as the International Maritime Organization and the secretariats of the United Nations Environment Programme and the Global Environmental Facility. Also included were detailed comparative studies of environmental treaty secretariats, including those of the United Nations Framework Convention on Climate Change, of the most important conventions on biodiversity, the United Nations Convention to Combat Desertification, the Vienna Convention for the Protection of the Ozone Layer and its Montreal Protocol, and the three main conventions on chemicals (Biermann and Pattberg 2012). This research documented three specific areas in which international bureaucracies are especially effective.

First, international bureaucracies exercise a significant cognitive influence on the global environmental agenda by "synthesizing scientific findings and distributing knowledge and information to all kinds of stakeholders, from national and local governments to scientists, citizens, environmental advocates, and the business sector" (Bauer, Andresen, and Biermann 2012, 33). This particular strength, in the area of agenda-setting, may be the singular advantage that international bureaucracies enjoy, both because of the importance of agendas in the policy process generally and because of the relative weakness of other potential agents in this respect (Bauer 2009b). Convention secretariats, for example, are able to capitalize on the unique technical expertise and institutional memory of their professional staffs to advance specific issues that are subsumed by their broad and generally stated mandates – exploiting the fact that international agreements often need to be stated in somewhat ambiguous terms for entirely political reasons.

Second, international bureaucracies have a demonstrated normative influence on global environmental governance. For instance, some bureaucracies initiate international conferences that often lead to negotiations regarding the institutionalization of environmental norms or to interventions in "processes pertaining to the implementation, revision, adaptation, or renegotiation of existent institutions" (Bauer, Andresen, and Biermann 2012, 34). This pattern of bureaucratic initiative is often most pronounced in the early years of an international bureaucracy's existence, but it generally persists as a low-profile feature of longer-term administrative practice. For example, while the United Nations Environment Programme's impact on the course of environmental governance may have been most prominent in the early years of its existence, the ongoing influence of its professional staff can be discerned in the significant role it continued to play in the administration of the Convention on Biological Diversity (Andresen and Rosendal 2014) and the Montreal Protocol (Bauer 2009a).

Third, research shows that international bureaucracies have a significant degree of autonomous executive influence in global environmental governance – evident most clearly in the capacity-building initiatives carried out by the World Bank, the United Nations Industrial Development Organization, and the United Nations Development Programme (Biermann and Siebenhüner 2009, 319–349). In these and other cases, international bureaucracies have gone beyond the mere implementation of technical provisions of international agreements "to develop and implement their own capacity-building policies" with a considerable degree of administrative autonomy (Bauer, Andresen, and Biermann 2012, 35). More generally, many international bureaucracies have stretched their mandates in other ways to embrace executive functions for which they lack a formal authorization. For example, United Nations Environment Programme has built joint programs with other UN agencies, initiated numerous public–private partnerships, and supported capacity development in developing nations (Bauer 2009a). This capacity is particularly important because it offers the opportunity to embrace various forms of what has come to be called "private governance," often consisting of certification schemes that hold both the promise of increasing sustainability and the peril of greenwashing, depending, at least in part, on how international bureaucrats manage them (van der Loos, Kalfagianni, and Biermann 2018).

In each of these ways, international bureaucracies bring cognitive, normative, and executive capacities to the challenge of global environmental governance that national governments cannot (or have chosen not to) develop. Over time, these capacities allow international organizations to become more effective collective agents as they engage in recursive interaction with multiple internal and external audiences (Dupont 2019). International bureaucracies have come to enjoy such a high level of autonomy as agents of global governance that further research – particularly systematic comparisons of international bureaucracies across policy areas and through time – is clearly warranted (Bauer and Weinlich 2011).

The potency (both latent and realized) of international bureaucracies as agents of global environmental governance makes it crucial that we better understand what form of agency these organizations actually represent.

3.2.2 Of Billionaires

There was a time when multi-national corporations could be counted on to greet global environmental initiatives with an attitude that fell somewhere between general suspicion and outright hostility. In contemporary global environmental governance, however, private companies have become more that the targets of the development and spread of environmental practices, norms, standards, and legislation – they have become substantial contributors to that development as well (Bouteligier 2011). For many years much of the work on "regime complexes" – loosely connected nonhierarchical institutions – excluded an important part of the institutional picture: the role of private authority (Green 2013, 2014; Zelli, Möller, and van Asselt 2017). But private global environmental standards are emerging as an increasingly important influence on the environmental performance of industry, resulting in increasingly complex multi-level and multi-actor governance structures featuring diverse groups of stakeholders and multi-level policy mixes (Anderton 2017). The growing interest in these private environmental standards has been shown to arise from processes of economic globalization as well as from increasing external pressure on firms and industries with respect to environmental concerns (Angel, Hamilton, and Huber 2007; van der Loos, Kalfagianni, and Biermann 2018). These standards can be categorized on the basis of the different agents involved in their development and the particular network architecture through which environmental standards achieve global reach. It is possible to distinguish between, for example, firm-based standards and those standards initiated by third-party organizations, such as nongovernmental organizations (NGOs) and industry associations.

The emergence of firm-based global environmental standards as an approach to managing the environmental performance of complex global production networks is illustrative of the promise of private standard-setting. Firm-based global environmental standards exist when a firm defines a uniform set of process and product environmental performance requirements that must be adhered to by all of a firm's facilities around the world, even if these firm-based standards exceed the requirements of local and national environmental regulations. These standards are often responses to increasingly stringent end-market environmental regulation, as well as growing concern over the need to protect a firm's reputational capital and operating legitimacy. These two key drivers of the adoption of firm-based environmental standards further suggest that firms are responding to these external drivers in part because of the characteristics of global production networks – a production form that depends on the ability to produce from any manufacturing plant to any end market. Case studies of the impact of firm-based environmental standards suggest that firm-based standards are providing a platform for learning and innovation within firms (Angel and Rock 2005). As an example, companies in the mining, oil, and gas industries operate in diverse institutional contexts, including developed and developing countries. These companies face significant environmental and social challenges ranging from pollution problems to community relation issues, and they must generally adhere to the requirements of several different national, international, and industry-wide institutional frameworks and standards. Mining, oil, and gas companies have responded to these challenges by developing corporate social responsibility practices. These standards can be understood as "regulatory scripts" – defined as the practices shared by a group of organizations in an industry in response to international frameworks and standards – which rely on the resulting "institutional expectations" within the industry's environment for their effectiveness (Raufflet, Cruz, and Bres 2014). A problem, of course, is that holding all of the various participants to the scripts that have been written for them presents significant accountability problems at the level of the firms within the complex supply chains (van der Ven 2019).

Private standard-setting beyond the firm offers an even wider scope of potential advantages. For instance, the harmonization of product standards and regulation in international trade is allowing the European Union, in partnership with coalitions of producers, to progressively rationalize its health, environmental, and labor standards (Casella 2001). Private standard-setting may also create the opportunity to both leverage and perpetuate whatever success the negotiation of intergovernmental standards may produce. For example, recent research on privately created standards within the regime complex for climate change and the relationship of those private standards to public authority suggests that public standards have the capacity to spin off private ones. Public rules in the Kyoto Protocol served as a "coral reef," attracting private rule-makers whose governance activities come to form part of the regime complex. A network analysis of public and private standards for carbon management has revealed evidence of policy convergence – around both public rules and a subset of privately created rules. In other words, there is an emerging order in the complex institutional landscape that governs climate change. This convergence arises from the desire of private standard-setters to demonstrate their credibility and provide benefits for users of their standards. Implementation of the Kyoto Protocol led to generation of public rules on carbon accounting, which have now outlasted the Protocol as they are perpetuated through private authority (Green 2013, 2014; van der Ven, Bernstein, and Hoffman 2017).

Private voluntary standards can also feed back into public agreements in positive ways. For example, the standards crafted by the International Organization for Standardization's (ISO) 14000 series have played an increasingly important role in encouraging corporations to adopt more sustainable business models on their own initiative and not in direct response to governmentally mandated requirements. ISO standards have a number of benefits, including promoting international uniformity, elevating environmental issues within an enterprise, promoting international trade, and providing a minimal level of environmental performance in countries with less than adequate regulatory infrastructure. Concerns about ISO standards include their relationship to public regulation and ISO 14001's essentially procedural (as opposed to performance-based) character. These concerns become all the more important when international trade agreements such as the North American Free Trade Agreement (NAFTA) and the World Trade Organization (WTO) Agreement on Technical Barriers to Trade inject ISO standards into public policy. Because of the structure of these agreements, ISO standards now have the ambiguous potential to operate either as a sword – a negative standard used to challenge a domestic regulatory action – or a shield – an internationally agreed-on reference point that bolsters the legitimacy of a national regulatory measure (Wirth 2009).

Private standards can have significant effects beyond the policy area they were purportedly designed to regulate – and often in ways that are difficult to discern, much less control. For instance, although not widely studied from a policy perspective, international accounting standards shape what information regarding a firm's environmental performance is communicated to international financial markets. Scholarship describing the influence of international accounting standards on private financial markets shows that nominally technical choices regarding how to recognize and measure firms' environmental impacts hold the potential to reduce these impacts. As a consequence, obscure accounting debates within the International Accounting Standards Board (IASB) often involve important political choices about what a firm must disclose to investors about its environmental liabilities and risks that are not readily available for public scrutiny. This demonstrates the authority of the IASB as an overlooked (one might even say "hidden") source of global environmental governance (Thistlewaite 2011). IASB decisions about how these data appear on corporate balance sheets change the link between a firm's environmental performance and its economic value and thereby contribute to steering private financial markets toward varying rewards for sustainable behavior within the global economy. In this way, private standards that are, putatively, designed to promote transparency can turn opaque at precisely the point where public inspection is most in order. Transparency is not the only concern regarding our growing reliance on private regulation. The existence of opaque spaces in the governance process allows for the commission of far more substantive sins to which we will return.

3.2.3 Of Academics

Scientists and other academicians have long played a role in thinking about the challenges of global environmental governance. Science certainly establishes much of the conceptual framework within which those challenges are discussed and supplies a good deal of the substance of those discussions. But "the role of science in global environmental governance has changed since the 1980s in the direction of greater institutionalization of scientific input into global policy fora, often through globally organized assessments or scientific advisory boards" (Gupta et al. 2012, 69). Scientists are now agents of environmental governance, playing formal and institutional roles across the entire spectrum of governance activities. This development poses two distinct but clearly related questions that are key to understanding the role of the scientist as agent of environmental governance. Does (or should) the influence of science in governance depend on whether the conditions of its production have a participatory and inclusive character? Does (or should) the influence of science in governance depend on whether the conditions of its production are insulated from political influences?

On first look, these two questions might seem to be two sides of the same coin. But they actually seek to address two distinct concerns about the role of science in governance. The first might be characterized as a concern that the objective of scientific research be not only generalizability but also applicability. In its classical form, science is pursued not only to accumulate accurate experimental data, "but also to *generalize* from them" (Kaplan 1964, 156, emphasis in the original). This experimental model (which is often taken to be coextensive with "science" per se) has as its objective the discovery of "a potentially lawlike variable" that accounts for the effect that we seek to understand (Diesing 1971). The austere and artificial quality of this account has led many to conclude that a "post-normal" form of science is required if scientists are ever adequately to address human concerns (Funtowicz and Ravertz 1993). Post-normal science would involve both a broadened concept of peer review (that combined both expert and lay perspectives in the production of knowledge) and reformed ways of communicating scientific knowledge from specialists to the general public and their institutions. In the realm of environmental governance, the objective would be the development of a "sustainability science" that attended to the entire scope of the relationship between humanity and nature, one that can reconcile the global perspective required by environmental policy with the ecological and social characteristics of particular places and people (Kates et al. 2001) without being distorted by the ambivalent role played by the international donor community (Blumstein 2017).

The concern that motivates the question about the insulation of science from the delegitimizing influence of politics has less to do with the problem of applicability than with that of efficacy. One view of the matter is that "objective scientific input that is separable from political considerations is neither attainable nor essential for the influence of policy relevant science" (Gupta et al. 2012, 88). This broad claim is only tenable with two important caveats. First, objectivity (as that word is generally understood) is an aim that scientists long ago should have foresworn. It has long been recognized that science relies not on objectivity but, rather, intersubjectivity. The question is not how can we achieve certainty but how we can "learn more than we know now" (Kaplan 1964, 173). The objectivity of modern science has never been dependent on our ability to arrive at value-free conclusions but, rather, to produce explanations that fit one of two possible models. Objectivity in scientific explanation pursued on the basis of a *deductive* model lies in the predictive power of the explanations one is able to construct. For science based on a *pattern* model of explanation, objectivity consists essentially in "that the pattern can be indefinitely filled in and extended" without causing the model to fail (335). So, to say that objective science is not attainable must be understood to refer to a "popular" and naïve conception of objectivity that does not actually describe science as it has ever been practiced.

The second important caveat is that policy-relevant science is attainable without naively construed objectivity, but only if it can make a persuasive claim to political impartiality. Impartiality has little to do with the broad valuative considerations that often contribute to decisions by scientists about which research questions to pursue and whether (and if so, how) to characterize their results to others. It has to do, rather, with the avoidance of bias. Bias can be usefully categorized as personal, class, and cultural (Diesing 1971), as well as, of course, gender. Scientists deal with personal bias in several ways. First, science is carried out by groups of scientists who submit their efforts for evaluation based on the standards of their disciplines by others who have demonstrated mastery of those standards. Second, all science is ultimately empirical. It uses observation that is controlled (in previously and consensually agreed on ways) to detect the biases that the mere act of observation involves. Third, scientists avail themselves of quantitative reasoning insofar as the nature of their study allows. Measurement is no panacea, but it does allow us to overcome some of the mistakes that human reasoning is prone to when estimation is our only guide (321–322). This process of review, based on shared disciplinary standards and grounded in empirical observation, is the basis for the scientific claim to intersubjective reliability – on the basis of which the special role of scientists in the policy process can be legitimated.

Class bias is more difficult to address. At one level, class bias is simply one more reason that every effort should be made to open the doors of the academy to all whose capacities might allow them reasonably to aspire to scientific careers – regardless of their class background. The more difficult "class" issue is the complaint that scientists (regardless of their backgrounds) become a class of their own. One often hears the complaint, for instance, that scientists are tools of the military-industrial complex (or some other equally ominous sounding complex). Although one can find capitalist-militarist elements in the sciences, "there are also anti-capitalist and anti-militarist tendencies as well as neutral elements" (Diesing 1971, 322). The sciences, after all, comprise large and diffuse assortments of people – characterized by the same diversity of personality and work environment that is typical of any other occupation. The answer to the problem of class bias in the sciences lies in both the consensus-oriented ethic of group work that has come to typify the life of science generally and in the variety of the people and places of science. In short, there is much to suggest that any tendency among scientists to form a class of their own is relentlessly undermined by both the intellectual and institutional circumstances of the activity itself.

Cultural and gender biases are difficult to address in the same ways that class bias is. Criticism can be especially pointed in the case of the social sciences, wherein cultural and gender variables often feature prominently in the explanatory models that are the disciplines' basic product. To some extent, "the social sciences have transcended the ethnocentric predicament by their extensive traditions of cross-cultural research, though sensitivity is still inadequately diffused" (Diesing 1971, 323). That this amount of progress has been made, however, clearly suggests that the ultimate solution to the problem is for these research traditions to strive for higher levels of rigorous and cross-cultural research, not to surrender to (much less embrace) subjectivity. The answer to the challenge of impartiality is not to deny that values are part of our lives – both as human beings and as scientists – but "to face those valuations and to introduce them as explicitly stated, specific, and sufficiently concretized value premises" (Kaplan 1964, 387) so that they can be subjected to the same critical analysis that all of the other premises of our various explanatory models must undergo. It is this form of objectivity (understood as impartiality) that is the foundation of whatever political efficacy science can legitimately enjoy. In its absence, the accusations of bias directed at science by climate change deniers, anti-vaccination polemicists, and other purveyors of irrationality can be met only with technocratic indifference, abstract theories, or inflexible ideologies – rather than the humane but tenacious form of reasoning required by the pursuit of knowledge in an uncertain and unpredictable world (Toulmin 2001).

3.2.4 Of Activists

Few policy arenas demonstrate the promise and peril of environmental activism as clearly as the regulation of food. The growing voice of civil society – together with changing legal and institutional frameworks, increased market concentration and buying power as well as their integration with financial markets – has provided the incentive for development of private standards in the global food system aimed squarely at satisfying the demands of consumers and food safety activists. Both economic and institutional incentives have driven major Organisation for Economic Co-operation and Development (OECD) food retailers to develop private voluntary standards that have played a growing role in shaping the global agri-food system. Research based on interviews with quality and safety directors of major OECD retailers and a survey of retailers' actual buyer practices suggests that, whereas food safety and quality standards are seen as key to maintaining and improving reputation as well as against legal liabilities, additional standards such as labor, environmental, and animal welfare are also gaining ground as strategies for customer loyalty and market share (Fulponi 2006). Moreover, the grass-roots retailer movement in the harmonization of food safety standards can be seen as an initial step toward a global approach to managing the food system, with harmonization of other food-related standards likely in the future. Given the buying power of an activist organized consumer community, these developments can be viewed as a way of governing the food system that will be increasingly important for both OECD and non-OECD food and agricultural sector evolution in the coming years (Fulponi 2006).

Notice, however, that ordinary citizens play a constrained role in this arena. As either consumers or activists (who serve as "consumers" of political messaging rather than of agricultural commodities), citizens are actors in the agri-food system and they may be agents of economic activity (expressing their own personal agency), but they are not agents of governance because they do not act authoritatively. Rising no higher in the governance structure than membership in voluntary associations places a severe upper limit on their influence. As political theorists have long recognized, "association is always a risk in liberal society. The boundaries of the group are not policed; people come and go, or they just fade into the distance without ever quite acknowledging that they have left" (Walzer 2007, 106). As a consequence of their institutional indeterminacy, the associations of civil society find themselves in break-out rooms adjacent to the halls of power, rather than at the conference tables where decisions of governance are actually made. The dangers of this marginalization can be demonstrated if we explore the governance of the agri-food system in greater detail, especially in light of the increasing financialization of the global food system and the agency-damaging ways that it exacerbates existing imbalances of power and wealth (Clapp and Isakson 2018; Clapp 2019). Examples of problematic activism in agricultural policy abound.

Criteria defining "good agricultural practices" (GAP) were originally developed for on-farm production methods and resource use (Burrell 2011). For over a decade, GAP principles have been applied throughout the entire agri-food supply chain by organizations promoting voluntary private standard schemes. Although the stated aim of such schemes is to provide consumers with guarantees of food safety and quality, they are strongly driven by the desire to reduce transaction costs within the chain and to limit the legal liability of chain operators and retailers in the wake of food safety lapses. This tendency raises a number of troubling issues: Are private standard schemes compatible with the polluter pays principle, is the standard-setting process itself legitimate, do private standards result in distorted public legislation, and to what extent do private standards erect barriers to market entry and impede competition? The potential for the extension of voluntary private standard schemes to global food chains raises further questions about their compatibility with sustainable development goals and with WTO rules regarding import restrictions based on production methods. Ultimately, these challenges include the operational coexistence of mandatory public standards and voluntary private standards in the agri-food arena and how they might be better harmonized within national and international legal frameworks (Burrell 2011).

Beyond these general and systemic difficulties, GAP standards raise questions of a more focused nature. The increasing prevalence of private standards governing food safety, food quality, and environmental and social impacts of agri-food systems has raised concerns about the effects on developing countries, as well as the governance of agri-food value chains more broadly. These debates have often been confounded by a failure to recognize the diversity of private standards in terms of their institutional form, who develops and adopts these standards, and why. In particular, there is a need to appreciate the close interrelationships between public regulations and private standards and the continuing ways in which private standards evolve (Henson and Humphrey 2010). For example, a series of focus groups with smallholders, together with semi-structured interviews and workshops held with actors at the national and international scales, was used to examine private standards initiatives operating in Kenyan export horticulture (Tallontire, Opondo, and Nelson 2014). This analysis suggests that, despite public announcements that these initiatives promote the voice of the farmer, the direct participation of farmers is largely absent from these policy spaces. This is a result of the ways that invitations to the spaces for participation are constructed, what are deemed to be appropriate subjects for discussion in private standards initiatives, and the practical challenges associated with the organization of farmers across spatial scales. The spaces for participation are located largely at the international and national scales with few connections to the local scale. Thus the use of private standards initiatives in agri-food value chains raises questions of democratic governance and accountability relating to the voice and agency of those whom the standards are designed to benefit – or whom they most affect (Tallontire, Opondo, and Nelson 2014).

These "agency" failures in private standard-setting manifest themselves in a variety of concrete ways (VanDeveer 2015). For example, the increased global trade in agricultural commodities that private standards initiatives are intended to promote has boosted fresh water consumption. The export of this "virtual water," embedded in products sold abroad, has increasingly affected local communities and ecosystems, especially in arid regions. Recent initiatives to certify agricultural production are showing a rapidly growing interest in considering water issues within schemes of quality assurance, sustainable production, and fair trade, and how agricultural production affects local water user communities. But these second-generation private standards generally reinforce the political and market power of private sector agro-food chains in local water management, to the detriment of local water user communities and national governments (Vos and Boelens 2014). Moreover, private standards initiatives have an impact on the sourcing behavior of export companies. Panel data for 1993–2011 from eighty-seven Peruvian asparagus export companies suggests that certification to private standards increases vertical integration and reduces sourcing from external producers, especially from small-scale producers. Perversely, especially high-level production standards lead to even stronger vertical integration (Schuster and Maertens 2013). Private regulation of ethical and environmental standards can also have serious implications for value chain structures and institutions in the smallholder agricultural systems. Global private regulation is driving structural changes in modes of farmer organization and trader–farmer relationships and is, for example, resulting in the increased upstream penetration of multinational trading companies into coffee-producing areas across Indonesia. An unintended consequence of these changes in the future may be to increase transaction costs along the value chain and to exert an overall downward pressure on farm prices (Neilson 2008). Private standards initiatives, therefore, stand accused of empowering the billionaires and bureaucrats (aided and abetted by standard-mongering academics) at the expense of activists who are increasingly margin-alized as regulation is privatized. These same risks repeat themselves across other policy domains that are subject to influences of commodification (Zelli, Nielsen, and Dubber 2019). But, does it necessarily have to be this way?

3.3 Agency beyond the Anthropocene: From the Legal and Political to the Moral

Obviously, the involvement of private actors in global politics is not a new phenomenon. But the creation of cooperative arrangements in the form of organizations that facilitate private regulation – thus complementing traditional ways of political influence – is relatively novel (Hickmann 2017a, b). An overview of private rule-setting organizations that have emerged in the global governance of sustainability suggests that, despite performing seemingly similar roles and functions, these organizations differ widely both in terms of outputs they produce and rules of participation and decision-making. In particular, a comparison of five private rule-setting organizations that emerged in the global governance of fisheries sustainability – the Marine Stewardship Council, Friend of the Sea, the Aquaculture Stewardship Council, the Global Aquaculture Alliance, and GlobalGAP – suggests that there is no correlation between democratic legitimacy and effectiveness (Kalfagianni and Pattberg 2013). Although a broadly inclusive and uncoerced rule-setting process tends to produce a more stringent set of proposed standards, these potentially more effective regimes are the least likely to be taken up and authoritatively implemented. So, addressing the shortfalls of private regulation, both in terms of democratic provenance and ecological effectiveness, is not simply a matter of more inclusiveness.

The conceptual framework of private governance has until recently been employed predominantly with reference to the OECD world. Despite this restricted view, a growing number of processes, organizations, and institutions are beginning to affect developing countries (Hickmann et al. 2017). New institutional settings open up avenues of influence for actors from the global South. This compels asking, what influences does private governance have on developing countries, their societies, and their economies (Kalfagianni 2013)? What influence do developing country actors have in and through private governance arrangements? Research on private governance in the global forest arena suggests that, while Southern actors have not benefited so much economically from private certification schemes, they have been partially empowered through cognitive and integrative processes of governance (Pattberg 2006). The development of politically meaningful cognitive resources has long been recognized as a result of participation in inclusive governance processes. Indeed, the ability of technical experts to facilitate this outcome is arguably one of the better justifications for the special role in governance processes enjoyed by academics (Baber and Bartlett 2005, 2009a). The integrative advantages of inclusion do not always accrue naturally and inevitably, although integrative options arise from other features of private governance.

An analysis of the organization of the fair trade flower industry, which examined the integration of Ecuadorian enterprises into these networks and the power of certification to address key environmental and social concerns on participating estates (Reynolds 2012), suggests that certain features of private governance have the potential to empower the previously powerless. This research locates fair trade within the field of new institutions that establish and enforce production criteria in international markets. Firm owners and managers support fair

3.3 Agency beyond the Anthropocene: From the Legal and Political to the Moral 65

trade's environmental and social goals, but these commitments are delimited by mainstream market expectations related to production efficiency and product quality. In environmental arenas, certification helps ensure that conditions exceed legal mandates and industry norms. In social arenas, certification helps ensure that labor standards exceed legal and industry expectations and funds important programs benefiting workers and their families. Most significantly, where unions are absent, fair trade's greatest impact may be in the establishment of workers' committees that can build collective capacity. Although these new labor organizations face numerous challenges, they have the potential to strengthen the social regulation of global standards networks, making firms accountable to their workers as well as to nongovernmental organizations, retailers, and consumers (Reynolds 2012). So there is at least the potential for private standards initiatives to redress some of this historical imbalance between capital and labor – even in the developing world. And this is not the end of the integrative potential of private standards initiatives.

A persistent question posed by private governance is, under what conditions can small suppliers and small-firm-dominated industries comply with stringent standards without compromising their trade competitiveness? This question is at the heart of an ongoing debate about the emergence of environmental standards as a variable in global trade and market access. There are few documented cases of success, and considerable scholarly skepticism remains about the ability of small supplier firms to comply with stringent environmental regulations. But research on the Indian leather industry`s relatively effective compliance with two German bans on Azo dyes and PCPs suggests that the supposed trade-off between environmental compliance and export competitiveness is not inevitable (Tewari and Pillai 2005). Critical to India's compliance with the PCP and Azo dye ban was not merely private governance mediated by lead firms and global buyers but also the institutionalization of compliance by the Indian state, which became deeply involved in diffusing the new standards in ways that generated – and sustained – a process of negotiated collective action and broad-based environmental compliance by the small-firm-dominated sector. This kind of government-led capacity building, allied with policies designed to protect nascent employing organizations created in the process of private standards development and implementation, provides the outline of a strong – and strongly progressive – role for bureaucrats in ensuring that the advantages of private governance are not bought at the expense of further disempowerment of those who are already politically disadvantaged. It suggests that empowerment of the previously disempowered might be purchased as a package deal – with the assent of bureaucrats offered as a tradeoff for the refocusing of academic research and the political forbearance of financial interests. This, however, suggests a further refinement of the understanding of agency in

3.3.1 Moral Agency

To reiterate: Legal agency can be likened to a form of servitude, in which the agent is a mere tool of the principal. Political agency, on the other hand, is understood to be a constituent element of the modern sense of self. Agents are individuals who enjoy the autonomy and capacity to act out the determinations of their own wills, to accept responsibility for those actions, and to judge the agency of others. These legal and political forms of agency, however, involve something of a dilemma – at least in one of their possible manifestations. One of the distinctive advantages of legal agency is that it empowers us to form corporate entities, the essence of which is that they protect their principals from liability for their collective actions. This, of course, turns the ancient tradition of principal liability on its head. It also suggests a conceptual conflict when applied to collective political action. Voluntary associations, both those that are overtly political and those only incidentally so, are formed by individuals seeking to act out their own agency. Part of that acting out is the acceptance of responsibility, but the corporate form of voluntary associations blunts that responsibility. These voluntary associations are (or can be) important agents of social inclusion. "Alongside their stated purpose . . . the associations of civil society provide recognition, empowerment, training, and even employment." They serve to open and to decentralize the spheres within which determinations of social justice are made, multiplying their "settings and agents" and "generating greater diversity in the interpretation of distributive criteria" (Walzer 2007, 90).

The responsibility for the acts of these corporate agents rarely runs to their original principals (the association members). It runs, instead, to the (emerged) principal who leads the association on behalf of its (submerged) members. When this inversion of agency occurs, it ultimately "makes little difference whether there is one principal and one agent, or one principal on the top of a tall bureaucratic pyramid. The preferences of the apex trickle down to the base" (Caplan 2007, 172). This is simply a particular manifestation of the broader problem of "agency costs" – wherein a (usually collective) principal lacks the capacity to dissuade its agents from substituting their own will for those of the principal (Posner 2008, 129). Government bureaucracies "minimize agency costs by laying down defined rules for bureaucrats to follow" (131) and business corporations rely on market signals to "determine the value" of their employees' actions and hold them accountable (130). Other voluntary associations enjoy neither of these options. They are not creatures of the market (other than the inchoate "marketplace" of ideas), and neither their members nor their employees are likely to support detailed rules of administrative oversight. For an answer to the quandary of how to hold voluntary associations (their principals and agents) responsible, we must add a third conception of agency – moral agency.

The literature on moral agency is far too extensive to review here. However, some key features of moral agency offer insight into the problem at hand – the empowerment of citizens as members of voluntary organizations and as agents of governance. An understanding of "citizenship as moral agency is one of the key sources of democratic idealism" (Walzer 2007, 117). Indeed, the question of "how it is best for me to act here and now in these particular circumstances" (MacIntyre 2006, 28) could be taken as the concrete and immediate quandary that gives rise to political theorizing generally. The construction of milieus that sustain systematic dialogue and critical scrutiny of moral judgments allows moral agents "to understand themselves as accountable to others." The challenge to the political theorist, therefore, is how to avoid "types of social structure that preclude the existence of such milieus, so that the very possibility of moral agency might be threatened" (196). This is essential if we are to identify the key prerequisites of moral agency. There is no better place to begin than with the requirement that a moral agent be possessed of knowledge.

3.3.2 Knowledge and Agency

Clearly, one social situation that undermines moral agency is ignorance. In order to achieve the "secure semantic references" that are critical to interpersonal communication (and, thus, to moral agency), it is essential that humans "as agents" be in contact with "the objects of everyday life and that they put themselves in contact with them repeatedly" (Habermas 2001, 17). For this reason, it is vitally important that new levels of policy-relevant research be achieved by the disciplines that contribute to knowledge of the environmental problematique (Setiadi and Lo 2019). Beyond this general and empirically based linguistic knowledge, moral agency requires that the individual possess an account of him or herself as an element within a causally related world. In modern, Western societies, much of this knowledge is (ideally) the product of the "scientific community," wherein an intellectual and ethical commitment to the ideal of "falsification" means that both error and deception are rooted out (MacIntyre 2006, 198). This does not mean, however, that moral agents must be scientists. An agent may be "guided by superstitious beliefs, be totally unreflective about his commitments, have conflicting desires and inconsistent beliefs, or live according to traditional roles simply because he has been brought up to. All these traits are consistent with being an agent – one who sees his actions as following from his own deliberations" (Gaus 2011, 338–339).

An agent who is thus burdened may be an ineffective one. His mistaken and unexamined beliefs may make him a failure if we assume (with many economists) that an agent is "a sort of punctate, Cartesian locus of well-being" (Dennett 2003, 180). But moral agency is far more than an exercise in need fulfillment. An agent is "aware of himself as a causal force" able to perform meaningful actions (Gaus 2011, 341), but a moral agent is aware that "there are certain kinds of actions that ought never to be performed" (MacIntyre 2006, 28). The ability to engage in "the efficient employment of appropriate means" is "far from sufficient for defining the status of the person deemed worthy of protection from the moral point of view" (Habermas 1993, 66). The capacity for moral agency is created socially – its powers can only be exercised by "those who are able to justify rational confidence in their judgments about the goodness or badness of human beings and this ability requires participation in social relationships and types of activities in which one's reflective judgments emerge from systematic dialogue with others and are subject to critical scrutiny by others" (MacIntyre 2006, 196). And moral agency is not merely social. It is also dialogic.

Moral agency is, to an important degree, about narratives. It requires that we engage in conversations that take "the subjectivity of respondents seriously" and that everyone have "the opportunity to talk about and think through their positions in terms of language they understand" (Dryzek 1990, 181). It recognizes that social meanings are "constructed, accepted, and revised for reasons, and that we have to engage those reasons," and that we do best (both morally and politically) when we try to find out what people "find valuable or satisfying" about their particular way of life (Walzer 2007, 56). In most social circumstances, the "established norms and values" within which we will judge and be judged as moral agents will be "to some large degree our own norms and values, the norms and values by which we have hitherto been guided" (MacIntyre 2006, 194). Moral agency has little to do with simple rule-following. Our narratives are far more compelling, and persuasive, if they involve a struggle with ambiguity. The idea that someone who "has been tested by serious dilemmas" of practical reasoning and who has "wrestled with temptations and quandaries" is more likely to be "a more responsible moral agent" is ubiquitous in popular culture – if not in moral philosophy (Dennett 2003, 125). Moral agency requires that people "learn not only how to occupy some determinant set of roles within their social order, but also how to think of their goods and of their character independently of those roles." Moral agents will unavoidably be inhabitants of at least two "moral systems" that are in tension with one another – the system of the "established order" and another that has developed within those social milieus in which that order has been put into question (MacIntyre 2006, 193). The normative structure of moral agency is, in this way, indeterminate. Although knowledge providers play various roles (Spruijt et al. 2016), none can resolve this

3.3 Agency beyond the Anthropocene: From the Legal and Political to the Moral 69

indeterminacy. Its principles must be worked out by agents themselves over time "so as to protect human agents and set them free for their creative (reiterative) tasks" (Walzer 2007, 192). A second vital prerequisite of moral agency is, therefore, autonomy.

3.3.3 Autonomy and Agency

That "the powers of moral agency can only be exercised by those who understand themselves as moral agents" (MacIntyre 2006, 195) determines the knowledge base of moral agency. This clearly involves knowing how their actions relate to their intentions as well as to events in the material world. In the absence of this understanding, those most negatively impacted by environmental change often show no more concern about that risk than others and, in fact, are sometimes less likely to perceive the benefit of measures to reduce or eliminate those risks (Ambrey et al. 2016).

Clearly, understanding themselves as agents requires that people have a particular kind of social knowledge, an ability to understand themselves as involved with and "accountable to others" (MacIntyre 2006, 196). On the other hand, moral agency also requires that people "understand their moral identity as to some degree distinct from and independent of their social roles" (195). This independence is the first building block of individual autonomy. While it is certainly true that not all of us place our status as autonomous agents at the core of our identities, it is still the case that "a conception of ourselves as agents is a fundamental aspect of our self-understanding and that no other conception is as widely shared and as deeply embedded in who we are" (Gaus 2011, 340–341). Freedom of thought and expression is certainly a part of this sense of autonomy. It will be a demand of moral agents "to deliberate freely and not to be coerced or conditioned in ways such that their deliberations and conclusions are determined by others." This freedom of discourse prohibits "not simply attempts to command belief" but also indirect efforts to induce belief "by constraining and controlling discourse" (353).

The autonomy requirements of moral agency are not limited to freedom of discourse and conscience. Moral agency requires a certain integrity and constancy – a refusal to be "one kind of person in one social context, while quite another in other contexts" (MacIntyre 2006, 192). This does not require a one-dimensional existence, eschewing the multiplicity of social roles that characterizes complex societies. Human beings "employ roles not as an alternative to agency but as a way to express and manage our presentation to others" of our selves (Gaus 2011, 337). Autonomous moral agency merely requires that people hold themselves to the same concept of the good "through extended periods of time, not allowing the requirements of social contexts to distract them from their commitments" (MacIntyre 2006, 192–193). This constancy across time and contexts, especially in the complex societies of today, requires an increasingly robust concept of autonomy. To protect human agency today "necessarily requires us to protect all individuals' right to choose the life they see fit to lead" (Ignatieff 2001, 57). Nothing less than a bundle of rights sufficient to secure personal self-determination will suffice, and that rights bundle derives "from our ideas about personality and moral agency, without reference to political processes and social circumstances" (Walzer 2007, 232).

The idea of human rights as "essentially designed to validate and enhance human agency" depends significantly "upon a culturally relative idea of human dignity and worth." But if you want to sustain any belief at all in human rights, some notion of "intrinsic human dignity" is necessary (Ignatieff 2001, 164). The potential for conflict over this notion is clear enough. For better or worse, the "nation" has become the chief representation of particularity among humans. When particularity finds expression in large enough groups, it often "makes for nastiness: groups like the nation, as soon as they are politically organized, eagerly take up the business of self-aggrandizement, seizing, dominating, destroying rival groups" (Walzer 2007, 202). Nevertheless, the universal commitments implied by human rights can be "compatible with a wide variety of ways of living" – but only if the universalism implied is "self-consciously minimalist" (Ignatieff 2001, 56). The key element of this compatibility is a particular kind of mutual recognition. Only when people encounter each other "in the context of an intersubjectively shared lifeworld with the goal of coming to a shared understanding about something can – and must – they mutually recognize each other as persons capable of taking responsibility for their actions" (Habermas 1993, 66). In the absence of this recognition, the sense of urgency, which is a primary element in effective communicative action, is difficult to achieve in even otherwise promising circumstances (Mees, Tijhus, and Dieperink 2018).

Under those circumstances of joint problem-solving, people "impute to each other the capacity to orient themselves to validity claims in their actions" (66). This focus on the facts of cases, rather than competing beliefs of groups, has meant that the argument for human rights "has gone global by going local, that is, by sustaining local demands by ordinary people for some exercise of free agency" (Ignatieff 2001, 169). This does not, of course, prove that the idea of dignity as agency is genuinely universal. It does, however, suggest two things. Even this thin universalism of rights recognizes that the creations of human agency are "greatly diverse and always particular, but there is something singular and universal about their creativity, some brute fact of agency" captured by the claim that all human agents have been created in the same image (Walzer 2007, 192). It also takes account of the fact that "rights are only enforceable within political communities" where they have been collectively recognized (232) and that the process by which they come to be recognized is a political one that requires a reasonably stable political arena if the rights are to become stable (Baber and Bartlett 2020). For this prerequisite of moral agency to be satisfied, autonomy must be supported by capability.

3.3.4 Capability and Agency

Rights may derive from our ideas about moral agency, but "enforcement of rights is another matter." If, as moral agents, we have rights, then we must also have "the right to have effective rights" (Walzer 2007, 232, 255). The path from passive and minimal to active and extensive rights can be seen replicated in a variety of areas. Freedom of conscience, for example, would strike most as absolutely fundamental to agency – to the right to be free in one's own thoughts. Freedom of conscience is "a core liberal right as it sums up the main grounds of free agency, uniting free deliberation and free action." It thus occupies "a basic place in the order of justification for agents" (Gaus 2011, 354). Indeed, the Universal Declaration of Human Rights (disparaged though it may be) can be regarded as an effort "to restore *agency*, to give individuals the civic courage to stand up when the state ordered them to do wrong" (Ignatieff 2001, 5, emphasis in the original). This invocation of universalism represents the characterization of "the rights of agency, including rights against being harmed," as both a common basic protection and as an assertion of (at least moral) jurisdiction (Gaus 2011, 385). But the demands of agency go beyond the freedom of conscience and expression. We are not able to engage in political life as moral agents "unless we sense that what we can do makes a difference, and an adequate political process must strive, against formidable obstacles, to preserve that potential power for each citizen" (Dworkin 2000, 202). The provision of that capability has at least three distinct but related dimensions, touching on issues of rights, justice, and virtue.

Human nature and human capabilities (or, capacities) are both "the results of human choices and actions" (Gould 1988, 19). If we subscribe to the view that humans enjoy an equal moral agency, then we must commit ourselves to choices and actions supporting the equality of rights that "have their origin" in that moral equality (68). Indeed, the recognition of human beings as free agents is the "moral principle from which rights are derived" (64). The political implication of this equality of agency is, of course, democracy. As central as democracy is to equal moral agency, however, its "political ontology" is problematic insofar as it holds individuals and their equal agency to be primary – which encourages a preoccupation with "abstract individualized self-interest" at the expense of sociality (97). This tendency is distinctly unhelpful because sociality is both a byproduct of agency and a result of the fact that human beings are "social from the start." Sociality is intrinsic to humans because "social relations are an essential mode of their individual self-development" and because humans "characteristically engage in common activities oriented to common and not merely individual ends" (71). The freedom of moral agents to realize their purposes requires not only that these social relations be free of domination but also that they "provide access to the positive conditions of agency" (110).

In addition to freedom, the other principal values of social ethics – equality, reciprocity, and democracy – can be seen "to have an ontological basis in the nature of human activity itself" (Gould 1988, 131). As equal moral agents, people "choose and can also transform many of their relations, either individually or jointly with others" (Gould 2004, 33). Indeed, to recognize others as human is to acknowledge their agency (either individually or jointly) and, correlatively, to "recognize that this capacity remains abstract and empty unless it is exercised in concrete cases; and furthermore, that this exercise requires conditions, both material and social, if it is to be realized as self-transforming activity" (34). From an extended analysis of human rights, we can therefore arrive at a conception of human agency as a value that goes beyond autonomy to "emphasize the concrete transformations of material and social conditions in varying historical contexts" as well as "equal access to these conditions for the emergence and self-development of people's goals and capacities over time" (72).

This emphasis on the conditions of people's development and their capacities to realize their projects over their lifetimes also leads naturally into a discussion of other views within the positive freedom tradition. For Sen (1992), the free moral agent is someone with the ability to promote the goals he or she finds reason to promote – which "can *inter alia* include goals other than the advancement of his or her own well-being" (Sen 2009, 287). Sen thus defines an agent as someone who acts and brings about change, whose achievements can and should be evaluated in terms of his or her own values and goals. This obviously differs from the legal use of the term we have described, which is also prevalent in economics and game theory (Sen 2001). This difference is crucial to understanding Sen's theory of justice, which does not view capabilities as instrumental to the achievement of well-being (or any other goal for that matter). Rather, capability is linked, centrally and inextricably, with the fundamental concept of freedom.

An agent is morally free only if he or she "has the power to make a difference that he or she can see will reduce injustice in the world." This freedom of agency is part of "an effective power that a person has, and it would be a mistake to see capability, linked with these ideas of freedom, only as a notion of human advantage: it is also a central concern in understanding our obligations"

3.3 Agency beyond the Anthropocene: From the Legal and Political to the Moral 73

(Sen 2009, 271). Moreover, this view of capability as an essential element of agency freedom "shifts the focus away from seeing a person as just a vehicle of well-being, ignoring the importance of a person's own values and priorities" (288). Crucially, the capabilities approach puts a justice argument at the center of the argument for sustainable development. Human development can be seen as fundamentally "an empowering process, and this power can be used to preserve and enrich the environment" rather than to decimate it. To reap this benefit, however, we must overcome the temptation to "think of the environment exclusively in terms of conserving pre-existing natural conditions, since the environment can also include the results of human creations" (249). As an example, water purification projects are exercises of agency that both contribute to human development through the elimination of disease and contribute to the enhancement of environmental quality. Although considerations of justice do not (as Sen recognizes) act as political trump cards, they can have significant impact when allied with prudential arguments and invocations of mutual obligation.

Nussbaum (2000) has compiled an extensive list of what she takes to be capabilities that are essential to the realization of human agency. As she recognizes, this list of capabilities corresponds closely to one that might be compiled of capacity deprivations that are central to Sophoclean and Aristotelian tragic predicaments (Nussbaum 2001). The particulars of the list (as careful and compelling as it is) are less important than what uses might be made of it. Nussbaum's capabilities are neither the expression of a set of basic rights (Gould) nor constituent elements of the ideas of freedom and justice (Sen). They are, rather, signposts on the road of a life worth living – a life, in other words, that acquits the dignity of each person's humanity. They show us the normative contours of a society in which "citizens would be informed from the beginning of life that there are certain entitlements that are particularly central, and deprivation of which is particularly tragic" (Nussbaum 2001, 418). Nothing less is implied than a substantive foundation for the human good. Moreover, there is a shared agenda. Much as there is an element of natural necessity involved in many of these tragedies (ill health and so forth), instead of resigning ourselves to tragic necessity, our normative commitment to the centrality of these capacities requires us "to react by asking what we can do so that such tragedies are less likely to happen" (419).

As with all substantive theories of the good, Nussbaum's dignity-oriented capabilities approach is subject to questions regarding the precise scope of the obligations it imposes as well as the degree of its universality. She is perfectly well aware that people will demand to know "what price dignity" and how universal the concept of dignity really is. The "price" of her capabilities approach is difficult to quantify because it does not understand capabilities as "instrumental to a life with human dignity: they are understood, instead, as ways of realizing a life with human

74   *Empowered Democratic Agency in the Anthropocene*

dignity, in different areas of life with which human beings typically engage" (Nussbaum 2006, 161). Therefore, these capabilities are neither fungible quantities that can be aggregated and traded off nor are they likely to be equally "expensive" in different areas of engagement. Actual equality, or even the Rawlsian difference principle, are plausible standards, but Nussbaum not unreasonably declines to go much beyond specifying an "ample minimum" for all the capacities (178), suggesting that we defer the process of developing further specifications pending the "yet unheard-of case" in which a society has fulfilled this relatively modest set of entitlements (179). Moreover, this "ample minimum" formulation of the capabilities approach grounds a modest but hopeful response to the question of universality. If the good, understood as a life of dignity, requires no more than this, then a combination of enlightened self-interest, the gradual but inexorable spread of self-governance, and increasingly "widespread" and "deeply rooted" acceptance of the idea of human rights makes it impossible to say of any nation that it cannot achieve its own "consensus" on this matter over time (204). This will, no doubt, be frustrating to those who seek a "covering law" answer to the problem of determining the content of the good. It is more likely to seem satisfactory to those who subscribe to the view that answering questions of this sort can only be a "reiterative" process, rather than a process of deductive reasoning to a determinate outcome (Walzer 2007).

3.4 Anthropogenic Agency: Nature in the Flesh

This lengthy discussion of capability as an element of moral agency was necessary to make an affirmative case that agency is not merely a matter of knowledge (beginning with self-knowledge) or autonomy (as the absence of restraint or coercion) or both. If a unit of agency is a "person or group or entity treated as the author of and held responsible" (Dworkin 2000, 224), we must attribute to that agent more than knowledge and autonomy. For an agent to be held responsible, the capability of effective action must exist. Moral agency involves making space for all to engage in practical reasoning (Lebel et al. 2019) in a form of *mindmade* politics (Milkoreit 2017). To be a moral agent is to have "the potentiality for living and acting in a state of tension or, if need be, conflict between two moral points of view." These points of view are never "simply or mainly" at the level of general or abstract theory. The choices confronting moral agents always involve a tension or conflict "between socially embodied points of view, between modes of practice" (MacIntyre 2006, 193). Effective practice presumes capability.

    A second reason that the issue of capability has played a crucial role in this discussion is that it offers a potential response to a puzzle regarding agency in the specific context of environmental governance. It has long been an ambition of

3.4 Anthropogenic Agency: Nature in the Flesh

environmentalism to achieve the "recognition of agency in nature." This would consist of a situation in which humans "listen to signals emanating from the natural world with the same sort of respect we accord communication emanating from human subjects, and as requiring equally careful interpretation" (Dryzek 2000, 149). This is, of course, a situation easier to describe than to achieve. For instance, a large number of those who work the land pursue self-initiated conservation activities without necessarily thinking of them as such (Runhaar, Polman, and Dijkshoorn-Dekker 2018). But trying to promote a higher level of environmental self-awareness in those circumstances can often have counterproductive results (Runhaar et al. 2019). This is due, at least in part, to the fact that humans are reluctant to engage with nature as something toward which they bear responsibilities (Fremaux and Barry 2019). For instance, "it seems to be a feature of our moral thinking that we are, or believe we are, more clearly obligated to deal with human wickedness or indifference than with natural disasters" (Walzer 2007, 257). This is likely due, at least in part, to the psychological fact that "people are naïve dualists about agency – they don't think physical things can have the properties required for agency and responsibility" (Roskies 2014, 118). But "thinking" is not the only thing that humans do when it comes to the agency of nature. We further confound our *thoughts* about the dualism between nature and agency with forms of *language* that conflate the two.

Human beings have a "general metaphor" in which the phenomena of nature are conceptualized as if they were agents (Lakoff and Johnson 1999, 212). When we say that the wind *blew* a door open, or that the waves *smashed* the pier, or that gravity pulled Icarus down to earth, we are equating natural events to the events *caused* by humans, tracing their causes back to the *agent* responsible. This metaphorical agency of nature leads us to "a notion of natural causes as forces" that are essential qualities of the natural world – essences that are themselves causes. It is these essences that grounded any ancient religious beliefs. These "essences" had specific identities that were the inhabitants of a polytheistic realm, with each natural phenomenon the responsibility of its own particular deity (225). The ability to hold someone responsible for the often-dire consequences *caused* by nature must have been (and may still be) a source of consolation for many whose life tragedies lack obvious human causes. But the universality of the capabilities element of moral agency offers an alternative consolation – the commitment of one's fellow human beings to prevent these tragedies where possible and to mitigate those that are unavoidable (Fremaux and Barry 2019). This commitment to accept responsibility for the nonhuman "actions" of nature is, of course, predicated on the "ample minimum" of capabilities that we have discussed and its ubiquity throughout the human part of nature. Indeed, there is historical evidence to suggest that this sort of commitment to others is a "moral consequence" of economic sufficiency (Friedman 2005). Here we have the opportunity to close the circle of human agency in the Anthropocene. We must resist the well-documented temptation to limit the agency of those outside of the core governance institutions and processes to a "support" role (Thaler and Seebauer 2019). Doing so both degrades the quality of decision-making and marginalizes those whose agency should be enhanced by self-governance.

If, indeed, there is no corner of the natural world that is beyond human influence, then no corner of the world lies beyond the human responsibility implied by our moral agency (Fremaux and Barry 2019). If moral agency requires that an ample minimum of capabilities across a wide range of human engagements with the world is (for reasons of political right, simple justice, or normative obligation) a fundamental entitlement, then the answer to the puzzle of how the agency of nature is to be grounded becomes clear. If no element of nature (anywhere) lies outside the responsibility of some humans, and if humans are uniformly *empowered* (with adequate knowledge, autonomy, and capability) to fulfill the requirements of *their* moral agency, then the agency of nature is borne (and born) in the flesh of humanity.

4

Embedded Governance Architecture in the Anthropocene

The Structure of Institutionalized Ecological Rationality

Piazza della Rotonda, in the heart of Rome, was laid out and paved in the mid-fifteenth century at the behest of Pope Eugenius IV (1431–1439), who had tired of hearing about the slovenly accretion of hovels that had grown up there since ancient times. Like most of Italy's piazze, della Rotonda is more than the intersection of two streets. No fewer than seven throughfares disgorge pedestrian traffic into its expanse, which one can only fully appreciate after emerging from the dense phalanx of four- and five-story buildings that enclose it. Most piazze present visitors with the challenge, once having entered them, of finding their way out again. On entering the typical piazza, newcomers are usually well advised to orient themselves well to their point of entry before exploring the festival of restaurants, shops, and gelaterias that make these shared living rooms so special. But Piazza della Rotonda offers the visitor its own unique landmark as an aid to navigation – the Pantheon.

The Pantheon is, in a word, remarkable. While precise dates for the building are difficult to come by, we know that it was commissioned by Marcus Agrippa during the reign of Augustus (27 BC–14 AD) and rebuilt in about 126AD by the emperor Hadrian (who, in an act of modesty uncommon for emperors of his time, declined to replace his predecessor's name with his own). The building is entered through a chunky portico, constructed of 12-meter granite columns supporting a pediment that was originally decorated with a relief sculpture, of which nothing remains but holes marking the location of clamps that held it (the arrangement of which suggests that its design was likely an eagle within a wreath, probably of gilded bronze).

Passing through huge bronze doors (which were replaced in the fifteenth century) the visitor discovers a rotunda in the form of a perfect hemisphere, 43.75 meters in both diameter and height. At ground level, all is the finest and most richly colored Roman marble. This level of the rotunda is adorned with altars, niches, artwork, and tombs that attest to the building's long and graceful transition – from pagan temple to Christian church, to burial site, to national symbol, and, finally, to world heritage treasure. In fact, this progression of human applications goes a long way toward explaining why this space still exists. Having never fallen into disuse, it has come down to us in far better condition than other ancient structures (such as the Coliseum) that were purpose-built for a narrower range of uses. Hovering above the level of its shifting human uses is an architectural marvel that is as it has been for two millennia – a glorious impossibility, made possible.

The interior surface of the rotunda's dome is far more subdued than its ground level, both in color and adornment. The softly monochromatic concrete surface features coffered panels arranged in five rows of twenty-eight panels each. The rotunda rises to an oculus, which measures precisely 20 percent of the dome's overall diameter, and which provides much of the light without which this luminous space would have entombed itself long before people decided to inter anyone here. These two design features (the oculus and coffered panels) combine to substantially reduce the overall weight of the dome. More important in this regard, however, is the fact that the concrete used in the dome's construction becomes progressively lighter as it ascends by incorporating increasing amounts of lightweight pumice as well as small pieces of pottery. The dome's weight is further reduced by its honeycomb construction, produced by incorporating hidden chambers into its structure.

Like all great pieces of architecture, the Pantheon is embedded in its cultural context – a structure based on principles that sustain human practices in a particular place. It is, of course, an aesthetic and engineering wonder. But it still exists today because it still means something to people in their lived experiences. Its *flexibility* and its *open texture* have allowed that meaning to both change and endure over time, as both the times and the people have changed, and to remain *embedded* in its cultural context. Therein lies a lesson for those who would craft policies (and institutions) that both protect the global environment and promote human security. In order to endure, such policies must have an architecture based on principles that are able to both create and maintain a rational relationship between human places and human practices. What are the criteria for environment and security policies that our architectural digression provides?

4.1 Governance Architecture in the Anthropocene: Principles, Practices, and Places

4.1.1 Flexibility

What does it mean for global environmental policy to be flexible and open textured? What does it mean for that architecture[1] to be embedded in a cultural context? Global environmental governance architecture stands today, as it long has, on the brink of major reform. Many discussions of reform continue to focus (directly or indirectly) on whether the United Nations Environment Programme (UNEP) should retain its institutional status as a subsidiary body of the UN General Assembly or be transformed into something else, such as a specialized agency – a World Environment Organization – of the UN. That choice of institutional form or any other, however, should not ultimately be made without reference to both the needs of global environmental governance and the factors impeding the effectiveness of the current governance architecture. Historical perspective on the question reveals the similarity between the current debate on institutional form, function, and financing of UNEP and the choices that the original designers of the current governance architecture made over forty years ago (Caldwell 1996). The fundamental global environmental problems and the functions of effective global environmental governance (though evolving in some ways) have remained generally unchanged. The largely political reasons for creating UNEP in its current form remain valid today. These longstanding concerns provide useful insight into the current debate. UNEP's shortcomings have little inherent connection to its institutional form but are, rather, linked to the underlying considerations that determined that form. These are issues that cannot be resolved, therefore, simply by a change in status. Addressing these issues directly will require deeper, yet probably easier to accomplish, reforms that focus on enabling UNEP to fulfill its intended role as an effective anchor institution for the global environmental governance architecture (Ivanova 2012). One effort in this direction has been to develop market-based policies that "govern" the global environment while avoiding the political overburden of global "government" by commodifying environmental goods and harms. The debate over climate change offers, perhaps, the leading example of this.

A growing body of academic literature is devoted to the evaluation of rival governance architectures and policy mechanisms designed to mitigate the risks associated with global climate change. The United Nations Framework Convention on Climate Change (UNFCCC) of 1992, the Kyoto Protocol to the UNFCCC of 1997, and the Paris Agreement of 2015 have all been subjected to intense analysis in this literature. Typically, these analyses of climate governance have focused on the environmental effectiveness, economic efficiency, and global distributive consequences of alternative climate architectures and policy mechanisms. A question often overlooked has been the performance of these climate architectures (and the policies they systematize) in terms of normative ideals whose meaning and significance cannot be fully captured in terms of goals and targets limited in their purpose to the improvement of environmental quality at the least economic cost and with minimal worsening of existing global inequalities.

These objectives can become disconnected from any shared agenda and detached from any coordinated and mutually binding mitigation efforts (Morseletto, Biermann, and Pattberg 2017). In the process, governance architecture loses its grounding in normative ideals of political legitimacy and procedural justice. One particularly important component of the emerging global climate architecture – greenhouse gas emissions trading – raises significant questions of legitimacy and justice. The well-understood cost and environmental quality benefits conferred by emissions trading schemes come at the price of imposing low levels of participation, accountability, and transparency on climate decision-making (damaging legitimacy) and producing results that, by ignoring the social complexity of carbon emissions, replicate the inequities of existing national and local economic structures (Page 2012). Not surprisingly, these issues have led to the collapse of discussion about the implementation of market- and nonmarket-based approaches under Article 6 of the Paris Agreement and to tensions regarding the inclusion of negotiating text safeguarding human rights in climate negotiations going forward (Cadman et al. 2019).

The institutional continuum of the architecture of climate governance has two ends. The focus on the UNFCCC and its progeny is the global end, but there is a growing awareness that climate change governance involves a wide range of both global and local issues related to questions of environmental security. Climate change governance poses seemingly insurmountable challenges for political, economic, social, and administrative systems at all levels of governance (Jamieson 2014; Newell and Bulkeley 2017; Edwards and Bulkeley 2018a) . Before condemning these existing systems for their inflexibility, we should remind ourselves that they evolved to handle other sorts of problems but are now being adapted to handle emerging issues of climate-warming mitigation and adaptation. Climate policy is commonly framed as a matter of international governance for which global policy strategies can be readily employed. Given the characteristics of the international system, practitioners view multilateral agreements negotiated by national governments without a viable institutional structure as the central mechanism for global environmental governance, leading some to advocate strengthening climate action through other better-established means such as preferential trade agreements (Morin and Jinnah 2018) and others to explore the governance issues associated with more speculative options for climate engineering (Jinnah 2018) and solar radiation management (Jinnah, Nicholson, and Flegal 2018). Climate-warming thus poses profound challenges to organizations of every type, requiring a wide variety of organizational responses. The drastic depth of cuts in emissions of greenhouse gasses proposed by many scientists, national government agencies, and nongovernmental organizations (NGOs) is likely to require radical shifts in sociopolitical structures, technological

4.1 Governance Architecture in the Anthropocene

and economic systems, organizational forms, and modes of organizing. As a result, climate change is more than just an environmental problem requiring technical and managerial solutions. It constitutes a political space in which a variety of organizations – subnational governments, state agencies, firms, industry associations, NGOs, and multilateral organizations – engage in contestation as well as collaboration over evolving regimes of good governance. There is, therefore, an urgent need to better comprehend the transformative impact of climate change on the human landscape and its policy architecture (Sarkar 2011; Matsumoto et al. 2017; Mah et al. 2018; Oberthür and Groen 2018; Patterson and Huitema 2019). To achieve this, we must overcome our habit of thinking globally.

After struggling for so long to promote global thinking, it might seem ironic to environmentalists that they might now be challenged to overcome their own success. At this time in our history "globalism" as a mode of thought, deriving from the practice of thinking globally (both literally and figuratively), not only informs major trends within governance and economics but also frames environmental issues – not least those related to global warming. Our efforts to counter (or adapt to) climate change may reveal a built-in contradiction between globalism and the interests of landscape as the diverse place of people, polity, and nature (Olwig 2011; Anderton and Setze 2018; Mees, Tijhus, and Dieperink 2018; Frantzeskaki et al. 2019). Overlooking the local dimensions of climate governance threatens to deprive us of many (most?) of our most potentially useful governance approaches (Hurlbert and Gupta 2019) as well as blind us to the connections between climate and other problems such as human rights and economic development – which are more complex and nuanced than is commonly imagined (Gupta and Arts 2018). For instance, the adoption of clean energy policies is becoming more common among localities, but is still far from universal. Policy innovation theory suggests that some shared internal characteristics should distinguish the localities that adopt those policies from others that do not. Based on a survey of US local government officials, and supplementary data from the US Census, Pitt and Bassett (2014) used multiple regression analysis to identify those distinguishing characteristics. They found that collaborative planning approaches (made possible by the absence of authoritative policy mandates) played a crucial role in helping localities build the local civic capacity necessary to adopt their innovative policies. These results are reinforced by other studies that have found that citizen participation and stakeholder participation in planning processes can help to foster the development of innovative local policies for sustainability and climate-warming adaptation (Kopela 2017; Hamilton and Lubell 2018). They also highlight the importance of having flexible and open-textured (here, nonauthoritative but supportive) policy structures at higher levels of governance.

In order to overcome the blind spots of global thinking, it is important for governance architects to remember a cardinal rule of architectural practice – form should follow function in this realm as in others. Different policy mixes are necessary in different geographical circumstances, and bottom-up reforms must be combined with policies based on more conventional institutional analysis (Hurlbert, Gupta, and Verrest 2019). By itself, organizational reform cannot achieve environmental protection, much less the broader goal of sustainable development (Young 2008; Young 2017). As an example, despite the substantial (and probably increasing) contribution of greenhouse gas (GHG) emissions from international shipping and the related adverse impacts on global climate change, GHG emissions from international shipping are not yet regulated by any legally binding, internationally accepted regulation aside from mandatory energy efficiency measures adopted by the International Maritime Organization (Hackman 2012; Kopela 2017; International Maritime Organization 2018). The governance architecture that is currently in place to regulate GHG emissions from international shipping is characterized by a high degree of institutional fragmentation within this architecture. It is generally understood that the degree and characteristics of fragmentation in the architecture of governance has a crucial impact on the effectiveness and performance of any governance system. But the current architecture of climate change governance in international shipping and the institutional interplay between its actors reveal an under-appreciated aspect of governance fragmentation.

International relations scholars increasingly address the phenomena of fragmentation by framing it with alternative concepts like regime complexes (Orsini, Oberthür, and Pożarowska 2014; Rabitz 2018) or polycentricity (Jordan et al. 2018). A considerable part of the existing debate remains focused on whether centralized or polycentric governance architecture is preferable (Dorsch and Flachsland 2017). Instead of continuing to pursue this debate, a more fruitful path might be to recognize that domains of global environmental governance – like climate change, biological diversity, renewable energy, and forestry – are already inherently fragmented when the policy architect takes them up (Zelli and Van Asselt 2013) and so will be the focus of continual efforts to achieve conceptual clarity and coherence (Dupont 2019). To continue the example, transportation-related GHG emissions are far from a unitary phenomenon. Commuters, farmers, shippers, first responders, relief workers, and virtually every other social and economic actor involved in the movement of goods or people are all contributors to the problem – regardless of the underlying social and economic reasons for the movement. The challenge lies not merely in the international, national, regional, and local occurrence of these activities. If the form of climate governance architecture is to follow its function, then it must be flexible enough to

4.1.2 Open Texture

An example of open-textured global governance policy is provided by the evolving architecture on reducing emissions from deforestation and forest degradation in developing countries commonly referred to as REDD+. As a mechanism supported by the United Nations Collaborative Programme on Reducing Emissions from Deforestation and Forest Degradation in Developing Countries, REDD+ is a vehicle for financially rewarding developing countries for their verified efforts to reduce emissions and enhance removals of greenhouse gases through a variety of forest management activities. As with other mechanisms under the UNFCCC, there are few prescriptions that specifically mandate how to implement the mechanism at national level. Principles of national sovereignty and subsidiarity suggest that the UN-REDD Programme can only establish what governance outputs it would reward, requiring that reports detailing those outputs be submitted in a specified format and made available for review. In essence, REDD+ is little more than a set of guidelines and offers of technical advice on how to report on forest resources and forest management strategies and their results in reducing emissions and enhancing removals of greenhouse gases. In spite of this somewhat casual approach, REDD+ has proven to be both popular and (potentially) groundbreaking. Its substantively indeterminant structure challenges many of the traditional concepts of centralization and decentralization in studies of environmental governance (Gallemore and Munroe 2013; Savaresi 2016; Schroeder and Gonzalez 2019; Zelli, Nielsen, and Dubber 2019).

The policy logic of REDD+ suggests that an "environmental subsidiarity principle" is and should be a guiding value in forestry governance. Although different trends in environmental management such as local participation, decentralization, and global governance have emerged in the last two decades at the global, national, and local levels, the conscious or unconscious application of subsidiarity has been a ruling principle in the development of REDD from its inception. The environmental subsidiarity principle, allocating governance tasks to the least centralized (or most local) actor competent to perform it, has become a critical conceptual tool for designing sustainable resource management. Environmental subsidiarity is the key principle that can link payment for ecosystem services with broader environmental public policies through more sophisticated strategies of multilevel policy integration that recognize the "circularity" of today's economies (Campbell-Johnson, Elfering-Petrovic, and Gupta 2019). Moreover, application of this principle has empowering political consequences for developing countries intent on reducing emissions from deforestation and forest degradation and enhancing forest carbon stocks. To the extent that the principle of environmental subsidiarity is realized, it has the potential to produce a highly *resilient* governance architecture by maximizing benefits to all stakeholders involved in payment for ecosystem services schemes such as REDD+ (Martinez de Anguita, Martin, and Clare 2014).

But experience with REDD also shows that transnational governance networks can easily become spatially centralized. Historical analysis of the development of REDD projects suggests that the evolution of REDD policy has been directed primarily from donor countries, especially in North America and Europe. Employing a social network analysis, Gallemore and Munroe (2013) present findings from a dataset of collaboration on 276 REDD, avoided deforestation, and sustainable forest management projects that began some form of actual operations between 1989 and June 2012. Their findings indicate that organizations in donor countries have from the beginning been the central actors in the REDD network. From this they conclude that REDD exhibits spatial centralization within transnational governance architectures despite institutional fragmentation, raising important normative questions about participation in transnational forest governance. Recognition of the inherent tension between this centralizing tendency within transnational governance networks and the principle of environmental subsidiarity is an essential element of the open-textured architecture of REDD+. In addition to contributing to the resilience of REDD+'s architecture, this tension is a constant reminder that climate change confronts humanity with *thresholds* (both environmental and socio-economic) at multiple levels of governance. Another element of that openness, however, is the recognition of the limits of the REDD+ range of applications.

By its very nature, REDD+ depends for its effectiveness on the social and economic characteristics of developing nations. The challenge in developing countries is not so much the absence of appropriate incentives, or even of well-considered regulation. It is, rather, to devise mechanisms that give a transnational effect to national timber policies (Cadman et al. 2019). There is an emerging transnational timber legality assurance regime consisting of a set of interrelated policy instruments, both public and private, aimed at controlling trade in illegally logged wood and wood products. The potentially productive interactions among these instruments in the emerging forestry regime have the potential to engender social learning, stimulate cross-fertilization, and enhance public accountability. In this respect, the EU's Forest Law Enforcement Governance and Trade (FLEGT) initiative provides a useful example of the interaction of public legal timber regulations and private certification schemes as the core of an emerging transnational regime with a distinctly experimentalist character. An experimentalist regime of this type is a promising approach to addressing contentious transnational environmental issues like forest governance where there is no global hegemon to impose a single set of rules (Overdevest and Zeitlin 2014b).

Experience with FLEGT implementation suggests that there are also a number of outstanding challenges to constructing an effective timber legality assurance regime, which if unresolved could undermine its promise. Chief among these is the difficulty that timber-producing nations in the developing world have had in creating the timber legality assurance systems called for by their voluntary partnership agreements with the EU (Overdevest and Zeitlin 2014b, 12). This problem is an example of the difficulties of regime complexity increasingly faced by architects of global governance in which a proliferation of regulatory schemes operate in the same policy domain, supported by varying combinations of public and private actors. Such regime complexity can lead to forum shopping and other self-interested strategies, which undermine the effectiveness of transnational regulation. These problems also make all the clearer the critical importance of the experimentalist governance approach that characterizes the FLEGT initiative. The scheme's interaction with private certification programs and public legal timber regulations, including those of third countries such as the United States and China, demonstrates how an increasingly comprehensive transnational regime can be assembled by linking together distinct components of a regime complex – thus achieving a high level of institutional *connectivity* in its governance architecture.

The experimentalist features of the FLEGT initiative and its regulatory interactions – which accommodate local diversity and foster recursive learning through *feedback* from decentralized implementation experience – make it possible to build up a flexible and adaptive transnational governance regime from an assemblage of previously existing but newly interconnected pieces, even in situations where interests diverge and no hegemon can impose its own will (Overdevest and Zeitlin 2014a). It also identifies an important additional characteristic of open-textured governance architecture. Because of the broad connectivity and constant feedback produced by such institutional structures, the structures themselves must always be regarded as incomplete – as perpetually unfinished.

This brief overview of REDD+ and FLEGT suggests four essential qualities of open-textured governance architectures – they are highly *resilient* structures that recognize *threshold* effects at multiple levels and allow dealing with those effects through high levels of institutional *connectivity* and *feedback*-driven experiential learning. These four themes also have been identified as the common core themes shared by the fields of geomorphology, ecology, and environmental governance.[2] More effective management of landscapes and ecosystems, better interdisciplinary

4.1.3 Embeddedness

While the qualities of flexibility and open-texture undoubtedly contribute to the ability of any piece of architecture to remain embedded in its cultural context, embeddedness cannot be reduced to these two characteristics. It is now widely recognized that environmental governance must be collaborative. It is an enterprise that involves collaboration between a diversity of private, public, and nongovernment stakeholders who, acting together toward commonly agreed goals, hope to achieve far more collectively than they could individually (Edwards and Bulkeley 2018b; Hurlbert, Gupta, and Verrest 2019). This approach appears to blur the familiar sharp boundaries that separate "the state" from civil society, yet we still know very little about exactly what this blurring of public and private adds up to, and what its implications are (Gunningham 2009b).

As an example, environmental movement organizations in Australia have experienced a frustrating (if prolonged) honeymoon with participatory governance. Conservationists have had increasing access to decision-making processes and forums. Since the 1980s, environmental decisions have generally involved public consultation and community engagement. Activist participants in these processes have tended, however, to overestimate their potential to achieve conservation objectives through deliberative governance. In many instances, environmental advocates have been coopted, institutionalized, and neutralized. A case study of the major and successful campaign to control widespread land clearing in Queensland, Australia, is also an example of failed community engagement. By rejecting both hierarchical, centralized decision-making and the inadequate engagement practices proposed by the state, activist groups mobilized community opinion and action to bring about a historic conservation win (Whelan and Lyons 2005).

Another empirical investigation, based on the analysis of Strategic Environmental Assessment documents produced during twenty-five municipal spatial planning processes in Italy between 2004 and 2010, makes a similar point (Bonfazi, Rega, and Gazzola 2011). The study found that advances resulting from community-based planning mechanisms were more evident in the creation of cross-sectoral governance networks (strengthening technocratic effectiveness) than in the involvement of citizens and civil-society organizations. Strategic environmental assessment seems to be able to increase the transparency and expand the scope (if not the strength) of democratic control over spatial planning decisions. Strengthening the democratization processes requires that *all* participants should consider themselves equally responsible within strategic environmental assessment networks and be ready to challenge the environmental value systems that underpin spatial planning processes (Bonfazi, Rega, and Gazzola 2011). But the boundaries between experts, decision-makers, and citizens remain clearly demarcated and their roles differentiated.

With respect to climate-warming, it is increasingly evident that the notions of collective "ownership," such as used in analyzing institutional arrangements that govern the use of large-scale environmental resources such as atmospheric sinks, need to be broadened. Neither the cost-minimizing features of emissions trading nor perfunctory efforts to decentralize policy implementation are sufficient (van Asselt and Zelli 2014; Torney 2019). Crucial parts of the institutional framework for governing atmospheric sinks are still missing, a shortcoming that maintains both the tragedy of the commons and gross distributional inequities in their use. A workable governance solution for global atmospheric sinks will ultimately need to (1) actually regulate the use of atmospheric sinks; (2) provide for genuinely equitable sharing of costs and benefits; (3) provide adequate compensation for climate change impacts and assistance for adaptation to climate change; and (4) create institutional solutions for enhancing participation in environmental decisions in order to guarantee progress in and legitimacy of the governance framework (Paavola 2008). This insight is particularly valuable in an age when the concept of governance is eclipsing that of government (Gupta and Möller 2019). Even though it is certainly true that law is no longer center stage in global environmental governance but simply one instrument among others in the environmental regulator's toolkit (Gunningham 2009a), the strong embeddedness of law – as both a cultural production and a constituting element of that culture – gives an unmistakable indication of the degree to which effective environmental governance must originate at the level of the human community rather than being transmitted there from "above" for implementation.

4.2 Governance Architecture in the Anthropocene: Of People and Their Food

What does the right to adequate nutrition have to do with global environmental governance issues like climate-warming? There are many connections. Climate change is increasingly recognized as a threat to human food security, a threat that can be planned for and responded to intelligently only with foresight. Carbon emissions in production and processing of agricultural commodities have not gone unnoticed. The challenge of meeting the global need for agricultural output without exacerbating climate change is not introduced here for the first time (Food and Agriculture Organization 2017; Newall, Taylor, and Touni 2018). The

88   *Embedded Governance Architecture in the Anthropocene*

imperative to improve human food security worldwide has led to the creation of governance architecture with distinctly local orientations. In addition to the normal amount of regime fragmentation, the existing food security architecture comes to the environmental policy specialist with a considerable level of embeddedness already built into it. Its flexibility and textural openness (and, therefore, its potential application to the problem of climate warming) is best evaluated by an examination of one of its most important elements – the emerging architecture of local foods.

4.2.1 Embeddedness

A number of policy models exist for the promotion of local food systems. They can usefully be categorized as either grants driven or grassroots in origin. An example of the grants-driven policy architecture is the Farmers Marketing and Local Food Promotion Program (FMLFPP) of the US Department of Agriculture.[3] Under FMLFPP, two competitive grant programs are available: the Local Food Promotion Program (LFPP) and the Farmers' Market Promotion Program (FMPP). The enterprise-oriented LFPP offers grant funds (with a 25 percent match) to support the development and expansion of local and regional food business enterprises to increase domestic consumption of, and access to, locally and regionally produced agricultural products and to develop new market opportunities for farm and ranch operations serving local markets. Eligible entities may apply if they support local and regional food business enterprises that process, distribute, aggregate, or store locally or regionally produced food products. Such entities may include agricultural businesses, agricultural cooperatives, producer networks, producer associations, community supported agriculture networks, community supported agriculture associations, and other agricultural business entities (for-profit groups); nonprofit corporations; public benefit corporations; economic development corporations; regional farmers' market authorities; and local and tribal governments.[4]

The goals of FMPP grants, on the other hand, are to increase domestic consumption of, and access to, locally and regionally produced agricultural products, and to develop new market opportunities for farm and ranch operations serving local markets by developing, improving, expanding, and providing outreach, training, and technical assistance to, or assisting in the development, improvement, and expansion of, domestic farmers markets, roadside stands, community-supported agriculture programs, agri-tourism activities, and other direct producer-to-consumer market opportunities. Eligible entities include: agricultural businesses, agricultural cooperatives, community-supported agriculture networks, community-supported agriculture associations, economic

4.2 Governance Architecture in the Anthropocene: Of People and Their Food   89

development corporations, local governments, nonprofit corporations, producer networks, producer associations, public benefit corporations, regional famers market authorities, and tribal governments.[5]

A transnational example of the grants-driven architecture is the European Union's Rural Development Policy, which it operates under the auspices of its Common Agricultural Policy (CAP). Under the 2014–2020 RDP, the EU contributed over €95 billion to investments that aim at fostering the competitiveness of agriculture; ensuring the sustainable management of natural resources; combating climate change; and achieving a balanced territorial development of rural economies and communities including the creation and maintenance of employment. Funds for rural development are disbursed through programs run by national governments: Each government appoints the Managing Authority, whose task is to inform potential beneficiaries of the support that is available, the rules that apply, and the level of the EU contribution. The agricultural expenditure is financed by two funds that form part of the EU's general budget: the European Agricultural Guarantee Fund (EAGF), which primarily finances direct payments to farmers and measures to regulate agricultural markets, and the European Agricultural Fund for Rural Development (EAFRD), which co-finances the rural development programs of the member states.[6] The parallels between the EU's Rural Development Policy and the United States' FMLFPP are evident. The Rural Development Policy is somewhat more open-textured than the FMLFPP, due largely to its transnational (as opposed to national) character.

An example of grass roots governance architecture in food policy is the robust, if spontaneous and rather piecemeal, growth in short food supply chain (SFSC) projects – which have become especially prominent at the local level in Italy (Mastronardi et al. 2015; Demartini, Gaviglio, and Pirani 2017; Sellitto, Vial, and Viegas 2018). This phenomenon is of considerable interest because it responds to a number of needs and opportunities of both farmers and consumers. SFSCs contribute to diversifying and increasing sources of income for farmers, help develop closer links between consumers and farmers (thereby reinforcing a sense of the importance of the agricultural sector for a sustainable society), and increase the supply of fresh, high quality, relatively unprocessed food at the local level – thereby promoting healthy eating without necessarily weighing down consumers' budgets. Moreover, SFSC systems are particularly suited to the highly fragmented nature of agricultural production in Italy and to Italy's cultural preferences for the promotion of a wide range of local food specialties that are closely linked to the diversity of the Italian nation. SFSC techniques include direct farm sales, agricultural markets, collective selling outlets, buying groups, home delivery (box schemes or community-supported agriculture), local festivals, direct farm pick-up, and even vending machines.

This recent proliferation of SFSCs, particularly the direct sale aspect, also meets farmers' needs to valorize local food production and increase their profitability. In addition, SFSC architecture addresses the important concept of sustainability in economic, environmental, and social terms – bringing a quality of multi-functionality to local agriculture. As an example, in the Italian agro-food sector, the sale of extra virgin olive oil is largely conducted in short supply chains. Economic analysis of direct selling in short supply chains for the extra virgin olive oil has found it to be profitable for farmers. Research also demonstrates the importance (and viability) of using a farm costs analysis for the identification of a selling price that valorizes the quality of the local products and at the same time ensures fair revenue to farmers (Finco et al. 2013). In short, research shows SFSC architecture to be a valid design for the (not atypical) Italian olive-oil market, capable of improving both local food production economics and environmental sustainability.

US examples of grass roots local food architecture abound – ironically, because of funding made available as partial settlement of the 1988 master settlement of the tobacco–Medicaid law suit (Cobb 2011). One such project, of particular interest inasmuch as it serves one of the nation's least prosperous regions, is ASAP, the Appalachian Sustainable Agriculture Project. The mission of ASAP (Appalachian Sustainable Agriculture Project 2018) is to help local farms thrive, link farmers to markets and supporters, and build healthy communities through connections to local food. ASAP's core activities include providing marketing support and training to area farmers, connecting area chef and foodservice buyers with the farmers who suit their needs, spearheading a Local Food Campaign (which includes a *Local Food Guide* and local food bumper sticker), certifying local products grown/raised in the Southern Appalachians as Appalachian Grown[TM], running a Growing Minds Farm to School Program (which focuses on reconnecting children with where their food comes from), organizing the Asheville City Market, and coordinating the Mountain Tailgate Market Association.

Moreover, ASAP's Local Food Research Center examines the social, economic, and environmental impacts of localizing food systems. The Center researches and tests the theory of food system change: that localizing food systems strengthens local economies, boosts farm profitability, increases sustainable production practices, and improves individual and public health. This theory is the core of ASAP's conviction that when the distance between consumer and producer decreases, transparency in the food system increases and drives changes that increase public health, build local economies, and sustain family farms. In addition to its research efforts, ASAP also maintains the Appalachian Grown[TM] logo, which is displayed with farm products grown or raised in western North Carolina and the Southern Appalachian Mountains.

The Appalachian Grown logo is a trademark owned by ASAP. To protect the integrity of the logo and the local food market, producers and retailers must agree to comply with certain logo-use restrictions and agree to a binding License Agreement. The requirements and agreement are meant to protect the logo and state that the logo may only be used to represent food and agricultural products grown or raised by Appalachian Grown-certified farms. Through support from the North Carolina Tobacco Trust Fund Commission, ASAP offers funds for Appalachian Grown-certified farms in North Carolina to be used in the promotion of locally grown food. These funds can be used for design and production of labels, packaging, or promotional materials featuring the Appalachian Grown logo. The promotion must reach the public and must support farmers within one or more of the Appalachian Grown counties in North Carolina (Appalachian Sustainable Agriculture Project 2018).

4.2.2 Flexibility

Local foods architecture exhibits a high level of embeddedness. Local food systems, however, should not be thought about in isolation. There is a growing awareness that agricultural systems exist within a wider network of social-ecological processes with other components including governance agreements, rural household and community norms, local associations, markets, and agricultural ministries, among many others. This entire institutional ecology must be considered in any thorough discussion of sustainable agriculture. Just as climatic profiles will influence the future viability of crops, human institutions create the conditions that foster sustainable food systems. Sustainable agriculture is the subject of a relatively weak and fragmented regulatory structure (Urrutia, Dias, and Clapp 2019) and is prone to the hazards of corporatization (Clapp 2019) and financialization (Clapp and Isakson 2018). Discussions of agricultural sustainability must, therefore, address agriculture concepts such as diversified farming systems within a broader context that is sensitive to concerns regarding human health, labor, democratic participation, resiliency, biological and cultural diversity, equity, and ethics, in order to assess social outcomes of agricultural activity (Bacon et al. 2012). The Agenda 2000 reform of the EU's Common Agricultural Policy (CAP) introduced comprehensive rural development as an integrated part of agricultural policy (Granvik et al. 2012).

Recent comparative research on agricultural diversification suggests the importance of this broader perspective. Analysis of case studies from California's Central Valley, Mesoamerican coffee agroforestry systems, and European Union agricultural parks finds that diversified farming system practices are unevenly adopted within and among these systems and are significantly interdependent with institutional environments that specifically promote diversified farming practices. Influential institutions in these cases include state policies, farmers' cooperatives and associations, and organized civic efforts to influence agro-environmental policy, share knowledge, and shape markets for more "sustainable" products. The Californian and Mesoamerican cases, considering organic and fair-trade certifications, show that although they promote several diversified farming system practices and generate social benefits, they are inadequate as a single strategy to promote agricultural sustainability. Alternatively, the complex governance and multifunctional management of Europe's peri-urban agricultural parks show unexpected potential for promoting a more comprehensive diversified farming system architecture. This is of singular importance, because unless diversified farming systems are anchored in supportive institutions and evaluated against an inclusive set of social and environmental criteria, short-term investments to advance diversified agriculture can miss valuable opportunities to connect ecological benefits with social benefits in the medium and long terms (Bacon et al. 2012).

The relatively better performance of Europe's peri-urban agricultural parks reveals the promise of the emergent concept of multifunctional farming. Multifunctional farming (combining both agricultural and non-agricultural diversification into a single policy architecture) has, more than any other rural practice, a positive role to play in integrating the natural environment with the cultural landscape and socioeconomic development. Comparative case study of six multifunctional farming development projects show that this comprehensive approach to agricultural diversification made it possible for rural inhabitants to continue living in rural areas and that the more institutionally integrated agricultural architectures are effective in identifying and supporting new opportunities for farm diversification. From this broader perspective, traditional agricultural practices can be seen as a key component in various diversification activities in rural areas, contributing to economic as well as social and environmental sustainability (Granvik et al. 2012).

Farmers in at least some locales undertake nature conservation measures at their own initiative (Runhaar, Polman, and Dijkshoorn-Dekker 2018) and arguments in favor of agricultural biodiversity find receptive audiences when properly framed (Runhaar et al. 2019). Nevertheless, critics of modern agriculture decry the dominance of monocultural landscapes and strongly advocate multifunctionality as a desirable alternative in facilitating the production of public goods. Harden, Ashwood, and Bland (2013) examine opportunities for multifunctional agriculture through participatory research led by farmers, landowners, and other local actors. They find that agriculture typically fosters some degree of multifunctionality that arises simply from the divergent intentions of actors. The result is a scattered arrangement of what they term "patchwork multifunctionality" – a ubiquitous status quo in which individuals provide public goods without coordination. In contrast, "interwoven multifunctionality" describes deliberate collaboration to provide public goods, especially those cases where landowners work across fence lines to create a synergistic landscape. This research demonstrates that a wide spectrum of both patchwork and interwoven multifunctionality currently exists, and it presents underutilized opportunities for public good creation. This last observation is a key to understanding the potential flexibility offered by the concepts of diversified farming systems and multifunctional farming. Their public benefits do not have to be "incentivized" in the way that other public-regarding behaviors often must be. These pieces of architecture are flexible because they are, to a significant degree, emergent qualities of existing patterns of agricultural practice and of rural life more generally. Indeed, it is the inherent flexibility of these concepts that will eventually allow them to become culturally embedded and to be embraced as constituent elements of the local foods architecture more generally.

4.2.3 Open Texture

In addition to their embeddedness and flexibility, the architectures of local foods, agricultural diversification, and multifunctional agriculture are open-textured to a significant degree. By this we mean simply that these architectures are not so densely structured that they can neither fully determine governance outcomes nor be penetrated by considerations originating in many other policy domains. For instance, the liberalization of agricultural trade is strongly contested as an international policy project. This resistance has been expressed in terms of perceived threats to the "multifunctionality" of agriculture and its ability to provide public environmental and social benefits. The result has been the emergence of neoliberalization as a policy agenda, reshaped in different states and regions through processes of resistance and accommodation arising from particular geographical, historical, political, and institutional contexts (Dibden, Potter, and Cocklin 2009). The contestation met by this neoliberalism should not be regarded as rejectionist in character, but rather it should be interpreted as an illustration of the importance of open-textured governance.

As an example, there is a dominant technocratic, neoliberal agenda for agricultural development and hunger alleviation in Africa. African agricultural and food security policy in the post-colonial period has been characterized by a "productionist" approach – a strategy comprising the use of hybrid seeds, fertilizers, and pesticides to boost crop production that has become entrenched in the New Green Revolution for Africa. This approach is underpinned by a new and unprecedented level of public–private partnership as donors actively work to promote the private sector and build links between African farmers, input suppliers, agro-dealers, agro-processors, and retailers. On the consumer end, increased supermarket penetration into poorer neighborhoods is proffered as a solution to urban food insecurity (Moseley, Schnurr, and Kerr 2015).

There are valid reasons for a renewed interest in adapting the lessons of the Green Revolution to the African setting, but research must go further in identifying any unique drivers of agricultural intensification within and across African countries. A case study of Ghana, for instance, sought to determine whether fast population growth and the remarkable agricultural performance the country has enjoyed in recent years have resulted in favorable conditions for the adoption of Green Revolution approaches – particularly their reliance on low-cost labor and intensive agricultural inputs (Nin-Pratt and McBride 2014). An analysis of the economic efficiency of agriculture in different production systems and agro-ecologies identified the limits of Green Revolution technologies for agricultural production in Ghana. In particular, an analysis of whether fertilizer use in Ghana is associated with high population density and intensive cereal production and whether land-intensive innovations are associated with more efficient production practices shows no evidence of Green Revolution agricultural intensification in Ghana. Moreover, no correlation was found between population density and input intensity. In contrast to neoliberal models, labor costs still play a major role in Ghanaian agricultural development by limiting the adoption of labor-intensive technologies (even in relatively high population density areas) without under-mining agricultural performance (Nin-Pratt and McBride 2014). The fact that neoliberal agricultural governance is contested by potentially successful alternatives is critical to the harmonization of food security to other important human values – to the multifunctionality of agricultural practice.

Paths to food security other than intensive commercialization exist – a reconciliation of agricultural productivity and a living wage is possible – and this is vital if the many distributional inequities that can accompany the commercialization of agricultural governance are to be addressed. As an example, expanded irrigation farming is envisaged to play a progressively larger role in rural development and to help reduce some inequalities in South Africa's agricultural economy (Tapela 2008). Since the late 1990s, the government has aimed to revitalize government-owned irrigation schemes, many located in the former homelands. This macro-policy shift seems intent on the creation of a black farming elite. An important question, however, is whether neoliberal agricultural policies will harm the poorest and most vulnerable in irrigation farming communities, and whether a new class of commodity producers can establish themselves in global commodity chains. An examination of vulnerability and marginalization in selected small-scale irrigation schemes in South Africa's Limpopo Province suggests that existing approaches to agricultural commercialization may fail to reduce overall rural poverty and inequality. Although these approaches help to integrate resource-poor irrigation farmers into globalized commodity production sectors, they threaten to undermine the livelihoods of the poorest and most vulnerable in these communities by reducing their relative competitiveness within their own communities (Tapela 2008).

This realization, that agricultural practices must be improved in ways that contribute to both food security and to socioeconomic equity, makes it clear that the right to adequate nutrition cannot be acquitted through governance architectures that sacrifice other fundamental human concerns (Gore 2019). Moreover, this realization is most vivid when we look at governance architectures from the ground up. Appropriate balances between these different, and sometimes competing, values are most likely to develop at the point where architecture meets the ground – where it is embedded in the human experience. Happily enough, there is a template for this kind of governance architecture, which can readily be deployed in the agricultural arena – the stakeholder partnership.

4.3 Governance Architecture in the Anthropocene: The "Foodshed" Partnership

One of the most pressing problems confronting global governance today is whether it has democratic legitimacy. In the wake of the World Summit for Sustainable Development in Johannesburg in 2002, stakeholder democracy has been advanced as an ideal-typical model of a new approach to key areas of global environmental governance. Stakeholder partnerships are standard fare in the governance of natural resources (Baber and Bartlett 2009a). Sustainability is an arena in which innovative experiments with new hybrid, pluri-lateral forms of governance, such as stakeholder forums and partnership agreements institutionalizing relations between state and nonstate actors, are taking place (Bäckstrand 2006). A leading example of this trend is the prevalence of the watershed partnership.

As the paradigm shift away from command-and-control statutory architecture toward collaborative institutional arrangements has progressed, public administrators, policy-makers, and watershed stakeholders have become more dependent on collaborative partnerships to solve complex environmental problems. Watershed management partnerships can be categorized as belonging to three basic types: (1) interagency governance, (2) cross-sector governance, and (3) grassroots governance. Each of these architectural types has its own strengths and weaknesses as a mode of governance, and experience has shown that the best approach for addressing a particular watershed goal is a highly contingent question

(Diaz-Kope and Miller-Stevens 2015). Not only does a focus on specific watershed goals help in determining which specific form of this architecture is called for under a given set of circumstances but it also provides an appropriate orientation to determining the value of efforts.

Collaborative governance critics continually call for evidence to support the widespread use of watershed partnerships. As is so often the case in environmental policy, the environmental outcomes of watershed partnerships emerge in their own time and context, making the evaluation of the provenance difficult. Moreover, the multitude of possibly confounding variables makes it difficult to correlate collaborative governance processes with specific governance results. But Biddle and Koontz (2014) offer empirical evidence that collaborative processes have a measurable, beneficial effect on environmental outcomes. Through the use of a paired-waterbody design, they created a dataset that reduced the potential for confounding variables to affect environmental outcome measurements. The results of their path analysis indicate that the setting specific pollutant reduction goals is significantly related to a watershed partnership's level of attainment of environmental improvement. Moreover, the action of setting specific goals (e.g. percentage of load reductions in pollutant levels) is fostered by sustained participation from partnership members throughout the lifecycle of the collaborative – clearly indicating the value of such de-centered and participatory governance architectures. The increasing stress that climate change will impose on water systems, and the risk of scalar mismatches between competing water management frameworks (van den Brandler, Gupta, and Hordijk 2019), are likely to make these flexible and participatory approaches increasingly important to the maintenance of water quality globally.

It is not only the environment that benefits from watershed partnerships. Partnerships have proven their human benefits around the world. A key component of collaboration is social learning. Through deliberation, stakeholders with different perspectives and information can learn from each other and develop a shared vision and plan for moving forward. Koontz (2014) compared social learning in collaborative watershed partnerships across two states within federal systems: Ohio (USA) and Niedersachsen (Germany). His analysis indicated that, although deliberative processes in both cases generated social learning, Ohio partnerships exhibited learning to a significantly higher degree. A key difference linked to these results was the higher levels of local process control and individual efficacy in Ohio. This offers an affirmative answer to the question of whether, if a little democracy is good, more democracy might be better still.

Adapting the architecture of watershed partnerships to agricultural policy at the local level should seem an obvious step. The local foods movement, short food supply chains, local food security activism, and agricultural multifunctionality are all socioeconomic phenomena that focus our attention on the concept of a *foodshed* – a region of food flows, from the area where it is produced, to the place where it is consumed, including the land it grows on, the route it travels, the markets it passes through, and the tables on which it ends up.[7] A foodshed can be described as a sociogeographic space: human activity embedded in the natural integument of a particular place (Feagan 2007). Whereas the extent of a watershed partnership can be defined in topographic terms with relative precision, the shape and size of a foodshed – like an ecological footprint – is determined by human behavior, usually little of which is undertaken with the specific intent of defining the limits of a place.

The intentional and self-conscious development of a foodshed partnership would have to overcome the built-in ambiguities of its scope. There is reason to think that the deliberate (and deliberative) process of forming such a partnership brings with it a complex of incentives and constraints that should allow for a continual renegotiation and redrawing of its boundaries. For instance, a farm-to-market system whose principal members contemplated expanding its scope to create a new farm-to-restaurant element would have to consider whether the boundaries of their current system contained a sufficient number of target businesses to justify the effort. By the same token, such a system would be constrained in its growth by the simple fact that extending its geographical territory would increase transportation costs as well, as the complexity of their product delivery procedures increase. In these ways, the counter pressures to expand or restrict the territorial reach of a foodshed partnership would be a recurring topic of conscious deliberation among its members. Similar complexes of incentives and constraints would continually order the deliberation among foodshed partners with respect to questions about expanding its membership and the scope of its operations. That does not mean, however, that foodshed partnerships would come easily, or naturally, under any given set of circumstances. Consider, for example, the case of San Diego County, located in the southwestern corner of the United States in the state of California.

As of the 2010 census, the population was just over 3 million, making it the second-most populous county in California and the fifth-most populous in the United States. Its county seat is San Diego, the eighth-most populous city in the United States. The county has a total area of 4,526 square miles with a varied topography. On its western side is 70 miles of Pacific coastline. Most of San Diego between the coast and the Laguna Mountains consists of hills, mesas, and small canyons. Mountains (sometimes snow-capped in winter) rise in the northeast, with the Sonoran Desert far to the east. The Cleveland National Forest is spread across the central portion of the county, while the Anza-Borrego Desert State Park occupies most of the northeast. Although the western third of the county is primarily urban, the mountains and deserts in the eastern two-thirds of the county consist primarily of undeveloped backcountry. These backcountry areas are home to a native plant community known as chaparral and to nearly all of the county's agricultural activities.

San Diego County's agriculture industry was worth $1.85 billion in 2013. The County is one of the top five egg-producing counties in the United States and is a leading producer of avocados, nursery crops (ornamental plants), and various fruits and nuts. In 2013, San Diego County also had the highest number of small farms of any county in the United States and the nineteenth-largest agricultural economy among US counties. The County's Farm Bureau sponsors a Community Supported Agriculture (CSA) initiative, which organizes farmers' markets and a subscription farming program. The Bureau also administers a locally grown branding project – San Diego Grown 365 – that exploits the region's ability to produce year-round harvests. The County is also home to a number of food security programs, administered by various nongovernmental organizations, as well as an informal but growing farm-to-table movement. To date, however, the County has not produced a group that has the breadth of scope of Italy's SFSC projects or the level of organizational sophistication of the Appalachian Sustainable Agriculture Project. A number of reasons for this suggest themselves.

First, San Diego County, though relatively isolated from the rest of California by a large area of federally owned land to its north, is part of a far larger economy than its 3 million population would suggest. Much of the County's agricultural production flows out into that larger market, serving California's population of over 38 million. Of course, far more developed local food systems have grown up in areas of Europe that are every bit as integrated in their larger surrounding economies. A second possible explanation is the political conservatism for which this area of Southern California has traditionally been known. The importance of that factor can be put in perspective by comparing political attitudes in San Diego to their far more conservative counterparts in the areas of Appalachia served by the ASAP. A third possibility is that climate variations across the county lead to an agricultural form of balkanization. It is true that climate variations across the County are impressive. While heavy snowfalls are typical in the higher elevations inland, some weather stations along the coast have never recorded a freezing temperature. With its many microclimates, the County's farmers raise a large number of different crops. Yet Italian climates are remarkably similar to those of California, as is the range of Italian agricultural products, and this has presented no obstacle to the development of foodshed-level organizations there.

A more useful explanation for the absence of "foodshed consciousness" in San Diego might begin with the observation that the County may present a relatively homogenous and integrated area of food consumption, but the same cannot be said of it as an area of agricultural production. Under such circumstances, consumer-oriented initiatives (which have already appeared in San Diego) might be more easily created than producer-based projects. A particular example is the variability within the county of the costs of irrigation. Although some parts of the county have ample groundwater supplies, many farmers must rely on high-cost water that is piped in from the Colorado River and Northern California. In fact, agricultural water rates in the County Water Authority are more than thirty times those of California's Central Valley Project or the Imperial Irrigation District. As a consequence, San Diego growers cannot compete with other areas in growing water-intensive crops like alfalfa and Sudan hay, two of the largest crops grown in neighboring Imperial County, where water is cheap (County of San Diego Department of Agriculture 2017). The absence of groundwater in some areas of the County commits farmers in those areas to water conservation pressures that are fundamentally different from those of their neighbors.

This geographic variation has influenced the decisions that farmers have had to make about diversified and multifunctional farming. For instance, the hillsides in the County's northern areas that used to be covered with citrus have gradually been converted to viniculture. Not only are grape vines less thirsty than citrus trees but they can be used to produce a high-value-added product instead of a bulk agricultural commodity. The resulting winery development has been so robust in the County that the United States Department of the Treasury Alcohol and Tobacco Tax and Trade has created two new American Viticultural Areas (AVAs) in the region (the first in 1981 and the second in 2006). These AVAs have become important foci of agricultural activity in the County, and suggest a more or less natural regional basis for creation of foodshed partnership areas. The impetus for such a development may eventually come from the rediscovery of another agricultural activity that, during the time of the Spanish missionaries, animated every settlement in California – the growing of olives and the production of olive oil. Like wine production, the pressing of olive oil allows producers to capture a far larger share of the value of the end product of their labors. Like winery operations, olive oil production is multifunctional, involving harvesting and processing as well as (potentially) numerous forms of marketing and branding. Olive oil production is already beginning to experience something of a renaissance in California (Downing 2006) and local production in the County is on the increase.

Even this brief discussion of San Diego County agricultural practices, and the comparisons one can draw between them and the other examples of local food networks, is sufficient to make one point with unmistakable clarity. The advent of foodshed partnerships may be, in some general way, an inevitable consequence of local food initiatives of the kinds discussed here. The incentives to form umbrella organizations of this sort are significant – offering to take food policy from the level of food security issues into a new arena of environmental governance. For instance, local short food supply chain accomplishments might eventually be rewarded by the earning of saleable certified emission reduction credits under the UNFCCC Clean Development Mechanism by reducing the carbon emission involved in the transportation of food products. Once these connections begin being made, higher levels of institutional integration in local foods policy (whatever they are called) may follow. But there is no one inevitable form that these institutions must (or are likely to) take. The highly contingent character of this potential future is key to anticipating it. The parallels between issues in the food policy arena and the problems associated with the management of riparian resources through the use of watershed partnerships suggest that the concept of foodshed partnerships offers a useful starting point. Food policy is in significant need of the stakeholder perspective (Kalfagianni and Kuik 2017), even at the risk of limiting the scalability of any architectural innovations that result (Buijs et al. 2019).

4.4 Governance Architecture in the Anthropocene: Lessons of the Oculus

A great deal of ink has been spilt in arguments about the architecture of global environmental governance focused on institution matters, such as the question of whether UNEP should change from its current form into something else. This debate continues in spite of the fact that, by itself, organizational reform cannot achieve environmental protection, much less the broader goal of sustainable development (Young 2008). A neo-institutional analysis suggests that this is a question we are destined to ponder for the foreseeable future. Through the notion of path dependency, historical institutionalism explains how the self-reinforcing cycle of a diffused development of the international environmental governance system, characterized by incremental changes, has made the system more complicated and prevented substantial institutional change. Historical institutionalism also highlights power inequalities and lack of trust between nation-states, as well as turf wars between international organizations, as key explanatory factors hampering governance reform. Rational choice institutionalism complements these explanations by showing how incremental institutional changes that do not add up to substantial reform are the result of neither nation-states nor international organizations being interested in establishing a powerful environment organization that might encroach on their sovereignty. Finally, discursive institutionalism suggests that the norm to do at least something to improve the international environmental governance system has prompted nation-states to create "symbolic" institutions, with the result that incremental institutional developments within the UN system are always more likely than substantial reform (Vijge 2013). All this notwithstanding, we find ourselves at a

4.4 Governance Architecture in the Anthropocene: Lessons of the Oculus 101

critical juncture – a moment when a highly dynamic, human-dominated earth system confronts us with nonlinear, abrupt and irreversible changes in the circumstances of our survival (Kanie et al. 2012). At a bare minimum, such a moment requires clarification of institutional hopes and expectations with regard to the future of environmental governance institutions.

Much of the current institutional discussion concerns the challenge of environmental policy integration – a concept so far mainly applied to domestic and European politics – at the global level (Bührs 2009). After exploring the options for organizational change, including clustering, upgrading, streamlining, and hierarchical steering (with a focus on whether the reform proposals can bring about environmental policy integration), one analysis concluded that in the longer term, an upgrading of the UN Environment Programme to a UN specialized agency, with additional and increasing streamlining of other institutions and bureaucracies, offers the most potential for environmental policy integration and does not appear to be unrealistic (Biermann, Davies, and Grijp 2009). This approach has the clear merit of starting with the status quo and moving it in the direction of higher levels of policy integration through opportunistic and small-scale reforms, taking into account that environmental regimes do not operate in isolation (Morin and Blouin 2019) and that policy innovations diffuse according to their own logic and circumstances (Meadowcroft and Fiorino 2017; Morin et al. 2019).

Another vision for the future seems less incremental in its approach (Kanie et al. 2012). It focuses more broadly on a proposal for an institutional framework for sustainable development in an effort to better address the critical issues and political dynamics in the twenty-first century. It calls for a fundamental restructuring of the institutional framework for sustainable development such that it (1) clearly articulates the "aspirations" of governance for sustainability, including objectives and underlying values and norms, (2) allows for meaningful and accountable participation by a wide range of actors to develop solutions from people for people, and (3) creates an architecture to include better configuration of actors, actor groups, and their networks, as well as improved institutions and decision-making mechanisms. This proposal would be instantiated through a series of "world café" discussions involving academic experts on global environmental governance and policy practitioners working at the local, national, and global levels. Armed with the resulting assessment of the current institutional framework for sustainable development and the challenges that we face, this vision suggests that a Sustainable Development Council in the United Nations and the use of "crowdsourced Delphi planning" (Coleman et al. 2017), as well as other proposals, warrant further consideration (Kanie et al. 2012).

This comprehensive and critical approach carries with it great promise. By focusing on sustainability values and norms to develop solutions from and for people, it echoes our basic working definition of architecture. It invokes the vision of a structure embedded in its cultural context and based on principles that sustain human practices in a particular place – offering the opportunity to construct a more coherent and functional edifice of governance. But that construction is projected to begin in a virtual café populated by academic experts on global environmental governance is a bit worrisome. How will the proposed conversations be grounded in human practices – in what cultural context will they be embedded? Starting construction of a new Pantheon with conversations among experts at the global level threatens that it will become yet another technocratic exercise, the creation of a dome before its foundation has been laid. Considering the mind-boggling variety of deities this temple will have to praise, its base needs to be of the densest possible material of human experience. Perhaps, however, the solution is simple, as obvious as the food on our plates.

In every corner of the globe, people have devised small pieces of institutional architecture that allow them to secure their daily bread. In many places, a few of which we have discussed, that architecture has shown remarkable creativity and potential for expansion. These dense and sturdy human experiences should become the topic of discussion in our governance cafés. The point of the discussion, moreover, should not be how we can replicate these experiences at grander and higher scales. Greater levels of consistency, or integration, in food architecture should not be our objective. Instead, we should seek consilience in our environmental governance architecture – a greater level of coherence in our knowledge achieved "by the linking of facts and fact-based theory across disciplines to create a common groundwork of explanation" (Wilson 1998, 8). For those who hope to determine governance outcomes by reforming its architecture, mere explanation might be too modest an objective. But it may be as dense a material as the structure of global governance can presently support. And it may be sufficiently dense to support the next higher level of the structure of governance. This next level of governance is the level of democratic discourse, which depends on the more solid and substantive level of explanation – grounded in holistic social experimentation – for both its subject matter and its evaluative criteria (Dryzek 1990).

It is worthwhile to remind ourselves of the dome of the Pantheon and the oculus at its apex. The dome grows less dense as it rises, putting less pressure on itself the higher it reaches. Moreover, the structure remains incomplete – as it has for two millennia. It is crowned by an oculus, both because air is lighter than even the lightest concrete and because the space within the building would be oppressively dark otherwise. Like all other products of humanity's ingenuity, the oculus is a mixed blessing. It allows the structure to stand and makes the space it encloses more habitable. But it lets in the rain. This disadvantage is managed successfully by a slight angle in the floor that leads rainwater to a grate at its center, allowing the water to flow out of a pipe beneath the building. The Pantheon has survived because it is embedded, flexible, and open-textured. Crucially, it is also subtle and ingenious.

The lessons are clear. The higher we build our governance architecture, the lighter should be the weight we impose on the structure beneath. We should never attempt to actually finish the building – an act of hubris that might well bring the entire edifice down and almost certainly would allow in less light. Adopting this approach means that the results of our efforts will remain, forever, incomplete. Our best course, then, is to enjoy the light, embrace the rain, and keep our drains clean.

5

Experimental Adaptiveness in the Anthropocene

Reconciling Communities and Institutions to Environmental Change

> ... as we know, there are known knowns; there are things we know we know. We also know there are known unknowns; that is to say we know there are some things we do not know. But there are also unknown unknowns – the ones we don't know we don't know. And if one looks throughout the history of our country and other free countries, it is the latter category that tend to be the difficult ones.
>
> *Rumsfeld 2002*

The tortured quality of Rumsfeld's comments should not blind us to the fact that he had a point. There are things that we know (or think we know) and there are other things about which we know that our knowledge is uncertain or lacking. And, regrettably, there are things about which even the depth of our ignorance is unknown to us. With respect to the disasters that might befall humanity if we continue to ignore ecological problems like anthropogenic climate change, both the popular and professional literatures provide a list of horribles for which we are unlikely ever to finish preparing. Environmental "unknown unknowns" is not a null set, but its members will reveal themselves only in their own time and, in any event, we have enough "known unknowns" to occupy our poor capacity to plan for the future. We should invest in thinking about how to prepare for the problems that we are able to imagine – while continuing to try to anticipate where the wild things might be.

This relatively more modest aspiration is challenging enough. Today, every aspect of governance is complicated by the inherent volatility of the times we live in (Conteh et al. 2014). As a result, the challenge of achieving some level of adaptiveness in global governance, particularly in environmental governance, has begun to draw significant scholarly attention (Kim and Mackey 2014). Much of this analysis has focused on the level of global governance, of entire regime systems. For example, a listing of the regimes that would have to be included in any assessment of the global challenge of climate change would inevitably include global governance of water systems, food security, health programs, and efforts to alleviate poverty. Climate impacts on economic governance and even international security would also have to be considered (Biermann 2014). These challenges, along with many others, already consume the days and complicate the lives of countless diplomats and elected officials around the world. But is it from this quarter that adaptiveness in global environmental governance can be really expected? Will the world's roughly 200 national governments forge master plans that are of sufficient scope and robustness to deal with the myriad implications of environmental degradation – or, in the alternative, will they allow the creation of a global government capable of doing so? Even to pose the question is to invite derision.

An implication of the inadequacy of existing political institutions for facing the challenge of adaptiveness in global environmental governance is that a likely source of innovation lies in the inchoate realm of global bureaucracy – understood to include administrators national, international, and increasingly subnational (Bernstein and Hoffmann 2018), both governmental and nongovernmental, across the entire range of policy arenas. This is not to say that administrative professionals at any level are apolitical, or that they are the only governance agents in the world capable of innovation. It is, rather, to point out that they enjoy the dual benefits of relative invisibility and administrative discretion. The dependence of national officials on broad delegations of authority to public and civil society administrators (both to implement specified policies and to develop policies where officials have chosen to avoid specificity) is both well-documented and well-theorized (Rosenbloom 2014). The central role of international bureaucrats in the creation of environmental regimes (Young 1998) and in the work of the formal institutions that they help mandate (Young, King, and Schroeder 2008) has long been recognized. Both of these features of the governance universe suggest that improving the insights of administrative professionals into the essential components of adaptiveness in environmental governance, and the role that they can play in promoting it, might pay considerable dividends. It is not as though administrators are strangers to the pressures imposed by change in either the governance of the environment or the environment of governance. Protected by both their relative anonymity and their institutional affiliations, they are (perhaps to a greater degree than any other agents of governance) in a position to engage in the best practice that humanity has discovered for learning from experience that we have not yet had – they can *experiment*.

5.1 A Brief History of the Future

"All social theories are based on some vision of the future. It is true, of course, that a theorist may choose to make such assumptions explicit or leave them unstated.

But the assumptions are always there" (Baber 1983, 1). It requires no great feat of theorizing to understand that the future is not what it used to be.

Entering the last quarter of the last century, the future that challenged was summed up by the term "post-industrial," popularized by Bell (1976). As the economy of a society undergoes a transition from the production of goods to the provision of services, knowledge becomes a valued form of capital. Consequently, producing ideas becomes the main way to grow the economy. As a consequence, the value and importance to the economy of blue-collar and unionized work (including manual labor and assembly-line work) declines and professional work (scientists, creative-industry professionals, IT workers, etc.) grows, both in value and prevalence. These developments promote and are reinforced by an increase in information production and in the international exchange of people, ideas, and financial capital.

In its time, post-industrialism confronted public administrators with a characteristic set of challenges. The replacement of laborers with professionals often changed the profile of demands placed on government by its citizens. The increasing value of information as a form of development capital, for instance, placed a greater emphasis than ever before on providing opportunities for higher education if state and local jurisdictions wished to promote continued economic growth. As the transportation of manufactured goods declined in importance relative to the transportation of people whose increasing incomes allowed for patterns of suburbanization to develop, transportation priorities shifted from railroads to streets and airports. As both human and financial capital became more portable, provinces and municipalities increasingly saw their economic development priorities focus beyond the boundaries of their own jurisdictions, or even those of the nation. All of these imperatives called for an approach to public management that emphasized advanced planning that would allow crafting *adaptive* responses to constantly shifting environments.

No sooner had administrative professionals begun coming to grips with the challenges of post-industrialism, however, than one of its constituent elements took on a life of its own. As early as the 1930s, scholars such as Machlup (1962) had begun to study the role of information per se as a commodity, introducing the concept of a knowledge industry. Later analysts built on this foundation the concept of an "information society." Although this concept of the future is, perhaps, less precise in its contours than the idea of post-industrialism, some of its essential features were provided by scholars of that other notion. For example, Bell (1976, 127 and 38) foresaw a future in which "what counts is not raw muscle power, or energy, but information . . . . A post-industrial society is one in which the majority of those employed are not involved in the production of tangible goods." This provides the occupational piece of the information-society puzzle. The entire pattern became fully visible later, when Toffler (1991) declared that knowledge (rather than military strength or capital) had become the essence of power in the information age. Toffler described what he terms as "info-wars" raging in such arenas as computers, high-definition TV, electronic networks, and industrial espionage, and the fight for control of customer data by retailers, manufacturers, banks, and credit-card issuers. The winners of these battles, fought both with and over information, would be the dominant powers in the twenty-first century and beyond.

The challenge for the administrative professionals in this new information society is to avoid getting caught behind the data curve. No longer can a manager treat his or her organization as if it is a closed system with predictable and manageable feedback loops. In particular, the overwhelming salience of information imposes a high level of functional interdependency on all governance operations. For example, when virtually every function becomes subject to contracting out, performance monitoring replaces direct administration. The use of private sector providers of both goods and services (both for profit and charity) may extend the reach and effectiveness of services but it also magnifies public or nongovernmental officials' information handling challenges and it increases their reliance on the cooperation of individuals not subject to their direct supervision. This sort of radical interdependency is a central feature of most accounts of our collective future and the collaborative forms of governance appropriate to it.

Finally, post-industrialism has bequeathed to us yet a third characteristic of the future – accelerated globalization, the increasing ease by which people, ideas, and capital can migrate around the world. In addition to the growth of international trade and the movement of investment capital, social and cultural globalization is well underway. Levels of migration have been on the rise, as is the rate at which new ideas are disseminated by the global communications network. Both entertainment and news coverage are becoming ubiquitous. All of these processes are contributing to the gradual consolidation of the Earth's human population into a single world society, not merely an integrated global economy (Albrow and King 1990; Albrow 1996; Steger 2017).

Two of the implications of globalization for governance are of the greatest importance. First, the escape of social, cultural, and economic processes from the limits imposed on them within national boundaries constitutes a direct challenge to the efficacy of government based on the institutions of the Westphalian nation-state (Slaughter 2004). If all are citizens of the world, no nation can enjoy an exclusive call on allegiance and obedience (or even our limited political attention). Therefore, to the extent that government institutions are structures based on political authority, their ability to work their will in a globalized environment is now constantly subject to question. Going forward, governance effectiveness will depend in large part on flexibility – the capacity to find alternative routes to its objective when the first choice among conceivable routes is blocked. Given the fact that the various routes available are often blocked by people outside of government – people who, inconveniently enough, have interests of their own – collaboration often becomes an essential of administrative flexibility.

Second, globalization is far from a politically neutral collection of social, economic, and environmental factors. Globalization does not mean that we find ourselves at the end of ideology and that democracy has won. Instead, the twenty-first century will be a period of intense ideological struggle (Steger 2001). The chief protagonist is the dominant neoliberal market ideology "globalism." Although much globalism constitutes little more than a shameless repackaging of old laissez-faire ideas, it deserves to be considered a "new market ideology" because its advocates have been able to link free-market concepts with cutting-edge "global talk." This ideology seeks to perpetuate certain self-serving myths – including assertions that "globalization is inevitable," "nobody is in charge of globalization," and "globalization benefits everyone." This old wolf in new sheep's clothing confronts governance administrators with a stark and unappealing choice. They must either content themselves with a radical libertarian dystopia, or commit themselves to the long, hard struggle for a *deliberative* consensus based on the considered judgment of the governed rather than on (the no longer available) aggregative majoritarian rule grounded only in outmoded authority structures. When the demands of flexibility, collaboration, and deliberation are considered together, it becomes clear that administrators will continue to spend a good deal of their time trying to adapt to a future that presents them with an ever-moving target.

5.2 Living in the Future: The Governance Administrator's Dilemma

Rapid change in the environment of governance, an escalating need for collaborative mechanisms of information-sharing and decision-making, and the sudden loss of authoritative institutional arrangements that had made bare majoritarian rule possible – these are certainly times that call for adaptiveness in governance. Happily enough, however, the real-life experiences of both citizens and governance professionals in every corner of the globe provide natural experiments that continually yield promising results. The crucial connection that must be forged is between those concrete experiences of average citizens, individual managers, and the collective wisdom of administrators as a group of widely spread and only loosely connected professionals. The processes of communication among administrators will be called on to deliver innovative responses to the challenges of flexibility, collaboration, and deliberation in governance.

5.2.1 Flexibility

The Daintree region of northeastern Australia is famous for its tropical rainforest and its unique combination of heavily forested mountains and inshore coral reefs. Among locals, it is also renowned for annual rain measured in meters, astonishingly steep slopes, and river crossings that are often more river than crossing. In the mid-1980s, the Queensland government, in the face of this hostile terrain and even more hostile protesters, cut a four-wheel-drive road called the Bloomfield Track across the Daintree. The resulting political disputes featured all the usual suspects – a development-oriented state government locked in combat with a more environmentalist federal authority; local land owners seeking easier access to their property asserting their rights against environmental activists concerned with the felling of trees, erosion, and the destruction of inshore reefs by increased sediment runoff; and media actors all too ready to advertise the day's most compelling exercise in symbolic politics (Niemeyer 2004).

Conducted in 2000, the independently funded Far North Queensland Citizen Jury (FNQCJ) was organized by scholars affiliated with the Australian National University. Jury participants were selected on a stratified random basis from the responses to a recruitment letter distributed throughout the region. Participants had the opportunity to inspect the location and to hear from and question both technical witnesses and community (interest group) representatives. They then were asked to discuss and choose from among five possible policies – upgrade the road by sealing the surface, upgrade it to a dirt road suitable for conventional vehicles, stabilize the road by repairing its trouble spots but leave at as a four-wheel-drive track, maintain the status quo but do no repairs, or close the road and rehabilitate the land.

Two outcomes of the FNQCJ are noteworthy. First, it changed people's positions. Prior to their deliberative experience, the aggregate preference of jury members (as revealed by a pre deliberative questionnaire) was for stabilization. But closure emerged as the clear post-deliberative choice, having risen from the position of least preferred in the pre-deliberative questionnaire. Second, there was convergence on a single "consensus" position, although a significant level of dissent remained (Niemeyer 2004). The drivers of these changes are summarized by Niemeyer (2004, 360):

First, the deliberative process provided the impetus for jurors to turn their minds to the issue. Second, the process assisted jurors in grappling with issues of significant complexity, about which their assessments and conclusions became comparably more sophisticated. Third, most importantly from the perspective of will transformation, deliberation served to dispel symbolic politics.

These results suggest that, where the task at hand is to resolve a specific public problem (rather than to formulate general policy), getting people to focus, think a problem through, and refrain from symbolic rhetoric are key elements of any successful outcome. Moreover, the technique employed by the FNQCJ organizers is *adaptive* in two different but equally important senses.

First, it is clear that this approach can be employed almost anywhere that the solution to a discrete public problem is blocked by public indifference, inattention to the facts, and distortion by interest groups – a fairly broad field of deployment, indeed. This sort of "policy jury" exercise is well understood, both at the theoretical level and as a matter of practice (Baber and Bartlett 2005; Fishkin 2011). Second, this technique supports flexibility, showing the capacity to actually move people away from their preexisting (and often ill-informed) preferences toward considered judgments based on better information and more careful consideration. Even when (as here) dissent remains, dissenters are far less able to argue that their views have been ignored or that they have been treated unfairly in some way. The potential of this approach for achieving broader public support for environmental governance initiatives is limited only by the ability and willingness of administrators charged with developing and leading such initiatives to put them to use. A growing database of case studies allows administrators in search of models for injecting flexibility into governance to find examples that parallel new concrete circumstances as they are confronted. But if the problem at hand is the formulation of broader policy, rather than the solution of discrete problems, what then?

5.2.2 Collaboration

Törbel is a village of about 500 people located at an elevation of nearly 1,500 meters in the Upper Valais canton of Switzerland. The area is notable for the steepness of its terrain, its wide range of microclimates (demarcated by dramatic variations of altitude), its relatively low precipitation, and its high exposure to sunlight (Netting 1972). For many centuries, the residents of Törbel have planted privately owned plots of land with grains, vegetables, fruit trees, and hay for winter fodder. Another important part of the local economy is communal. Cheese produced by a small group of herdsmen who tend village cattle pastured on the village's communally owned alpine meadow during the summer months have long provided a critical part of the villagers' livelihoods (Ostrom 1990).

Since at least the year 1224, the village of Törbel has had a set of land tenure rules regulating the use of five distinct types of communal lands; grazing meadows, forests, "waste" lands (unused areas), irrigation systems, and the system of paths and roads that connect privately and communally owned properties. Adopted and revisited in annual meetings (where all citizens enjoy the franchise), these rules address the widest variety of property and resource issues and are implemented by officials who are also chosen in the annual meetings. Far from being a quaint anachronism, this system represents the informed choice of citizens who are (and for at least five centuries have been) fully aware of the advantages and disadvantages of both private and communal land ownership systems and who have carefully matched particular types of land tenure to particular types of land usage (Netting 1976).

Everywhere across the alpine regions of Switzerland, farmers use private property for their particular agricultural pursuits but communal ownership is used to manage summer meadows, forests, and stony waste areas – all of which are subject to despoliation through overuse because their low potential yield and the difficulties of profitably managing them as private property leave them vulnerable. Moreover, all of the Swiss institutions that have evolved to govern common property resources (CPR) such as these share one thing in common – "the appropriators themselves make all major decisions about the use of the CPR" (Ostrom 1990, 64). The provincial and national governments of Switzerland have generally respected these systems of local governance. As a polity, the Swiss have chosen to focus on the logic of subsidiarity rather than the rhetoric of national supremacy. In part, this is a result of the particular character of the Swiss tradition of federalism. But there are better reasons than tradition for this policy.

Collaborative and decentralized systems for promoting the long-term sustainability of common pooled resources (like fragile alpine meadows and forests) are not unique to Switzerland. Nor are they poorly understood as a theoretical matter (Baber and Bartlett 2005; Baber 2010). In fact, it is widely recognized that they offer distinct advantages over more centralized approaches that emphasize the development of uniform, widely applicable rules. Those who appropriate local CPRs over a long period of time have usually developed a relatively accurate understanding of how their particular ecosystem operates because the long-term success of their endeavors has relied on it. They are also likely to have knowledge of the other locals and the norms of behavior that they would consider appropriate. Using these disaggregated forms of knowledge, they are more likely to craft rules that are better adapted to local CPR management than any general system of rules. These rules devised by locals increase the probability of trustworthy and reciprocal behavior, thus reducing the need for enforcement efforts. Because local appropriators of a CPR have to bear the costs of monitoring compliance, they are more likely to craft rules that make infractions obvious and easy to avoid. Finally, a system of local and collaborative CPR rules is more likely to be regarded as legitimate (producing greater rule conformance) and less likely to prove ineffective over a wide geographic region because of the use of parallel and autonomous systems of rule-making, interpretation, and enforcement.

In other words, a structure of local and collaborative policies in pursuit of a well-understood and widely accepted general objective is likely to work better than solutions brought to the problem from afar (Ostrom 2005, 279–282). Where indigenous systems for environmental management exist and work well in their particular context, the job of the environmental administrator is simple – don't fix what isn't broken. Moreover, customary land tenure rules (and other environmental policy solutions) can easily be accommodated by later, more formal rules if the value of custom is recognized and acknowledged. We do not have to wait centuries for these kinds of systems to develop on their own. Politicians and administrative professionals (both national and international) are fully capable of instigating collaborative policy planning. The potential universality of this approach is evident from the wide use of watershed partnerships in the United States and elsewhere (Sabatier et al. 2005) as well as in the increasing interest in the dynamics and potential of stakeholder partnerships generally (Orr 2013).

The potential for customary land tenure rules to be incorporated into more formalized and modern legal codes suggests that rule systems of this nature have an ongoing utility. The very process of incorporating such traditional land claims into statutory schemes can secure indigenous understandings of how natural resources should be husbanded and also order the relationships of indigenous peoples to the modern states in which they find themselves (Weiner and Glaskin 2011). Administrative actors will always be intimately involved in codification processes of this kind wherever and whenever they occur. How might they find and continually revise something like a general public will, especially among a diverse and largely disconnected collection of people who are not really conscious of themselves as belonging to an actual "public" in the first instance, such as at the transnational level?

5.2.3 Deliberation

It is often the case that answering the most fundamental questions is the hardest part of the process of making and implementing policy. Finding the general principles that can guide policy development is usually complicated (if not entirely prevented) by ideologies and by interests that imagine themselves to be so at odds that no common ground is even possible (Baber and Bartlett 2005). It is easier to wean people away from ideological arguments over symbolic politics if you ask them simply to resolve a concrete problem rather than craft a general principle. It is much simpler for people to reconcile competing interests if they come to see their task as a search for collaborative strategies to manage a shared resource. But what of public life's fundamental questions? How can we come to agreements about basic governing principles? A "just so" story can help illuminate how that knotty problem might be addressed.

5.2 Living in the Future: The Governance Administrator's Dilemma 113

In an imaginary hemisphere, there might be a continent called Terra (Baber and Bartlett 2015). Terra is dominated by a mountain range that runs nearly the entire length of its southern coast, often dropping abruptly into the sea. Terra's other dominant physical feature is the River Terra, which begins its course high in the Southern Mountains near their eastern terminus, drops swiftly into the broad central plains, and then turns west, finally forming a broad marshy estuary on the continent's northwestern coast. The River Terra serves a number of human purposes. It provides easy irrigation to the fertile high plains just north of the southern mountains. It is the only source of water in the arid regions further to the north and west of those plains. The river has become a thermal dump, and fish that are native to the river provide a rich source of food, constituting an increasingly high percentage of the protein consumed by human populations the further north those populations live.

The river provides the only national boundary on the continent that is not an arbitrary vestige of its colonial past. On the east and north of the river lies the continent's largest nation – Panterra, the population of which exceeds that of the continent's other nations combined. Its economy is similarly outsized and highly varied in composition. Small in population, Meerland is the neighboring country to Panterra's southeastern region. Meerland comprises the central half of the coast and Southern Mountains together with nearly all of the fertile plains to their immediate north. Meerland's economy is small, but it is growing rapidly as a consequence of its major investment in ecotourism. Arroya is a large and sparsely populated arid expanse across the River Terra from Panterra's central and north-central regions. Arroya's population is engaged almost exclusively in subsistence farming and is heavily dependent on River Terra fish for its protein.

Some years ago, the government of Panterra decided that the nation's electricity supplies were becoming inadequate to its needs and that the environmental hazards of increased reliance on fossil fuels made that option unattractive. The country enjoys significant geothermal resources along its border with Meerland and Arroya. Accordingly, Panterra began building geothermal electrical generating stations in that area. The clean wastewater produced by these stations is cooled to ambient air temperature and then dumped into the headwaters region of the River Terra. This has produced a significant warming of the water in the southern area of the River, which, in turn, began reducing fish populations. The stretch of the river that constitutes the border between Panterra and Arroya will be largely barren of its large fish species in the near future. In its desperation, Arroya has appealed for help to an international environmental panel.

Citizen panels, presented with this scenario, can be given the pleadings of the nations involved and the rationales offered in support of their requests. These "stories" contain the various arguments used by the proponents and opponents of international regulation of greenhouse gasses. Such a hypothetical deliberative exercise can be used to provide normative direction for a public that does not yet clearly recognize itself.

When this dispute is submitted to citizen panels (each consisting of eight to twenty persons) it is accompanied by background information on the history, population, society, and economy of each of the countries involved as well as briefs submitted by each disputant making specific requests of the panel and providing reasons in support of those requests. Each participant completes a pre-deliberative questionnaire and records a preferred resolution of the dispute. The members of the panel are then instructed to resolve the dispute as they see fit and to provide a concise statement of the reasons for their collective decision.

Based on many repetitions of this exercise using this scenario and others in multiple countries, a few general observations are possible. Participants take the experience quite seriously. They discuss the differences among the countries involved in considerable detail. In explaining their decisions, they tend to employ a mixture of the reasons included in the briefs as well as justifications of their own. As an example, there has been a marked tendency in the deliberations carried out so far to try to disentangle questions of distributive justice from those of environmental protection. Rather than adopting a regulatory standard that tries to allocate the burdens of regulation in ways that compensate for historical social and economic disadvantages, there is a preference for regulations that achieve desirable environmental results with other considerations resolved in side agreements or by the use of transfer programs that do not touch on the fundamental regulatory regime.

A few basic conclusions about hypothetical deliberations and their utility in global environmental governance are justified. First, the complexities involved in environmental regulation at the international level do not take the problem beyond our capacity for crafting deliberative models for that process. For those who wish to go beyond forced-choice response research techniques (that ask people merely to react to generalizations about the environment that are unavoidably tainted by interest and ideology), deliberative simulations offer the opportunity to allow ordinary citizens to grapple with the kind of concrete environmental problems that regulatory regimes are created to address. Moreover, requiring participants to confront the views of others and to defend their own tends to strips away ideological cant and individual bias, leaving fully "public" justifications for the decisions that are produced (Baber and Bartlett 2005).

Second, in sufficient numbers these hypothetical deliberations can be used in the same way that actual precedent is used in the development of law in common law systems. Based on a millennium or more of experience, common law systems have developed bodies of fundamental doctrine that represent social consensuses on a wide range of human concerns. Often, majority and minority views on a particular subject are revealed and in many cases that very process yields an eventual consensus. With sufficient repetition, patterns develop in deliberations like these that can serve to indicate how concrete environmental disputes ought to be resolved. These decisions can ultimately be summarized through a procedure similar to the "restatement" process as it has been developed in the United States by the American Law Institute (ALI). If this restatement can be accomplished in a way that analysts could agree is accurate and reliable, the result would be a body of global environmental proto-regulation that would be presumptively legitimate because of its deliberative and democratic provenance (Baber and Bartlett 2009a, 2020).

Third, a sufficiently far-reaching collection of restatements of deliberative simulations can provide the raw material necessary for codification. Just as ALI restatements eventually provide the foundation for statutory enactments, restatements of the deliberation of hypothetical cases would provide a populist foundation for regulatory regime formation. Mindful that there is all the difference in the world between the merely populist and the genuinely democratic, the modeling technique described here is conceived as merely one element in a broader pattern of policy-making designed to redress the "democratic deficit" in international law (Baber and Bartlett 2009a, 2011; Baber 2010).

The potential value of deliberative exercises in this pattern of decision-making is easily grasped if we recall that ordinary citizens are reluctant to complicate rules for environmental protection by trying to make them yield redistributive results. Armed with insights like that, perhaps the negotiators of international agreements can anticipate more of the troubles that their creations eventually encounter. Adaptive capacities could be improved and collaborative bona fides enhanced if they are able to ground their policy prescriptions in a body of deliberative exercises whereby ordinary citizens from around the world have revealed their normative commitments through the adjudication of concrete problems of common pool resource management. Clearly, a deliberative approach of this sort – juristic democracy – has a wide field of potential application – including any circumstance in which a polity faces ecological challenges that hinge on fundamental environmental values, the discussion of which tend to distort the decision process by opening the door for symbolic political debate.

5.3 Living in the Future: The Citizen's Dilemma

To focus on the adaptiveness of systems – systems of institutions, of laws, and of procedures – runs the risk of overlooking a wild and vital frontier of human adaptiveness. If it is largely administrative professionals who must manage these various systems with an adaptiveness sufficient to provide a sustainable future, it will be citizens who must find the adaptiveness within themselves that will be needed to live in that future. Is it reasonable to assume that citizens can actually produce discourses that are worthy of so much effort?

Social scientists, and their philosopher cousins, have long been caught on the horns of this particular dilemma. Is the average democrat actually up to the demands of genuine democracy? We have often tried to understand democracy by studying the history of democracies – by peering back at their birth through a lens that tends to focus most clearly on revolutions and revolutionaries. One of the many reasons that the observations of the first social scientist regarding democracy, Alexis de Tocqueville (Elster 2009), have proven to be enduring is that he managed to avoid this trap. His eye for detail, and his abiding interest in the everyday, set his work apart from anything that had come before – and from much of what has come since. Yet even he bemoaned the absence of great men and the dearth of true genius in America. Indeed, both we and he might be forgiven for thinking that the very concepts of greatness and genius fit poorly into the language of democracy. Many choose to regard it as a sad fact about the today rather than a timeless and depressing inevitability that "you campaign in poetry but you govern in prose" (Keyes 2006, 21). So what is it, from the democratic perspective, that is truest and best about human beings – their plodding goodness or their potential genius?

In discussing what he calls "the contingency of selfhood," Rorty (1989) contrasts the philosophical and the poetic understanding of the human self. The philosophical perspective, which Rorty associates with Kant, is "appalled at the Romantic attempt to make idiosyncratic poetic imagination, rather than what [Kant] called the 'common moral consciousness,' the center of the self" (Rorty 1989, 30). The Kantian sees the "unselfish, unselfconscious, unimaginative, decent, honest, dutiful person" as the paradigmatic human being. It was for the sake of such persons that Kant "distinguished practical from pure reason, and rational religion from enthusiasm" and conceived of "a single imperative under which morality could be subsumed" (34). For Nietzsche, on the other hand, nothing worth taking the trouble to understand could ever be subsumed under a single rule or proposition. The paradigmatic human enterprise was, for him, the effort to achieve self-knowledge through the heroic act of "self-creation" (27). To be fully human is to embrace one's own contingency, and that embrace expressed itself most naturally and appropriately in forms of expression that were poetic. Nietzsche's poet lives and strives for one purpose – to do to the past what the past has tried to do to the poet. To "make the past itself, including those very causal processes which blindly impressed all her own behavings, bear her impress" is the poet's heroic mission (29). What is the aspiring democrat to do – keep the nose to the moral grindstone and miss the chance at greatness, or take flight on poetic wings and risk that close encounter with the sun that awaits the high fliers of mythology?

Rorty offers a third option. Instead of choosing between eternal war against causality itself and an abject surrender to its whim of the moment, Rorty suggests a more therapeutic alternative. Freud, in Rorty's reading, allows us to accept, and put to work, the Nietzschean sense of what it is to be fully human without rejecting causality – precisely "by tracing our conscience back to its origin in the contingencies of our upbringing" (Rorty 1989, 30). The individual conscience, in the light of a "commonsense Freudianism," is nothing more or less than an experiment that we conduct in partnership with others within the social and natural boundaries that science (broadly conceived) helps us to discern (31). Freud's analytical insights make it possible "to see science and poetry, genius and psychosis – and, most importantly, morality and prudence – not as products of distinct faculties but as alternative modes of adaptation" (33). In this light, we can see the Swiss land tenure traditions and the resolution of the Bloomfield Track question as successful (if not entirely self-conscious) experiments in pragmatic adaptation, and the deliberative practice of juristic democracy is an effort to reflect those successes back into the shared consciousness of environmental protection in a useable form.

It remains to suggest how to think about the relationship between the problem-solving that people engage in (both personal and interpersonal) and the interventions by which professionals (therapists, social scientists, and others) make problem-solving a more self-conscious process. Freudian psychoanalysis, one might say, holds out the possibility of a poetic subconscious to those who have neither the time nor the inclination to engage poetry in their conscious lives. It has even been said that Freud "showed us the poetry indigenous to the very constitution of the mind" (Trilling 1965, 79). Likewise, legal restatement might reasonably be regarded as an analytical technique intended to render more explicit those forms of tacit knowledge that find their way into the various forms of dispute resolution problem-solving as it is practiced by people with little conscious concern for the precedents that they might establish (Baber and Bartlett 2015). The role played by organizers and moderators of planning cells, policy juries, and other deliberative exercises can plausibly be described as merely focusing the attention of citizens on more rigorously structured problems so that the solutions they arrive at can be compared across human groups. What all of these routines arguably have in common is that they are varieties of the broader practice of active listening or, more specifically, "reflective listening" (Sundararajan 1995).

Reflective listening involves (among other things) reducing the impact of extraneous details on a conversation, embracing the speaker's perspective without agreeing with it, and recapping the speaker's points to ensure that a faithful account of them has been created. The objective is to put the problem-oriented narratives that people develop more fully within their access and make them potentially available to others who may be similarly situated. The codes of professional responsibility and behavior of those who play this facilitative role in their relations with others will, of course, vary from one discipline to the next. But they would all embrace the fundamental point that the professional does not "speak for" the patient, client, citizen, respondent, or other. Their role is to assist others in finding their own voices such that the "private ethic of self-creation," which preoccupied Nietzsche, has the potential to become "a public ethic of mutual accommodation" that is ultimately more plausible than the bridge between humans built of "shared beliefs or desires" for which Kantians have long searched (Rorty 1989, 34). At stake, perhaps, is the achievement of Walt Whitman's dream of an "aesthetic democracy" in which we would, at last, hear the poetry of the people (Frank 2007).

This perspective seems to lead us, almost inevitably, to challenge the conventional understanding of change in the international order as a product of action by nation states as rational unitary actors. There is scant evidence that these particular policy actors hear, or are even trying to hear, the poetry of the people – as a literature on global regime change in environmental governance too vast to cite clearly suggests. Even within institutionalist and neoliberal traditions, some of the more sophisticated analyses reveal cracks in that simple account of change. As an example, Monheim (2015) confirms the main points of regime theory: Where state interests converge, environmental agreements are likely; where those interests collide, adaptive change is frustrated. But his in-depth analysis of three paired sets of international negotiations (climate change failure in Copenhagen followed by success in Cancun, Cartagena and Montreal on biosafety, and trade talks in Seattle and Doha) tells a far more nuanced story. It is not simply that later negotiations build on earlier ones. In these cases, the later negotiations were conducted more skillfully. The capabilities and authorities of the lead organizers, the transparency and inclusiveness of the process, and the promotion of argument over bargaining as the mode of negotiation allowed for both the adoption of positive-sum solutions and the generation of process legitimacy.

This finding dovetails with the findings in Gupta and Mason (2014) that, although transparency policies as mechanisms of adaptive change in environmental governance advantage nonstate actors by making information more freely available to them and opening new spaces for their activities, they also reinforce mechanisms of state-based international law and empower states and market actors as much as (or even more than) civil society activists. It is also suggestive of a tension between those who argue for empowering treaty secretariats (as international bureaucracies substantially independent of member states of a treaty) to pursue creative adaptations to environmental change in circumstances where the core remit of a treaty is ambiguous or permissive in some way (Jinnah 2014) and those who argue that adaptive change requires expansion of current bureaucratic structures such as a World Environment Organization or even the creation of entirely new political fora such as an international parliamentary assembly (Biermann 2014).

How such institutional initiatives address the need for adaptation in the face of ecological change and the environmental citizens' dilemma of living in the future is far from clear. How do these system-level initiatives address the contingency of our selfhood, our need for a deeper understanding of our own beliefs and desires, and the necessity for more reflective capacity in our political interactions? The answers still elude us. But if firm conclusions are impossible, some implications of the narrative fabric we have woven are becoming clear.

5.4 Implications

The times in which we live and the futures we face place ever-shifting demands on our public institutions, so flexible governance will be required to solve the problems that confront us. Ours is an era of a highly dynamic, human-dominated earth system in which nonlinear, abrupt, and irreversible changes are likely (Kanie, Betsill et al. 2012), often characterized by environmental tipping points that are intrinsically hard to detect (Galaz et al. 2016). It is important that this aspect of the Anthropocene be understood within a more context-dependent and localized framework of social understandings (Biermann et al. 2016). If our lives (both as individuals and as members of a civil society) are destined to be characterized by an ever-increasing level of fluidity and interdependence, then political, social, and economic processes of all sorts will need to become far more collaborative than they have been heretofore – amounting, ultimately, to a new "geopolitan" form of democracy, based on a radical extension of democratic horizons of space, time, community, and agency (Eckersley 2017). If globalization undermines the ability of electoral structures across the globe to respond to environmental change (Dryzek and Stevenson 2011; Dryzek and Pickering 2019; Dryzek et al. 2019) and institutional path-dependency constrains the adaptive capacity of governments and markets alike (Dryzek 2014), our interactions in public spaces will need to be increasingly deliberative if they are to be viewed as democratic and if the decisions they produce are to be seen as legitimate by those whose acceptance of them will determine their ultimate effectiveness.

Understood in this way (as a collection of flexible, collaborative, and deliberative governance processes), the day-to-day work of administrative professionals can become a path to social and political arrangements that are not only more adaptive but also more democratic and more effective in reconciling humans to their environment. The examples of the Bloomfield Track, the Swiss land tenure system, and the Terran hypothetical deliberations are illustrations of only a few of the forms that flexible, collaborative, and deliberative collective will formation, led by administrative professionals, might take. Admittedly, taking examples from the area of environmental protection runs the risk of stacking the deck. But if in this area humans cannot see the need to deal with rapid change, interdependencies, and challenges to the legitimacy of collective decisions, it is hard to imagine where they ever could. There are, in fact, at least two distinct explanations for why deliberative approaches might enjoy special advantages in the environmental context. First, these techniques may succeed in "de-moralizing" environmental issues (Miller 1992) by elevating the status of ecological issues above that of individual interests. Deliberative techniques may enfranchise nature by giving it a voice in the political domain where before it was silent (Goodin 1996), giving it a seat at the table where games of symbolic politics are played. If this is true, the special success of deliberation in environmental decision-making might not recur in other issue arenas where public decisions are already fully "moralized."

A second alternative view of citizen juries and other techniques of collaborative deliberation is that they reveal an environmental consensus that had previously eluded people precisely because it had been distorted and concealed by politics as usual – by the overheated disputes between the competing claims of symbolic political debate (Niemeyer 2004). In effect, deliberative techniques succeed environmentally because their emphasis on solving concrete problems in particular circumstances removes environmental politics from the arena of moral disputes – effectively "de-moralizing" them (Haidt 2012). If this is the key to deliberation's success, that is good news for the technique. It suggests that collaborative deliberation is widely deployable, with good prospects wherever symbolic political debate is obscuring viable solutions. Developments in global environmental governance suggest that the logic of this approach is finding its way into new areas.

For example, the European Union has been involved in collaborative and place-based resilience-building in the Horn of Africa (Joseph 2014). This effort can be understood as part of a particular approach to governance. By focusing on the concept of governmentality (as opposed to government), it can be argued that this kind of project is part of a broader strategy that seeks to govern from a distance. This strategy is consistent with two other developments. First, it fits with new and more modest approaches to development and global governance. And it fits with the EU's own internal processes both in the field of risk and disaster preparedness, and in relation to things like the open method of coordination. Second, this new initiative also illustrates how the emergence of resilience governance has encouraged new administrative approaches that are transforming both internal and external EU relations (Joseph 2014). Government officials are far from the only source of decision-making in the environmental field. New actors play critical decision-making roles, and new mechanisms and forums for decision-making are becoming important – for instance, in some contexts regulation is supplemented or replaced by markets and cooperative arrangements (Armitage, de Loë, and Plummer 2012). But administrative professionals are essential as organizers and monitors of those processes. A considerable literature has grown up about initiatives of this sort, extolling the virtues of adaptive comanagement of natural resources. A case study of its implementation, however, shows the degree to which this approach is dependent on the attitudes that environmental administrators bring to it.

Adaptive comanagement is often suggested as a way of handling the modern challenges of environmental governance, which include uncertainty and complexity (Shinn 2016; Whitney 2019). Adaptive comanagement is a novel combination of the learning dimension of adaptive management and the linkage dimension of comanagement. It is not, however, a panacea. There is a need for more insight into the enabling policy environment for success and the contribution that administrators must make to it. A case study of the world famous Venice lagoon in Italy provides an illustration of the importance of these administrative insights (Munaretto and Huitema 2012). The analysis, based on interviews with stakeholders, participatory observation, and archive data, suggests that the prerequisites of adaptive comanagement were often understood imperfectly, if at all, in this case. Some levels of useful cognitive learning did take place (albeit very much within established administrative paradigms). Normative and relational learning, however, were much rarer, and when they occurred they seemed to have had relatively opportunistic motivations. Only low levels of collaboration were achieved because the governance system was deliberately set up in a hierarchical and mono-centric way. The limited possibilities for stakeholder participation resulted in low levels of social capital formation and an incapacity for handling disagreements and uncertainty (Munaretto and Huitema 2012). This reinforces the broader conclusion that adaptive comanagement encourages adaptation that emerges organically among multiple centers of agency and authority as a relatively self-organized process of experimentation that governments can promote by creating enabling conditions but cannot produce by command (De Caro et al. 2017).

Flexible, collaborative, and deliberative techniques are effective in environmental decision-making precisely because they have the potential to defuse the symbolic politics associated with those decisions – allowing for flexible and collaborative problem-solving. This explanation for the success of collaborative deliberation suggests that those techniques are not dependent on the special circumstances of environmental decision-making. There is, of course, no guarantee that these techniques will be taken up by administrators in order to deal with the volatility of policy-making across policy domains. The thought that symbolic politics and administrative intransigence may end up swamping Venice is profoundly depressing – both to students of environmental governance and to lovers of *seppie al nero*. The possibility of such disappointment will remain as long as executives and policy professionals are reluctant to actively involve and commit to interactive governance processes. Even when this reluctance can be overcome, the organization of the interconnections between interactive processes and existing representative democratic institutions is very difficult and needs constant maintenance (Edellenbos, van Schie, and Gerrits 2010).

Grounds for a broader optimism in the future of adaptive governance lie in one of the most endearing characteristics of administrative professionals – they are scavengers *par excellence*. The volatility of their environment has meant that administrators face devolved responsibility in governance for both acquiring resources and achieving results. As the work of treaty secretariats demonstrates (Jinnah 2014), their challenge is increasingly strategic, a search for strategies that allow for the inclusion of administrative priorities and values in setting the direction of governance while coping with the conflicting desire of politicians to have more control over administrators (Llewellyn and Tappin 2003). Placing policy administrators (both national and international) in this kind of bind ensures that an approach that works well *anywhere* is destined to eventually be tried *everywhere* (Meadowcroft and Fiorino 2017). In the context of environmental governance today, *experimentation* is no longer merely a virtue. It is a basic survival skill.

6

Equivocal Democratic Accountability in the Anthropocene

Where Effective Legislatures Do Not Exist

Administrative and policy professionals are especially well-situated to plan, manage, and evaluate the experimental approaches to environmental governance needed under the circumstances of the Anthropocene. But if our governance efforts become heavily reliant on professionals, we risk creating an "accountability trap," in which institutional goals for addressing environmental problems are placed in tension with the need to hold unelected officials (and private actors) to account for their actions (Park and Kramarz 2019). Usually, the primary mechanism for holding administrative agencies accountable in any democratic polity is the practice of legislative oversight, a mechanism that is severely challenged by the globalization and modernization that characterize the Anthropocene. Globalization and modernization amplify humankind's ability to disturb ecosystems in fundamental ways, creating an urgent and growing need for responses that will yield, and constitute, effective governance. Meeting the need for effective governance requires the development of institutional arrangements that involve strong administrative capacities (Bauer, Andresen, and Biermann 2012). But neither globalization nor modernization, nor anything else, seems to be moving humankind toward creation of anything resembling a global legislature that could ever effectively exert oversight over even the still grossly insufficient earth system administrative capacities already developed over the last century. The same forces of modernization and globalization (such as the internationalization of capital and hollowing out of the nation-state) that give rise to the ecological challenges of the Anthropocene also prevent effective global legislative oversight by national legislatures acting individually or in concert. Should some sort of legislative body or collection of democratic authorities ever emerge and attempt to assume responsibility for oversight of administered environmental governance (the prospects of which are vanishingly low), it would be overwhelmed by the immense and growing complexity of the fragmented, multi-level proliferation of institutions, networks, and relationships that will necessarily constitute the evolving governance system of the Anthropocene. The demand for accountability has led to a proliferation of accountability mechanisms for private, voluntary, and hybrid institutions (Kramarz and Park 2016; Park and Kramarz 2019). But the challenge of accountability is especially acute for international governance institutions, which are often insulated from democratic accountability by architectures that have bureaucrats unanswerable even to other bureaucrats, much less to any kind of global public or judicial authority or to officials or institutions with themselves any kind of democratic provenance.

Yet only democratic processes have the potential to inform and legitimate environmental governance at every level in ways that respond to the challenges of ecological rationality, popular participation, and globalization (Dryzek 2016; Dryzek and Pickering 2017; Baber and Bartlett 2020). Accountability is central to all democratic practice. So what hope can there be for the urgent task of cultivating global public accountability mechanisms in the Anthropocene if global legislative oversight of public administrative capacities is unlikely, if not impossible? What alternative form of public democratic accountability could fit the political circumstances of global governance in the Anthropocene? A more urgent task for future theorizing, innovation, and experimentation is hard to imagine.

Prior experience may have something to teach us. A substantial source of global administrative experience has been accumulated by the United Nations system and by the many international intergovernmental agencies that have been established in the last century. Unfortunately, most of these agencies suffer from overall accountability deficit issues and none offer a model of real democratic accountability. There is, however, one real-world organization (or system) that does offer some promise of being a fruitful subject of investigation, namely, the world's the most fully developed example of transnational government: the European Union. Even with decades of treaty tinkering and the evolution of practice – on a limited continental rather than a world scale – the EU has been unable to design and authorize legislative bodies that can exercise broad and effectual legislative oversight. Given this failure to establish meaningful legislative oversight, it should not be surprising that the EU has also experimented with alternative mechanisms of accountability that do not rely on legislative oversight. The EU is a pioneer of transnational democratic oversight and administrative accountability and, as such, its incremental and trial and error innovations, as inadequate as they still are, offer lessons for the problem of accountability of global governance in the absence of effective legislative authority.

6.1 Earth System Governance Accountability in the EU: The Challenges

Earth system interactions can, in fact, be governed – with the proviso that doing so requires comprehensive packages of governance responses across both eco-social subsystems and levels of governance (Nilsson and Persson 2012). The United Kingdom's separation from the European Union highlighted how dense and extensive the frameworks for governance and law are that have found their way into national legal orders as a result of membership in the EU. A seceding nation needs to replace them with domestic environmental governance standards if it wishes to maintain environmental governance accountability (Lee 2018).

Governance policy packages of this sort are likely to comprise a complex set of interrelated policy instruments. As an example, the EU's Forest Law Enforcement Governance and Trade initiative mixes legally grounded timber regulations with private certification schemes as the core elements of an emerging transnational experimental regime (Overdevest and Zeitlin 2014b). An experimentalist regime of this sort provides a promising approach to environmental governance that, by its nature, has no global (or even regional) hegemon to impose a uniform set of administrative rules. This is precisely the crux of the accountability problem in earth system governance – a need to rely on administrative mechanisms in the absence of conventional administrative accountability. The problem can manifest itself in several ways.

First, the "regulated parties" within such a governance system are going to be differentially situated when it comes to taking advantage of the opportunities to promote policy-relevant learning, stimulate cross-fertilization, and enhance accountability that experimentalist regimes offer (Overdevest and Zeitlin 2014b). Sometimes, this is the result of flaws in the underlying architecture of the regime. With regard to the EU's transnational biofuel governance efforts, for example, Thiel and Moser (2018) found a relatively inefficient governance of public goods resulted from legal mechanisms that required insufficient transparency and accountability at national government levels. In other areas of earth system governance, compliance capacity is a bigger issue. In the area of biodiversity governance, for instance, EU policies can be frustrated by the inability at the national level to incorporate all relevant concerns in the decision-making process, difficulties in responding to the demands of multiple levels of government, or the invisibility of the issue to the public (Suškevičs 2012).

Second, at least some level of difficulty in EU accountability policy is implicit in the very structure of the Anthropocene. It has long been an adage of environmentalism that there is no such thing as doing just one thing. The notion of interdependence underlying that adage may have achieved its radical fulfillment in an era when no human action is without environmental consequence and no change in the environment lacks a human dimension. Governance in such an era is bound to be polycentric (Thiel and Moser 2018). In recognition of this new level of governance complexity, EU countries are increasingly opting for a mix of voluntary and mandatory measures in areas such as environmental, social, and governance disclosures (Camilleri 2015a). Member states are transposing EU directives on this subject, but their success in creating specific administrative standards for non-financial corporate disclosures is decidedly mixed. Where those efforts have met with success, full engagement of relevant stakeholders has fostered a constructive environment leading to continuous improvement in environmental, social, and governance disclosure practices.

This echoes the conclusion of Overdevest and Zeitlin (2014b) that the successful construction of transnational environmental regimes is likely to depend on national compliance capacities and the tolerance for standards of continuous improvement rather than strict performance. While some may still worry about the "open-ended" nature of disclosure as a regulatory tool, it is probably best to work toward its improvement. There is every indication that reliance on the approach is likely to increase (Vukić, Vuković, and Calace 2017) and at least some reason to hope that (as with corporate social responsibility policies) more proactive government involvement will lead the private sector toward more conscientious performance (Camilleri 2015b).

Third, it would be foolhardy to ignore the problem that political power poses for effective earth system governance through environmental administration. Political modernization presents one form of this problem, a form especially relevant to the EU experience. It has long been possible to discern a shift of modern societies away from thinking strictly in terms of the institutions of government and toward a diversity of processes and activities of governance in conceptualizing regulatory action. This trend contributes both to the polycentricity of modern society and to the creeping de-legitimization of public institutions as mechanisms for regulating that diversity. The impact of this trend can be seen in the increasing reliance on private standards, such as for the protection of animal welfare in the European food market (Maciel and Bock 2013). Stakeholder participation has included citizens, farmers, unions, and NGOs, but the overweening power of food retailers has cast significant doubt on the long-term desirability of political modernization in this regulatory arena.

It is not entirely clear, however, that direct and authoritative intervention by the EU would be helpful in such circumstances. The processes of modernization weaken nearly every state, but consider the problem of environmental governance in nation-states that have been weakened even more dramatically, or even a state whose very existence is contested. A study of regulation of the energy sector in Kosovo, for example, suggested that the intervention of the EU and other external actors to build regulatory capacity has actually weakened that nation's domestic institutions and reduced its ability to respond to domestic nonstate actors who might otherwise have been a source of pressure for improved regulatory performance (Obradovic-Wochnik and Dodds 2015).

Happily, the experience of Kosovo stands in stark contrast to the broader European experience with respect to administrative accountability policies. Analysis of the emerging administrative practices of the European Union, including review of the peculiarities of the delegation of administrative discretion, the obstacles to direct legislative oversight, and attempts to achieve oversight through the evolving "open method of coordination" (OMC), suggests opportunities for further EU reforms to create a deliberative framework capable of producing the independent norms needed to constrain the substantial administrative discretion vested in the EU Commission (Nedergaard 2009). A deliberative model of administrative accountability could be grafted onto these existing nonlegislative accountability mechanisms to accomplish just that at each level and stage of the policy process by identifying normative principles, choosing policy models, and adopting action plans and implementation strategies. The resulting model of transnational democratic accountability is one that could be fully transferable to the broader global transnational accountability challenges of environmental governance in the Anthropocene. It is a model that does not rely on new legislative inputs or continuous monitoring by elected officials (the fantasy of global legislative oversight), but it can accommodate augmentation of existing administrative competencies. Moreover, it fits the continuing political circumstances of the Anthropocene – that is, it can constitute an accountability system responsive to the urgency of achieving greater democratic accountability, be adaptable to the complexity of (mostly nonhierarchical) future governance, and can build on responsibilities that both nongovernmental and intergovernmental organizations already exercise well.

6.2 Delegation and Oversight in the European Union

If one were to listen only to the sharpest of Eurocritics, one would conclude that the European Union presents a remarkable paradox. It is alleged, on the one hand, to be a feckless and fragile creation – accomplishing little or nothing and ready to fly apart at any instant. This criticism is heard especially loudly on the subject of European foreign policy (Toje 2008; Helwig 2013). On the other hand, the EU is often chastised for what is alleged to be its overbearing and intrusive behavior – displacing local initiative and threatening national sovereignty (Adam and Maier 2011). Before dismissing the skeptics (as officials of the EU Commission have sometimes been inclined to do) as inveterate complainers who want to have it both ways, we should ask ourselves whether these two strands of criticism ever converge without self-contradiction.

Were Euroskeptics to squarely face the challenge of reconciling their apparently contradictory criticisms, they could credibly say something like the following: It is entirely possible for a government (or set of governing institutions) to be simultaneously intrusive and ineffectual – to threaten national sovereignty without offering a credible replacement for it. All it need do is interrupt existing processes of democratic governance without itself being sufficiently democratic. The result would be a politics that is ineffective *precisely because* it is undemocratic (Baber and Bartlett 2005). Other ways of reconciling the apparent contradictions in Euroskepticism are undoubtedly available. But among the various arguments that skeptics might offer, this one is probably the most substantively plausible and certainly the most normatively important.

Framing the problem in terms of the differences between Eurosceptics and advocates of continued European integration serves to focus attention on a central tendency of government – the inclination of legislators to leave the details of lawmaking to bureaucrats (or, more charitably, the inability of legislators to do otherwise). This tendency has long been recognized as problematic, and it is one further exacerbated by legislators inevitably being overwhelmed by the complexity and urgency of the challenges of the Anthropocene. More recently, this practice has even been criticized as a threat to the existence of constitutional government itself (Iancu 2012). A standard defense of legislative delegation is that governmental efficiency is improved and the effectiveness of policy outcomes enhanced by the practice of leaving policy details to substantive specialists and technical experts. At its strongest, this defense amounts to an entirely plausible argument that legislative delegation is not merely prudent but (given the complexity of the modern state) a practical necessity (Shane 2010). As a subsidiary element within this general argument, criticisms of legislative delegation grounded in democratic theory are additionally answered by reference to the democratic potential of the practice of legislative oversight (Pelizzo and Stapenhurst 2013).

In the United States, the enterprise of legitimating legislative delegation and the administrative discretion that results from it has been a central focus of administrative law scholars. In his landmark statement on discretionary justice, Davis (1969) was careful to distinguish legislative delegation of authority (guided by principles inherent in the delegation) from areas of administrative discretion (wherein the limits of administrative powers leave the administrator free to choose among alternative courses of action). It is with these normatively unconstrained choices that the democrat must be primarily concerned. Much administrative law scholarship has focused precisely on this problem. In spite of promising early efforts, American and European scholars of administrative law have not embraced comparative approaches in ways that have been typical of other areas of legal research and practice (Boughey 2013). As a result, scholarship addressing the problem of administrative accountability in global governance is especially deficient. But this problem must be addressed because accountability is a central element of the political legitimacy to which both global governance and the EU aspire. This aspiration of global governance for legitimacy may also be thwarted by factors similar to "structural factors in the EU that have made it especially difficult to devise a satisfactory solution in pragmatic and normative terms to the dilemma of legitimating secondary rules of a legislative nature" (Craig 2012, 111).

It is critically important to the legitimacy of democratic government (at any level) that the discretionary acts of bureaucratic officials be guided and constrained by normative principles not of their own devising (Habermas 1996). Where unelected government officials are judged only by standards of their own creation, no genuine accountability is possible and democracy is ever at risk. The problem is exacerbated by the fact that much modern legislation, and especially that of the EU, is framed in "relatively open-textured terms, thereby necessitating greater specification through subsequent action" (Craig 2012, 109). Dubious claims regarding the adequacy of so-called outcome legitimacy notwithstanding (Scharpf 1999), behavioral norms that are not the result of, or at least consistent with, fundamentally democratic processes are (from a democratic perspective) of deeply problematic provenance. Detailed legislative oversight, to the extent that competent authorities can exercise it, is one potential response to that problem.

In this respect the European Union has a significant problem. The three institutions that share legislative power in the EU – the European Parliament, the European Council, and the Council of Ministers – all are structurally incapable of exercising much legislative oversight of European Commission actions. These bodies have three basic ways to exercise legislative power – the Community method, Comitology, and treaty reform. To put matters succinctly, each of these methods requires the cooperation of Commission administrators for elected officials to legislate, making significant legislative changes of administrative decisions nearly impossible. The Community method vests the power of initiating an act of legislation in the European Commission, whose administrative actions would be the subject of any legislative oversight. Comitology (to the extent that it is still a viable option) is a process carried out through rule-making committees that are chaired by Commission representatives empowered to set the committees' agendas. Treaty reform, though not subject to unilateral obstruction by the Commission, requires a unanimous vote from both an intergovernmental conference and the member states themselves (Miller 2011), all of which are proceedings in which the Commission can involve itself politically. It would be remarkable indeed if a decision were ever to be reached over significant Commission objections. In short, the EU legislative process is fundamentally flawed in terms of administrative accountability – "the actors who make the Union legitimate cannot overrule the EU's regulators, the actors who make it functional" (Miller 2011, 325).

130 *Equivocal Democratic Accountability in the Anthropocene*

The independent norms needed to constrain the administrative discretion of European Commission decision-making are unlikely to be provided by elected EU officials (at least, as the Union is now constituted). It is important, however, that this situation be viewed against the backdrop of the EU's overall policy objectives. In 2000, pursuant to its general goals of becoming the world's most competitive and dynamic knowledge-based economy (European Council 2000a), the European Council adopted the "open method of coordination." The Council described the open method of coordination as a decentralized process in which member states, regional and local governments, and social partners and civil society would be actively involved (European Council 2000b). The general components of the open method of coordination included the establishment of guidelines for the Union (including specific timelines for achieving short-, medium-, and long-term policy goals); qualitative as well as quantitative benchmarks based on global best practices but tailored to the needs of the various member states; translation of these European guidelines into national and regional policy objectives (including specific performance targets and adopting measures); and periodic monitoring, evaluation, and peer review (conceived of and organized as a mutual learning process).

The OMC process was reaffirmed in 2005. A new three-year planning cycle was introduced, the starting point of which is an EU Commission synoptic document – the strategic report. Based on its consideration of this report, the European Council adopts integrated guidelines. Acting on the basis of these guidelines, member states then draw up national reform programs, after consultation with all stakeholders (European Council 2005). Whether or not this "re-launched" version of the OMC will achieve the economic and social objectives of the EU remains to be seen. This much, however, is clear: The Commission still plays its historic role as the initiator of the process of establishing the general goals and policy objectives of the EU. Member states are charged with tailoring these policies to their needs, and subnational governments continue to be imagined as an important part of the implementation process. Fundamental normative values are still established at the level of the Union and on the basis of an agenda devised by unelected officials of the EU Commission and other EU agencies. By any measure, this represents a massive delegation of legislative authority, creating an expansive zone of administrative discretion within which the future direction of the EU is charted. Elected officials of the EU can then exercise some (conventionally understood) limited oversight of how this discretion is exercised, but they are poorly situated to do so.

The legitimacy of legislative oversight requires that "administration does not have access to the normative premises underlying its decisions" and that administrative power "may not be used to intervene in, or substitute for, processes of legislation and adjudication" (Habermas 1996, 173). By this standard, the situation of the European Commission as we have here described it is clearly problematic. Circumstances are further complicated by the fact that "democratic self-control and self-realization has until now been credibly realized only in the context of the nation-state" (Habermas 1998, 61). Even the capacity for "democratic self-steering within the national society" is being seriously degraded by the "disempowerment of the nation-state" that results from globalization's impact on national regulatory and fiscal independence of action (Habermas 1998, 67, 69). If this degradation of the nation-state conspires with the transnational character of environmental risks to make it necessary to address environmental protection at the global level, it becomes all the more imperative that the democratic deficit of international politics be addressed.

6.3 In Search of Policy Norms: A Deliberative Model of Administrative Accountability

Changes in the EU's official legislative processes have so far not fundamentally altered the fact that it is "an elite project above the heads of the people concerned" and continues to operate with democratic deficits resulting from its "essentially intergovernmental and bureaucratic" characteristics (Habermas 2009, 80). Adoption of a deliberative model of administrative accountability, summarized in Table 2.1, suggests several additional accountability mechanisms that could be added to what the EU already does to better address the problem of providing governing norms to constrain the exercise of administrative discretion by the Commission, and to do so in a way that satisfies the requirement that those norms not be the creation of the Commission itself. Ultimately, a deliberative democratic approach is preferable to other approaches because it contains within itself the means of revising both its procedures and its products at the initiative of either organizers or participants (Gutmann and Thompson 2004). Deliberation is central to achieving this reflexive quality in governance because only it can reconcile many if not most of the sometimes contradictory claims that are made about the drivers of ecosystem reflexivity (Dryzek and Pickering 2017). If such a model were adopted, instead of generating the normative principles that guide its own use of administrative discretion, the European Commission would serve as the convener of deliberative conferences, juries, and panels to perform that task. To put it most simply, the Commission (either directly or through other EU agencies) would commission rather than create the principles needed to constrain its use of administrative discretion.

Prior to ratification of the Lisbon Treaty in 2009, the democratic theorist in search of an accountability mechanism at this stage of the EU policy process would have encountered significant frustration. But two innovations adopted in the Lisbon Treaty suggest new institutional opportunities for this kind of deliberative uptake. A new category of administrative law, the delegated act, was created by the Lisbon Treaty. This form of law is best thought of as an amendment (often technical in nature) to a preexisting piece of EU legislation. Given the general, often aspirational, nature of EU law, even so significant a choice as between command-and-control regulations and market-based incentive systems could well fall within the ambit of this new process. The Lisbon Treaty also authorized a process of citizen initiative, designed to allow what amounts to a petition drive to place a legislative proposal before the European Parliament (Miller 2011). These innovations clearly offer at least the possibility for the European Commission to secure external normative standards for the exercise of its discretionary authority.

One concrete example of this approach has been described as "collaborative learning" (Cheng and Fiero 2005), an approach to policy development that is strongly reminiscent of the European Commission's mission to promote mutual learning at the level of local implementation decisions. Collaborative learning (Cheng and Fiero 2005), which is an innovation in public participation that departs from the traditional focus on issues and interests, is an approach designed specifically to address the complexity and rancorous conflict. Collaborative learning is characterized by a systems approach to understanding issues, the promotion (instead of avoidance) of dialogue about differences among stakeholders, and a focus on feasible improvements in concrete circumstances rather than ideal outcomes over the longer term. It is an approach to policy development that could help achieve the European Commission's mission to promote mutual learning at the level of local implementation decisions. The European Commission could, for example, sponsor and sustain collaborative learning through the kinds of transgovernmental networks that research has already shown to be effective in improving compliance effectiveness within the EU (Hobolth and Martinsen 2013). The potential for this sort of participatory planning to improve the accountability of the European Commission's use of its longstanding authority to promulgate implementing rules (Craig 2012) is unmistakable.

6.4 Deliberative Practice and Administrative Accountability in Global Environmental Governance

Analysis of an extension of the deliberative model of administrative accountability to the EU's embryonic nonlegislative accountability mechanisms yields four main observations about the problems of governance accountability in the political circumstances of the Anthropocene: (1) deliberative techniques are readily deployable and offer significant advantages with respect to administrative accountability; (2) in part because of what deliberative democratic techniques make possible in the way of accountability, they can contribute much to political

6.4 Deliberative Practice and Administrative Accountability

legitimacy as well; (3) deliberative democracy can increase social capital for institution building and maintenance, such that loss of organizational effectiveness does not have to be an unavoidable cost of gains in legitimacy and accountability; and (4) properly designed deliberative mechanisms can produce normative premises independent of the bureaucratic institutions of governance and can in turn hold bureaucratic institutions accountable to those premises.

To elaborate, there is nothing about the issues of environmental governance that puts them out of the reach of democratic deliberation. New deliberative techniques like juristic deliberation can easily be imagined as tools for exploring the contours and limitations of normative consensus about both the exploitation and conservation of natural resources and the avoidance or amelioration of the results of that exploitation. Well-tested techniques like deliberative polling can readily be used to elicit a more reflective public opinion on contending models of environmental policy. Watershed partnerships are a preeminent example of stakeholder planning and the coproduction of regulatory implementation. At each successive step of the process of developing policies of environmental governance, deliberative techniques are readily deployable and offer significant advantages over less fully participatory approaches, particularly in terms of the political durability of the solutions that they produce and the administrative accountability being sought.

The fact that democratic deliberation is deployable at each stage of the process of environmental policy development leads to the observation that deliberative democracy has the potential to add significantly to the political legitimacy of global environmental governance. This is significant because issues of both natural resource management and environmental protection are likely to involve issues of distributive justice and significant levels of political conflict. This characteristic of environmental governance makes broadening involvement in the policy process to include representatives of historically underrepresented groups more difficult, and more essential. The experience of Native American tribes, for example, indicates that their political and economic disadvantages mean that they are not often involved in watershed decision-making. But their involvement in watershed partnerships (when it occurs) leads public officials to deploy financial and human resources in ways that better manage watersheds across a full range of social values, resulting in more equitable and more defensible regulatory outcomes (Cronin and Ostergren 2007). Thus, the realization that every step in the process of environmental governance can include significant citizen participation means that a virtuous circle of public confidence and public involvement can be created that can legitimize outcomes that are ecologically sound but that may disappoint some stakeholders and might otherwise have been rejected for that reason.

Recognizing that democratic deliberation has a role to play at every stage of the policy process is just a short step from realizing that the unidirectional assumption inherent in the very concept of the policy process, and the role of administrative agencies in it, needs to be overcome. In any broadly participatory political process, arriving at consensus is a recursive proposition. Yesterday's normative agreement can always be unwound by today's political dissent or tomorrow's social discord. To a greater degree than political theorists, the skilled policy analysts and experienced public professionals who populate administrative agencies are aware that all conclusions are tentative and no victory is final. That is why the leaders of collaborative watershed partnerships so often find themselves grappling with challenges of organization development and maintenance rather than the environmental issues that originally brought them to the table (Bonnell and Koontz 2007). Collaborative environmental governance is at least as much a matter of organization building as it is environmental protection.

A long recognized strength of deliberative democracy is its tendency to increase the social capital necessary for institution building and maintenance (Shandas and Messer 2008). It does so in at least two ways. First, well-implemented democratic deliberation makes it possible to achieve an "economy of moral disagreement." Democratic deliberation requires citizens to justify their political positions to one another by seeking a rationale that is fully public, a rationale that all deliberators could (at least in principle) accept. This requirement minimizes the outright rejection by deliberators of positions that they oppose by discouraging reliance on comprehensive moral or religious doctrines in favor of more limited rationales that allow for the eventual convergence of their views with those of others (Gutmann and Thompson 2004). Second, democratic deliberation has the tendency to turn a collection of separate individuals into a self-identified group whose members see one another as cooperators in a shared project rather than as opponents in a zero-sum contest. Among the norms that deliberation promotes is a norm of cooperation within the group that is often strong enough to discourage members from clinging to their positions for transient or entirely personal reasons (Miller 2003). Deliberative exercises conducted iteratively in any given community are likely to increase that community's ability to resolve problems in a collaborative way.

Together, these two features of democratic deliberation (its tendency to reduce moral disputes and to promote consensus) can reduce the costs of organization maintenance in a stakeholder community by narrowing the grounds of disagreement among participants, thereby reducing the range of possible policy outcomes with which any final decision procedure must deal. When this result is achieved, more of the resources of environmental professionals can be turned to solving environmental problems as less time is spent overcoming the forces of organizational entropy. Ultimately, a tipping point is reached where gains in democratic legitimacy are no longer paid for with losses in organizational effectiveness. In the process, administrative agencies involved in environmental governance become the subjects of externally generated normative constraints that impose new patterns of accountability on their use of the administrative discretion with which they are unavoidably invested.

From a thoroughly political perspective, what is still needed is more than merely *popular* participation but, rather, fully *public* participation. The distinction, obviously, is between those outside of government who have a direct stake in the issue at hand and those outside of government who have only that interest in the issue that all other citizens have. The resolution of a particular issue by a committee of stakeholders (aided by, for example, an administrative law judge) may be reasonably stable over time. It may also be immediately defensible as a reasonable *modus vivendi*. If it is the result of a well-crafted process of administrative rule-making, there may even be a record of the decision sufficient to allow a court to subsequently evaluate whether the action has harmed the interests of persons not party to the discretionary process or exceeded the legitimate authority of the agency that issued the ruling. Given the way the term "stakeholder" is commonly understood and defined in these processes (Whitman 2008), none of these advantages over unrestrained exercises of administrative discretion are sufficient to satisfy the demands of democratic legitimacy – namely, that all decisions result from fair and open participatory processes, that the majority of the broad community be the source of sovereign power, and that outcomes give citizens reason to continue to participate (Baber and Bartlett 2005; Whitman 2008). The challenge, then, is to develop mechanisms of rule-making that will address the democratic deficit without compromising the advantages these mechanisms enjoy over the option of regulation by detailed legislation (which is well out of reach at the international level in any event).

It might well be objected that even if the European Commission pursued some or all of the deliberative initiatives suggested, the results would still fall short of promoting accountability by enforcing external normative standards on its use of administrative discretion. After all, might not the Commission ignore any results that failed to advance its own agenda? Were no other EU entities concerned with assuring accountability in the continuing process of Union integration, this objection would be quite a serious one. But the existence of some democratically generated external normative standards should be expected at least to marginally strengthen the ability, if not the resolve, of institutions such as the European Council, the European Parliament, and the Council of Ministers to hold the Commission to account. In addition, European courts exercise significant powers of judicial review over actions of the Commission and are clearly motivated to advance the cause of uniformity in the application of EU legislative rules – but it is unlikely that they can hold the Commission to account on their own, simply by applying general principles of law to legislative enactments (Schwarze 2012).

In reviewing any administrative action the Commission might take in response to deliberatively generated norms, courts are quite capable of comparing the reasons given by the Commission for its actions to the normative principles that it claims to be pursuing. Lest we conclude that, in relying on European courts to hold the European Commission and other EU agencies accountable, we have merely substituted one unelected form of decision-making for another, we should remember this. Normative principles generated by properly designed deliberative mechanisms are both heterologous to the appointed institutions of governance and directly democratic in their provenance. So here we have a means of addressing both the problem of administrative accountability in the EU and the broader democratic deficit in the legislative institutions of earth system governance generally.

6.5 Equivocal Accountability in the Anthropocene

Making sense of the Anthopocene involves using that concept to capture many ideas in one word. Part of the appeal of "Anthropocene" is that, among other things, it provides a way of making sense of, and appreciating reflexively, (1) the immense complexity of the physical and cultural worlds and the minimal but growing human understanding of it; (2) the unthinking and often inadvertent human assumption of responsibility for directing the ill-understood relationship with this environment and even for controlling the environment itself; and (3) the inkling, barely dawning, of just how complex and urgent various transformations need to be if humans are to govern themselves onto trajectories that promise environmental richness and equitable prosperity for future generations (Linnér and Wibeck 2019). For many reasons, including the generation, dissemination, and incorporation of knowledge, the necessary ubiquity of action, implementation effectiveness, openness to learning and adaptation, and the need for nearly universal normative buy-in, among others, this governance must evolve quickly, in a matter of a few decades rather than a few centuries, and it must be democratic. Much of the needed action – regulative, allocative, distributive – cannot be accomplished in a timely way and on an adequate scale other than by delegating considerable discretion to administrative agents and agencies. If such governance is to be at all democratic, these agencies must be seen as democratically legitimate and they must be held accountable by mechanisms that are clearly democratic in their provenance.

Legislative oversight, the primary mechanism for accountability responsibility within nation-states, provides no prospective answer to the immense and complex accountability needs of global governance in the Anthropocene. But democratically responsible accountability is still possible in a governance world of diffused power and complex relationships. In struggling forward with this transnational accountability challenge, the EU has laid a foundation for employing a set of deliberative democratic practices that can achieve significant democratic oversight in the absence of an effectively empowered and engaged legislature. Additional deliberative democratic techniques can contribute to norm mapping and building, to choosing among policy models, and to developing and implementing policy action plans. By establishing new democratic responsibilities and the expectation that policies and actions must be consistent with democratically embraced normative principles, appropriately institutionalized deliberative democracy in the Anthropocene has the potential to add significantly to the accountability, and therefore the political legitimacy, of global environmental governance.

7

Equitable Access and Allocation in the Anthropocene

Reconciling Today and Tomorrow

Consider what it means for human beings to enjoy security. Were we able (for analytical purposes, at least) to set aside the human tragedies involved in terrorist attacks and the sorry history of terrorism, we might be able to see that the distortive effect of terrorism on our collective thinking about security has been one of its most lamentable results. As merely one among many threats to human security, terrorism displays "a cockeyed ratio of fear to harm" (Pinker 2012, 344). From 2006 to 2018, the annual death toll from terrorism (both international terrorism and its more liberally defined cousin, domestic terrorism) ranged from 11,000 to 33,000 globally (statista.com). In 2017 alone, there were 110,000 entirely preventable deaths worldwide just from the measles (Dabbagh et al. 2018). The economic harm and deaths, direct and indirect, that resulted from the virus-transmitted Covid-19 pandemic in 2020 may never be fully accounted. If we were really serious about fighting mass murder, the seven million people who die annually from tobacco use (World Health Organization 2017) would elicit far more attention than the Islamic State and Al-Qaeda combined. It is no exaggeration to say that compared to the number of deaths from far more easily preventable causes, the worldwide toll from terrorism is lost in the statistical noise (Pinker 2012).

Because of the radical discrepancy between the insecurity generated by terrorists and the actual threat that they pose, the United States spent 6 trillion dollars in two wars trying (as yet, unsuccessfully) to secure its population from terrorism (Crawford 2018). National priorities in other countries throughout the developed world have been similarly, if not always so severely, distorted. This is no accident. It is precisely the kind of self-inflicted defeat that terrorists set out to impose (Pinker 2012, 344–361). But this is not the only manifestation of the contemporary national security fixation. Global military spending continues to increase even though international battle deaths in war have dropped from around a half million per year in the late 1940s to around thirty thousand per year in the early 2000s.

One would never guess that the dream of the 1960s folk songs has very nearly come true: "the world has (almost) put an end to war" (302).

In light of this history of skewed reasoning and squandered resources, perhaps it is time to begin weaning ourselves away from the very concept of "national" security. Perhaps a broader concept such as "human" security should become more prominent as an organizing principle of governance (Lautensach and Lautensach 2014). What changes in orientation might this involve? A useful hint can be found in the same statistics of global conflict that, when carefully examined, warn us away from our preoccupation with terrorism and war among nations. While it is true that interstate war has very nearly joined colonial war in the dustbin of history, civil wars appear to be more popular than ever (Themnér and Wallensteen 2014). If wars between nations are clashes of egos or of civilizations, then what leads to civil wars? The experience of post-colonial Africa serves as a guide.

There is a popular belief that Africa's civil wars are caused by its ethnic and religious diversity. But models of the overall incidence of civil wars in 161 countries between 1960 and 1999 (Elbadawi and Sambanis 2000) show that the relatively higher incidence of civil war in Africa is not due to the ethno-linguistic fragmentation of its countries, but rather to high levels of poverty, failed political institutions, and economic dependence on shrinking natural resources. The best and fastest strategy to reduce the incidence of civil war in Africa and prevent future civil wars is to institute democratic reforms that effectively manage the developmental challenges facing Africa's diverse societies. In fact, Africa's ethnic diversity helps – rather than impedes – the emergence of stable development as it necessitates inter-group bargaining processes (Elbadawi and Sambanis 2000). These processes can be peaceful and positive if ethnic groups feel adequately represented by their national political institutions and if national and regional economies provide opportunities for productive activity to all. These two values, access to the halls of government and an equitable allocation of economic opportunity, firmly ground the concept of human security in the larger context of social justice. They also provide the normative context for any examination of issues of access and allocation in earth system governance.

7.1 Access and Earth System Governance

Environmental goods are supplied by nature, but how they are received is a matter decided by people. Even so ubiquitous a good as a sustainable human relationship to the global climate is, at least potentially, subject to appropriation by those with disproportionate financial means (Biermann and Möller 2019). Therefore, any assessment of how environmental goods are accessed and allocated that is intended to influence decisions people make regarding their interactions with nature needs to take account of how equitably distributed is the ability to actually benefit from different ecosystem services (or, suffer from the deprivation of those services). Posing questions of this sort is particularly important in light of the fact that environmental inequity has been preserved in climate negotiations between the global North and South (Ciplet, Roberts, and Khan 2015). Although power relationships in the low-carbon transitions that are necessary to address climate change are distinctly asymmetrical, they are also promisingly unstable (Sovacool and Brisbois 2019). Climate solutions, therefore, always need justification from the perspective of equity.

This kind of justification is now invited from every country submitting intended nationally determined contributions under provisions of the 2015 Paris Agreement (Winkler et al. 2018). But the critical question remains, what determines the distribution of ecosystem services benefits between different sections of society? Some insights into this question are available in the existing literature. For instance, an "entitlements approach" was used to examine how people perceive ecosystem services benefits across twenty-eight coral reef fishing communities in four countries (Elbadawi and Sambanis 2000). This research showed that access to environmental benefits is mediated by key access mechanisms, which can be rights-based, economic, knowledge-based, social, or institutional. Specific access mechanisms influence which ecosystem services (ES) people prioritize. But local context strongly determines whether specific access mechanisms enable or constrain benefits. For example, local ecological knowledge enabled people to prioritize a certain habitat benefit in Kenya, but constrained people from prioritizing the same benefit in Madagascar (Hicks and Cinner 2014). "People perceive ES benefits in bundles rather than as discrete individual benefits and . . . access mechanisms are strongly related to which ES benefits people perceive" (17794). From this observation, Hicks and Cinner conclude that ecological services assessments, and the policies that they support, need to take account of the broad suite of access mechanisms that enable different people to benefit from a supply of ecosystem services if they are to be both locally grounded and ecologically effective. This depth of analysis is especially important given the high level of path dependency in institutions that are complicit in the destabilization of major earth systems (Dryzek 2016).

In order to understand the development of and subsequent changes in the institutional mechanisms that determine access to ecosystem services, it is important to account for historical changes in rules, norms, and conventions composing those mechanisms. It is equally important to access the highly particular knowledge of local informants in order to assess the scales at which ecosystem services are supplied, demanded, and governed, as well as to discover any scale misfits in relation to historical conflicts over access to ecosystem

services. Particularly in an age of modernization, it will generally be possible to identify at least two major threads of institutional change in these institutions – one characterized by conflicts between a central state and local users arising from enclosures of communal resources and associated restrictions in ecosystem services, and another involving a clash between customary governance institutions and new ones emerging with increasing levels of central state intervention and market integration. These threads interact to challenge, and yet render more essential, the maintenance of multilevel governance regimes that promote coordination and institutional diversity across governmental levels while respecting local sovereignty over ecosystem management. Institutions that achieve and maintain this balance are more likely to prevent environmental conflicts and to produce better outcomes regarding the long-term sustainable use of ecosystem services (Gómez-Baggethun et al. 2013).

Insights such as these have, over recent decades, resulted in a paradigm shift in how natural resources management is conceived. The shift has been away from state-centered control toward community-based approaches in which local people play a much more active role – approaches situated in theoretical frameworks seeking to empower local communities through decentralization policies. Many case studies have examined the organizational frameworks within which decentralization is implemented. Generally speaking, they find that at the local level there is a complex interface between traditional and modern authority structures, with both complimentary and conflicting jurisdictions and mandates. Given this multiplicity of institutional features, most observers argue that access to environmental goods should be determined at this level and for a systematic determination of the appropriate organizations and individuals to be involved in each specific decentralization process (Nemarundewe 2004). There are, however, several obvious challenges to this approach that also relate to the problem of access.

Access to the institutions of governance will be worth little without a concomitant access to information. Social and economic development in any country depends heavily on that country's scientific strength and its ability to resolve problems in such areas as public health, infectious disease, environmental management, and industrial progress. Access to research information historically depends on ability to pay, a form of dependence that has a negative impact on the populations of developing countries. A number of new initiatives (ranging from consortial licensing and new publishing models to the Open Access Initiative) address this imbalance and have the potential to meet the needs of research in financially constrained countries. The advent of the Open Access strategies, particularly interoperable institutional archives, also has the potential to revolutionize access to essential research (Kirsop and Chan 2005). Even more important, however, is the notion that those affected by decisions about access to environmental services and the process of making those decisions should have access to the processes of generating environmental information, as for instance in a project to engage researchers and fishers together in adapting social science approaches to the purposes and the constraints of community-based fisher organizations (Wiber et al. 2004). This project's rationale reflected increasingly popular arguments that (1) effective community-based environmental management requires that managers must be able to pose and address social science questions; (2) participatory research (involving true cooperation in all stages) can support this process; and (3) there is a need to overcome practical and methodological barriers faced in developing participatory research protocols that will serve the needs of community-based management while not imposing excessive transaction costs. The project's work with fisher organizations, both aboriginal and non-aboriginal – in which social science priorities were set by each organization, and small-scale research projects were designed and carried out to meet these needs – identified fisher interests in research on three different levels of meaning. These included practical livelihood concerns (including what, when, where, and how intensively to fish), social, economic, and political issues (such as institutional structures, politics of access and allocation, overlap and conflict between regulatory regimes), and the values and ethics that implicitly or explicitly guide policy development and implementation. As a result of the project, local fisher organizations were able to address several critical research themes – including sharing power, defining boundaries of a community-based group, achieving access and equity, designing effective management plans, enforcement, and scaling up for effective regional and ecosystem-wide management. This project (and others like it) has demonstrated the effectiveness of extending participatory methods to challenge traditional scientific notions of the research process but it also highlights the inherent tensions in participatory research between personal interests, systematic knowledge, and shared political values. These tensions are the sources of discord that often contribute to human security threats.

Users of environmental goods do not bring a scholar's level of dispassion to the practice of environmental policy research, which suggests two other challenges faced by those who would democratize and decentralize the processes of environmental decision-making. First, enhanced local involvement in environmental decision-making is not guaranteed to result in outcomes that actually improve the environment. As an example, in the United States there is a complex (and not always positive) relationship between local autonomy in land-use planning and management, economic development, and federal efforts to restrict land use on and around identified hazardous waste sites. Specifically, the successful implementation of the federal government's Superfund program is increasingly dependent on the willingness of local governments to create institutional controls that restrict access to and use of certain properties, often in ways that are inconsistent with local economic interests. Within the context of intergovernmental competition for economic development opportunities in a decentralized system of government, it is often difficult for local governments to comply with national institutional controls that impose restrictions of this sort without alienating their own constituencies (Ellison 2001). Likewise, at the international level, globalization can lead to either conservation or depletion of the natural resources that are used in the production of traded goods. Rising prices may lead to better resource management as the value of a resource increases, making the costs of management appear to be a better investment. Alternatively, stronger incentives to extract these resources may exacerbate their decline – especially in open access institutional frameworks. For example, an examination of the impact of agricultural trade promotion on the groundwater extraction in India using nationally representative data from 1996 to 2005 found evidence that trade promotion led to significant depletion of groundwater reserves (Sekhri and Landefeld 2013). Access to world markets in a liberalized trade regime may both appeal to local interests and hold out the promise of increased national incomes, but it cannot be relied on to produce the kind of environmental governance institutions that are needed to protect limited natural resources and to diminish the sources of tension that give rise to human security risks.

Second, initiatives to decentralize and democratize access to environmental goods and the decision-making processes regarding them may have the perverse effect of reproducing patterns of differentiated power that result in an inequitable allocation of those same resources. Insight into this problem can be gained by a comparison of institutional approaches that address questions of access to forest resources and issues of redistributive justice for indigenous peoples in Australia and India. For over three decades, both countries have seen the emergence of claims to forest access and ownership made by indigenous communities that historically have been disadvantaged and marginalized from the benefits of mainstream social and economic development. The result has been a series of regional forest agreements in Australia and a collection of joint forest management experiments in India (Rangan and Lane 2001). Australian regional forest agreements are twenty-year plans for the conservation and sustainable management of native forests and are intended to provide "certainty" to commercial forestry operations while protecting environmental values. They rely on a mix of community and industry consultation combined with scientific research. The regional forest agreements are supported by the forestry industry, but they are widely criticized by environmental groups as green lights for uncontrolled cutting. In Tasmania, for example, a forestry operation that is undertaken in accordance with a regional forest agreement is not required to obtain the environmental approvals otherwise required by the Environment Protection and Biodiversity Conservation Act, nor to protect rare or threatened species listed in the CAR (comprehensive, adequate, representative) Reserve System. In contrast, Indian Joint Forest Management relies on partnerships involving both the state forest departments and local communities (Gupte and Bartlett 2007). The policies and objectives of Joint Forest Management are detailed in the Indian comprehensive National Forest Policy of 1988 and the Joint Forest Management Guidelines of 1990. Although schemes vary somewhat from state to state and are sometimes known by different names, a village committee usually known as the Forest Protection Committee and the Indian Forest Department enter into a joint forest management agreement. Villagers agree to assist in the safeguarding of forest resources through protection from fire, grazing, illegal harvesting, and other management tasks, in exchange for which they receive non-timber forest products as well as a share of the revenue from the sale of timber products. Unlike Australian regional forest agreements, joint forest management agreements directly link forest resource conservation to the economic advancement of the region's indigenous population (Rangan and Lane 2001) – overcoming (at least in principle) the tendency of other governance institutions to replicate existing social and economic inequities while sacrificing environmental values to the cause of economic growth (which often happens beyond the boundaries of the community in question).

Inequitable allocation of environmental goods is a potential consequence of inappropriately designed institutions of access to both environmental resources and the authoritative decision processes that manage those resources. The wider question of the allocation of environmental goods is yet another aspect of environmental inequity that threatens human security.

7.2 Allocation and Earth System Governance

Decentralization of environmental policy-making can be a mixed blessing. All too often, decentralization of decision-making reproduces at the local level precisely those differential power relationships that impoverished people in the first place, as exemplified by forest management. The literature on natural resource decentralization with respect to forests in developing countries is located at the intersection between discussions of, on the one hand, good governance and democracy, development, and poverty alleviation, and on the other, common property resources, community-based resource management, and local resource rights. This literature shows that policies implemented in the name of decentralization are often applied in ways that are incompatible with the democratic potential usually associated with decentralization. Only rarely have these policies resulted in pro-poor outcomes or challenged underlying structures of inequity. This gap between promise and performance often results from inattention to the issues of who receives decentralized powers, the role played by property rights regimes, the notion of "the local" at work in particular situations, and how the interaction of expert and local knowledge poses institutional contradictions and structures key issues. Fundamental differences in conceptions of democracy, participation, and development lie behind these contradictions. These differences highlight the need for strategies for the redistribution of access to political power and resources as an integral part of decentralized decision-making (Larson and Soto 2008).

The necessity for developing strategies for the redistribution of social, political, and economic power is easier to see in some circumstances than in others. For instance, the problems of achieving either human security or environmental quality in the resource-rich nations of the developing world are well-known. Corruption (both private and public) is one of the main reasons why resource-rich countries often perform badly in both economic and environmental terms. Corruption in resource-rich countries takes two main forms – rent-seeking and patronage. Apparent availability of resource rents induces rent-seeking, as individuals compete for a share of the rents rather than using their time and skills more productively. Resource revenues induce patronage as governments pay off supporters to stay in power, resulting in reduced accountability and an inferior allocation of public funds. The existing scholarly literature on natural resources and corruption supports a conclusion that both international donors and domestic policy-makers should give priority to policies that address rent-seeking and patronage (Kolstad and Søreide 2009). In other words, policy in resource-rich countries, and the development aid given to them, should be less about macro-economic management and more about building institutions to prevent rent-seeking and patronage and providing the right incentives to players in the resource sector. But what are the dynamics of environmental policy making in the far more common circumstance of resource scarcity? Must there be a different logic at work under those conditions?

Perhaps not. For example, the particular form of inequitable allocation of natural resources that is water poverty is a serious threat to human security throughout the world. This particular form of inequitable allocation of natural resources is a function of both physical constraints (affecting access and supply of water) and institutional arrangements (affecting access to decision-making regarding the utilization of water). This distinction reflects the complexity of water poverty and highlights the need to look beyond technical and financial means that are admittedly necessary (but not sufficient) to reduce its prevalence and severity. Policy decisions affecting water resources are generally made at a provincial or national level. But hydrological and socioeconomic evaluations at these levels (or at the water basin level) cannot be presumed to be in accord with the reality of water poverty or livelihood vulnerability at more local levels. An approach more likely to account for such local inequities would include an initial mapping of observed water poverty, the estimation of factors that potentially influence the observed poverty patterns, and, finally, a consideration of the correlates of water poverty in the places where their effects appear most severe. A potentially serious political challenge arises from comparative analyses of correlates of poverty at basin, national, and local levels, which often show only limited congruence with more fine-grained analyses.

Variation in water quantity and the presence of irrigation and dams have no or limited correlation with observed variation in water poverty measures across these geopolitical levels. Research has shown that education and access to improved water quality are the only variables consistently significant and spatially stable across entire water basins. At all levels, education is a consistent non-water correlate of water poverty, while access to protected water sources is the strongest water-related correlate (Ward and Kaczan 2014). In other words, investments in human development and targeted uses of public authority to protect water quality in disadvantaged regions are both necessary to alleviate water poverty. The technocratic development responses so often favored by national and international elites and their financial and industrial supporters fail to address water poverty as it occurs locally. Landscape and scale matter for understanding water–poverty linkages and for devising policy concerned with alleviating water poverty. Interactions between environmental, social, and institutional factors are complex and consequently a comprehensive understanding of water poverty and its causes requires analysis at multiple levels of governance (Ward and Kaczan 2014). Actually dealing with water poverty in effective ways requires that both donor and developing countries resist the corrupting pressures to invest in brick-and-mortar policies that may enrich multinational corporations but produce national infrastructures that fail to address local needs and distributional inequities.

Experiences with environmental conservation in the developing world suggest that a healthy environment is required to achieve sustainable economic development. The factors most often cited as responsible for policy failure in addressing environmental degradation in developing nations include income inequality, weak institutional capacity, and lack of access to information and public participation. Strengthening of law, increasing respect for human rights, and promoting democratic governance are widely regarded as measures through which human security, in both economic and environmental terms, can be achieved (Amechi 2009). The distributional dimension of this challenge is also well understood. A significant percentage of the global population does not have access to safe drinking water, sufficient food, or the energy supplies necessary to live in dignity or to realize basic human capabilities. There is a continuous struggle to allocate the earth's resources among users and uses. These distributional problems have two faces: access to basic resources and allocation of the environmental resources, risks, burdens, and responsibilities for remediating environmental damage. Addressing problems of access and allocation often requires intervention in such social processes as science, political movements, and law. Analysts (both environmental and economic) have tended to take a narrow, disciplinary approach even though an integrated conceptual approach could yield better results. What is required is a multi-disciplinary perspective on the problem of access and allocation (Gupta and Lebel 2010). The consequences of ignoring this imperative can be seen clearly in the case of global biofuel policy.

The large-scale production of crop-based biofuels has been one of the fastest and most controversial global changes of recent years. Global biofuel outputs increased sixfold between 2000 and 2010, and a growing number of countries adopted biofuel promotion policies. Meanwhile, multilateral bodies were created and a patchwork of biofuel policies emerged. Clearly, rigorous, cross-disciplinary analysis of the global biofuel policy context – its nature, its institutional architecture, and issues of access and allocation – is in order. Assessment of existing policy in this area reveals a density of national policies but an absence of international consensus on norms and rules. The global biofuel context remains a non-regime, in spite of the fact that serious issues of access are overlooked – even as a risky North–South allocation pattern is being created. Although biofuel governance is not completely absent, existing international institutions and initiatives fail to take account of the different voices in the debate and leave a large vacuum of unaddressed social and environmental issues (Lima and Gupta 2013). Even a cursory examination of biofuel politics in key countries suggests that this is likely to remain an arena of nongovernance at the international level, barring a fundamental realignment in how the normative and environmental implications of this fast-growing industry are perceived.

7.3 Access and Allocation in the Anthropocene

Both access and allocation pose serious challenges for earth system governance. Both are potential sources of human insecurity and both raise questions of justice, corresponding as they do to the procedural and distributive dimensions of that concept. Critically analyzing access and allocation and how they relate to each other will illuminate and, ultimately, make possible institutionalization of the duality implicit in the idea of environmental justice. The relationship between them is obviously reciprocal, but just making that observation does not get us very far. The question of allocation is primary in the sense that it provides an evaluative standard for whether or not sufficient access has been achieved. If independently established norms of distributive justice are not being met, then whatever is being done in terms of access is falling short (no matter how good it otherwise looks). But traditional legislative, judicial, and executive tools of the liberal democratic state have so far proved inadequate to the task of identifying, much less achieving, environmental justice – and they remain almost wholly inapplicable to any issues of justice and security that extend beyond the state (Coolsaet 2015a).

At the level of the nation-state, significant disparities in the allocation of environmental goods and harms betray an inequity in access to environmental decision-making. The dominance of special interests in the halls of legislatures around the world is routinely cited as a major contribution to ecologically unsound public policies. Redressing those inequities is a major plank in reform-oriented party platforms in any number of countries. But where does one go, at the international level, to redress inequitable environmental allocations by increasing access to environmental decision-making? As has long been appreciated, legislatures at the international level are severely stunted in their development – unlike international networks of policy specialists (Slaughter 2004). To what other institutions should those who have been inequitably treated demand access? Perhaps it is necessary to turn away from the hope for a cosmopolitan revolution in global public opinion and pursue a less imaginative and ambitious alternative.

A deliberative approach can lend a substantive cast to the largely procedural notion of equal access. Principles such as equitable use in the area of riparian rights clearly link process to outcome by highlighting the degree to which procedural choices determine fundamental human capabilities. The focus on capabilities brings together a range of ideas that have previously been excluded from (or were inadequately addressed in) traditional approaches to the economics of welfare. The core focus of the capabilities approach, as formulated by Sen (1992, 2003) and Nussbaum (2011), is on what individuals are able to do. The capabilities approach highlights the importance of real freedoms in the assessment of a person's relative level of advantage. This focuses attention on individual differences in the ability to transform resources into valuable activities as well as the multivariate nature of activities giving rise to human satisfaction. The focus on capabilities promotes a more realistic balance of materialistic and nonmaterialistic factors in evaluating human welfare and a concern for the distribution of substantive opportunities within society.

The capabilities approach emphasizes functional capabilities or "substantive freedoms," such as the ability to live to old age, engage in economic transactions, or participate in political activities. These are construed in terms of the substantive freedoms people have reason to value, instead of utility (happiness, desire fulfillment) or access to resources (income, commodities, or other assets). Poverty is thus understood as capability-deprivation. The emphasis is not only on how humans actually function but also on their having capabilities, which makes possible practical choices to achieve outcomes that they value and have reason to value. Someone could be deprived of such capabilities in many ways – ignorance, government oppression, lack of financial resources, or false consciousness, and so forth. The deliberative democratic approach to access and allocation improves the knowledge that citizens have of issues affecting their capabilities in life, opens access to processes of governance, encourages more equitable allocations of resources, and facilitates the communicative rationality that Habermas (1996) has identified as essential to the legitimacy of governance. An equitable foundation for governance, therefore, consists of these two virtues – access to decision-making on an equal footing is afforded to all, and the equity of allocations is judged by their tendency to equalize fundamental capabilities.

7.4 Democratic Conceptualizations

Research on access to and allocation of environmental resources in a deliberative system of democratic governance builds on and extends an existing, albeit limited, research literature on the implications of deliberative democratic practices for environmental justice policy and governance. Whether conceived of as general principles of law, international soft law, or global administrative law, structures of rules generated democratically and deliberatively would have the potential to improve human security by making access to environmental goods more open and the allocation of those goods among various elements of the population more equitable. Perhaps of even greater importance, this approach to collective will formation presents a concept of equitable allocation to the world of political discourse that originates not in the halls of power, but in the common experience of people like those whose fate will be determined by the policies developed. In this uniquely democratic form of equity may lie a new and potentially powerful answer to humanity's security dilemma.

The substantively equitable access and allocations described here represent a particular conceptualization of democratic governance. It is a form of democratic practice in which people accept an equivocal form of citizenship by agreeing to justify themselves to one another by offering reasons for their positions that are (for them) true but not total. The objective is to allow citizens to interact dialogically, to engage the argument of the other, rather than self. Moreover, both the mutual respect that democracy requires and the adaptiveness that environmental governance in the Anthropocene demands are best served if these arguments are adjudicated (in so far as possible) through experimentation, by a comparison of peoples' ideas with intersubjectively reliable observations – by the substitution of testing validity claims (Habermas 1984) for the testing of political influence. When the commitments to refrain from imposing political marginalization on people based on their identities and to resolve disagreement among citizens based on the soundness (and empirical validation) of their arguments are combined with a concept of equal opportunity that guarantees fundamental capacities to all, we probably will have gone as far in the development of substantively equitable access and allocations as democratic conceptualization can take us.

To venture further than this, the dialogical engagement of citizens needs to take the shape of a recognizable normative consensus. In manifestation of consensus, some environmental goods (and bads) can usefully be conceptualized and prioritized as bundles of human rights (Baber and Bartlett 2020). Many narratives involving environmental human rights have derived largely from environmental justice discourses and have generally concentrated on environmental inequities related to race (Zimring 2016), indigeneity (Gilio-Whitaker 2019), and class (Robertson and Westerman 2015). That these narratives derive primarily from inequities experienced at the level of the nation-state has impeded their uptake in international environmental discourse. Particularly among those who see the development of an international environmental regime as a plausible and desirable approach to securing environmental rights, national experiences might seem to be of limited utility. But there are at least two reasons to attend to environmental rights at the national level.

First, there is much to celebrate in the recent history of environmental human rights at the level of the nation-state. Not only have environmental rights been entrenched in a large and still-growing majority of the earth's countries (Boyd 2012) but there is also evidence that constitutionalized environmental rights are correlated with both environmental and human rights outcomes (Jeffords and Gellers 2017). Moreover, when procedural environmental rights are paired with substantive environmental rights provision, the resulting human rights/environmental protection synergy (environmental democracy) is especially potent (Gellers and Jeffords 2018). Recent work in this field has already brought into clearer focus the need for a redesign of participatory institutions (Baber and Bartlett 2005; Bäckstrand et al. 2010), more assertive grassroots politics (Schlosberg and Craven 2019), and higher levels of democratic engagement in earth system governance (Dryzek and Stevenson 2011; Eckersley 2017; Dryzek and Pickering 2019; Dryzek et al. 2019). Moreover, in-depth analysis of previous instances of deliberative environmental governance narratives shows that they can usefully address many of the most challenging problems of securing environmental rights. They have the potential to establish a set of environmental rights principles – a new social consensus – grounded in an at least moderately progressive account of our history, a moderately pragmatic view of our present, and a moderately optimistic vision of our future (Wironen, Bartlett, and Erickson 2019).

7.4 Democratic Conceptualizations

Second, beyond the general argument against putting all of our eggs in one international basket, there may be reasons to think that focusing on the pursuit of an international environmental regime generally might be a misallocation of resources. The potential of environmental constitutionalism to form a new social consensus in support of environmental rights is precisely the point at which a global pact for the environment (such as the one envisioned by the UN General Assembly) may prove its inherent weakness. Beyond the structural complicity of much existing international environmental law in causing and exacerbating the Anthropocene's socioecological crises (Kotzé 2019), international environmental law generally lacks higher-order global constitutional-type norms that could help to constrain sovereign states in their relations with the environment (Kotzé and Muzangaza 2018; Kotzé and Kim 2019). In addition to its factual and technical gaps, international environmental law is plagued by a glaring but widely ignored weakness in precisely this normative arena (French and Kotzé 2019). If this weakness continues to go unaddressed, any global pact for the environment that conventional international environmental law produces will ultimately fail in its ambition to strengthen the public and private governance efforts aimed at halting the ongoing deterioration of earth system integrity (Kotzé and French 2018). If any international regime initiative in the more specific area of environmental human rights inherited this general (genetic?) flaw in international environmental law, the resulting institutions might be stunted from the moment of their birth.

This quandary occurs at such a grand level that it is difficult to know even where to begin addressing it. But if human rights are best understood as regions of consensus in various policy spaces (Baber and Bartlett 2020), then efforts to understand those phenomena in greater detail cannot be wasted effort. More equitable access to and allocation of environmental "goods" should be a focus for a next generation of environmental research characterized by improved normative understanding as well as more meaningful and reflexive potential for sustainability transformation (van der Hel 2018, 256). Acquiring better knowledge of the ways environmental rights (both procedural and substantive) produce positive results for both humans and the environment is the first step.

In so doing, we may be able to enhance the authority and influence of science in processes of sustainability governance (van der Hel and Biermann 2017; Berg and Lidskog 2018), opening avenues for local knowledge and norms to guide access and allocation in our collective future (Elmer, Lutz, and Schuren 2016).

8

Earth System Democracy

Governing Humanity in the Anthropocene

Over the course of a little more than a decade, an unusually coherent and comprehensive literature has emerged on the demands of effective earth system governance. Informed by the insight that humanity is no longer (and can no longer be) a spectator with respect to global environmental change, the concept of earth system governance recognizes that human actions have had an impact on our planet that has driven, and is driving, its primary ecological systems beyond the range of their natural variability. As a result, humans face a challenge like no other – the necessity to actively and self-consciously govern the environment that sustains us.

In the face of this pressing necessity, the very concept of global governance has become hotly contested. To some, it is a "panacea for the evils of economic and ecological globalization." To others, it is a "global menace" that threatens to create a "universal hegemony of the powerful few over the disenfranchised masses" (Biermann and Pattberg 2012, 1). But in the hands of a growing number of social and environmental scientists, the concept of global environmental governance is an analytical construct that allows thinking more rigorously about the essential elements of effective environmental policy-making. In the first decade or so, that research focused on five critical dimensions of earth system governance: the concept of *agency* (particularly agency beyond that of state actors); the *architecture* of governance (from local to global levels); issues of *accountability* and legitimacy; the equitable *allocation* of and access to resources; and the *adaptiveness* of governance systems (Biermann 2014).

These foci have continued into a second decade, accompanied by greater attention and focus on democracy, power, justice, anticipation, imagination, and reflexivity (Burch et al. 2019) – six additional research lenses that all also relate intimately to empowerment, embeddedness, experimentation, equivocality, and equity. These essential five normative elements necessary for effective democracy apply across all of the analytical research lenses found in both the first and second

152

Earth System Governance Science Plans. The analysis herein is an effort to close some of the concentric circles that describe work on deliberative environmental governance and the wider earth system governance literature that has accumulated contemporaneously. The ways that the minimal conditions for environmental governance can be truly sustainable, ecologically sound, and genuinely democratic are perhaps best summarized by reviewing the five research lenses and five normative prerequisites as a series of pairs.

8.1 Agency and Empowerment

The earth's agents of governance were once thought to be a collection solely of nation-states – entities possessing a permanent population, defined territory, singular government, and the capacity to enter into relations with other such entities. It is that last characteristic – the capacity of nations to create and maintain relations among themselves – that combines with the various national legal orders to constitute what was once thought to be the entirety of global governance (Betsill, Pattberg, and Dellas 2011).

The earliest cracks in this structure appeared at the national level, most notably in the form of private regulation (industry-based standards intended to serve the regulatory functions of governance without resorting to actual government). Today, recognized agents in earth system governance are a far more varied collection of actors. Ranging from governments to science networks, from environmentalist NGOs to industry associations, and from faith-based organizations to intergovernmental organizations, agents of global governance have become a highly diverse group. This is because, in part, agents of governance are not merely political actors. They are, rather, authoritative actors – groups and individuals having both the legitimacy and the capacity to act in ways that influence environmental governance (Biermann 2010). An understanding of the concept of moral agency is necessary in order to fully appreciate the challenge to democracy posed by this new formulation of agency.

Moral agency is not merely a matter of knowledge (beginning with self-knowledge) and autonomy (as the absence of restraint or coercion) but it also includes an element of capability. If we understand a "unit" of agency as a person or group that is appropriately treated as the author of its actions and consequently the entity to be held responsible for them, we must attribute to that agent more than knowledge and autonomy. For an agent to be held responsible, the capability of effective action must exist (Dellas, Pattberg, and Betsill 2011). Moral agency involves a mode of practical reasoning. To be a moral agent is to have the potential for living and acting in a state of tension or, if need be, conflict between competing moral points of view. These points of view rarely exist at the level of general or abstract theory alone. The choices confronting moral agents always involve a tension or conflict between socially embodied points of view, between modes of practice. Effective practice presumes *capability*.

A second reason that the issue of capability plays a crucial role in agency is that it offers a potential response to a question regarding agency in the specific context of environmental governance. It has long been an ambition within the environmental movement to achieve the recognition of agency in nature itself (Boyd 2017; Baber and Bartlett 2020). In terms of agency, this would suggest a situation in which humans listened to signals emanating from the natural world with the same respect we accord communication coming from other humans. This is, of course, a more difficult situation to achieve than to describe. Humans are generally reluctant to engage with nature as a source of responsibilities – much less obligations. It seems to be a feature of our moral thinking that we are more clearly obligated to deal with human evil or indifference than with natural disasters. This attitude can be traced to the psychological fact that people tend to be naïve dualists about agency – thinking that physical objects lack the properties that give rise to issues of moral agency and responsibility *for us* – in the same way that the we/they of distance and difference make it difficult for us to recognize the agency of indigenous populations (Schroeder 2010). To this kind of dualist thinking humans add particular ways of talking about the agency of nature. We further confound our *thoughts* about the dualism between nature and agency with forms of *language* that conflate the two.

Humans have a general metaphor in which the phenomena of nature are discussed as if they were themselves agents. When we say that the wind blew open a door, we are equating natural events to the events caused by humans, tracing their causes back to the agent responsible. This metaphorical agency of nature leads us to a notion of natural causes as forces that are essential qualities of the natural world. It is these essences that grounded ancient religious beliefs. These essences often have anthropomorphic identities in a polytheistic realm, with every culturally important natural phenomenon falling within the responsibility of its own particular deity. Holding some agent responsible for the often-dire consequences "caused" by nature must have been (and may still be) a source of consolation for many whose life tragedies lack obvious human causes. But it sets up an oppositional relationship between humans and a hostile "other." The capabilities element of moral agency offers a different form of consolation – one less likely to alienate us from the nonhuman environment – in the commitment of one's fellow humans to prevent "natural" tragedies where possible and to mitigate those that are unavoidable. This commitment to accept responsibility for the nonhuman "actions" of nature is, of course, predicated on the ample minimum of capabilities and its ubiquity in human societies. But there is historical evidence to suggest that this sort of commitment to others is one moral consequence of economic sufficiency. Therein lies the opportunity to close the circle of human agency in the Anthropocene through concepts of sustainable development that are practice-guiding rather than merely aspirational (Stevens and Kanie 2016; Gore 2019; Betsill, Benney, and Gerlak 2020).

If, indeed, there is no corner of the natural world that is untouched by human influence, then no corner of the world falls outside the realm of human responsibilities implied by our own moral agency (Biermann and Lövbrand 2019). If moral agency requires that an ample minimum of capabilities, across a wide range of human engagements with the world, is (for reasons of political right, simple justice, or normative obligation) a fundamental entitlement, then the answer to the puzzle of how the agency of nature is to be grounded becomes clear. If no element of nature (anywhere) lies outside the responsibility of some humans, and if humans are uniformly *empowered* (with adequate knowledge, autonomy, and capability) to fulfill the requirements of *their* moral agency, then the effective agency of nature is within our shared ability (and responsibility) to ensure.

8.2 Architecture and Embeddedness

A growing body of academic literature is devoted to the evaluation of rival governance architectures and policy mechanisms designed to mitigate the risks associated with global climate change as well as other environmental hazards (Biermann and Kim 2020). To offer but one example, the United Nations Framework Convention on Climate Change (UNFCCC) of 1992, the Kyoto Protocol to the UNFCCC of 1997, and the Paris Agreement of 2015 have all been subjected to intense analysis in this literature (Ferrara 2017).

Analyses of governance architecture have typically focused on issues such as the environmental effectiveness, economic efficiency, and the global distributive consequences of alternative architectures and policy mechanisms. Often overlooked has been the performance of the climate architectures (and the policies they systematize) in terms of the normative ideals whose meaning and significance cannot be fully captured without a domain-level perspective that transcends the improvement of environmental quality at the least economic cost, taking account of the sociopolitical norms of climate governance (Betsill and Hoffmann 2011). One particularly important component of the emerging global climate architecture – greenhouse gas emissions trading – raises significant questions of the norms of political legitimacy and procedural justice. The well-understood cost efficiency and environmental quality benefits conferred by emissions trading schemes come at the price of imposing low levels of participation, accountability, and transparency on climate decision-making (thus damaging legitimacy) and producing results that, by ignoring the social complexity of carbon emissions, replicate the inequities of existing national and local economic structures. Concerns such as these make it clear beyond reasonable doubt that the institutional assumptions of climate governance require rethinking in more dynamic, socioecological terms (Dryzek 2014).

Of vital importance is an observation that the institutional continuum of environmental governance architecture has two ends. In the arena of climate governance, the early focus on the UNFCCC and its progeny was the global end. But there has been a growing awareness that climate change governance involves a wide range of both global and local issues related to questions of environmental security (Fisher 2013). Climate change governance poses serious challenges for political, economic, social, and administrative systems at all levels of governance. These systems evolved to handle other sorts of problems but are now being adapted to handle emerging issues of climate change mitigation and adaptation. Climate governance is undergoing an ongoing reconfiguration, and patterns of institutional authority in climate policy are increasingly fluid. Yet the reliance on state-based forms of regulation persists (Hickmann 2017b).

To a worrisome degree, climate change policy is still commonly framed as primarily a matter of international governance, for which existing policy strategies can be readily employed. Given the present characteristics of the international system, multilateral agreements negotiated by national governments are the central mechanism for global environmental governance. But these agreements are generally born without the presence of viable institutional structures. Climate change thus poses profound challenges to organizations of every type, requiring a wide variety of organizational responses – especially in developing nations (Hickmann et al. 2017). The drastic depth of cuts in emissions of greenhouse gasses proposed by many scientists, national government agencies, and nongovernmental organizations is likely to require radical shifts in sociopolitical structures, technological and economic systems, organizational forms, and modes of organizing.

For this reason, climate change is more than just an environmental problem requiring technical and managerial solutions at the global level. It is a governance challenge arising in highly differentiated contexts within a political space in which a variety of organizations – state agencies, firms, industry associations, NGOs, and multilateral organizations – engage in contestation as well as collaboration over evolving regimes of climate governance. In order to better comprehend the transformative impact of climate change on the human landscape and the policy architecture necessary to adapt to those changes in fully democratic ways (Dryzek and Stevenson 2011), humans must actually overcome the hard-won habit of thinking (only or primarily) globally. Like all other forms of successful

8.3 Adaptation and Experimentation

architecture, the governance structures crafted to deal with climate change will have to display a high degree of flexibility and an open-textured quality if they are to remain effectively embedded in the human communities whose climate impacts are to be regulated. Fighting the normative contexts within which our governance architecture must function will, ultimately, prove as futile as it is undemocratic.

8.3 Adaptation and Experimentation

Every aspect of governance is complicated by the inherent volatility of the times we live in. As a result, the challenge of achieving some level of adaptiveness in global governance, particularly in environmental governance, has been one of the five core analytical problems of earth system governance. Much research has focused on the level of global governance where entire regime systems reside. For example, issues that would have to be included in any assessment of the global challenge of climate change would inevitably include the governance of water systems, food security, health programs, and efforts to alleviate poverty. Climate impacts on economic governance and even international security would also have to be considered, as would rapid change in the environment of governance, an escalating need for collaborative mechanisms of information-sharing and decision-making, and the ongoing loss of the authoritative institutional arrangements that had made bare majoritarian rule possible.

The inadequacy of existing political institutions for facing the challenge of adaptiveness in global environmental governance has been, of course, long and widely discussed. The persistent challenge is to recognize and take advantage of the brief windows of opportunity to make planned change in environmental and resource regimes, which tend to linger on long after their effectiveness has been undermined by the inherent fluidity of the policy environment (Young 2010). A less-widely discussed corollary is that a likely source of day-to-day innovation lies in the arena of the global bureaucracy – understood to include administrators at the national and international levels, both governmental and nongovernmental, interacting in expert networks across the entire range of policy arenas.

This is not to say, of course, that administrative professionals at any level are the only governance agents in the world capable of innovation. It is, rather, to point out that they enjoy the dual benefits of relative invisibility and administrative discretion. National governments depend on broad delegations of authority to public administrators and on the central role international bureaucrats play in the creation of environmental regimes and later in the work of the formal institutions that they helped create (Baber and Bartlett 2005, 2009a). As an example, the institutional space made available by such discretion allows for experimental efforts to add to the adaptive capacities of nation-states, such as the Lima-Paris

Action Agenda (LPAA) and the Non-State Actor Zone for Climate Action (NAZCA), that attempt to enlist the capacities of the corporate world in addressing climate change (Widerberg and Pattberg 2015).

This kind of administrative discretion allows policy professionals, both within and beyond government, to pursue a wider array of policy alternatives than ordinary political processes generally countenance, contributing to policy adaptiveness in at least three distinct ways. First, the ability to respond in flexible ways to novel circumstances allows for planning processes that permit assessment of system performance for various system configurations (adaptation options) under a range of external disturbances, and an exploratory modeling approach, developed to explore policy effectiveness and system operation under a very wide set of assumptions about future conditions (Thissen et al. 2017).

Second, administrative professionals are often in a position to pursue *collaborative* strategies in both policy development and implementation. For example, novel methodological approaches that highlight the ways in which sustainability projects and local knowledge are co-produced by a multiplicity of human and nonhuman actors are contributing to new indigenous-led approaches to address coupled socioecological crises. Efforts such as these allow us to access conceptualizations of environmental norms produced by indigenous scholars and to propose alternative bodies of thought, methods, and practices that can support the wider sustainability agenda (Parsons, Nalau, and Fisher 2017).

Third, the opportunity to take a deliberative (and deliberate) approach to policy choice is all too rare in modern politics (both national and global). When administrative professionals are afforded that opportunity, space is created for social learning that can reduce normative uncertainty, help cope with informational uncertainty, build consensus on criteria for monitoring and evaluation, empower stakeholders to take adaptive actions, reduce conflicts and identify synergies between adaptations, and improve fairness of decisions and actions (Lebel, Grothmann, and Siebenhüner 2010).

These features of global environmental governance suggest that the insights of administrators and other policy professionals into the essential components of adaptiveness in environmental governance, and the role that they can play in promoting it, will be crucial to our ability to adapt to environmental change. After all, it is not as if administrators are strangers to the pressures imposed by change in either the governance of the environment or the environment of governance. Protected by both their relative anonymity and the nature of their institutional affiliations, they are in a position to enhance the democratic quality of our adaptive responses through one of humanity's most inherently open and participatory activities – they can experiment (Baber 2014). It is this experimental quality that is

8.4 Accountability and Equivocality

likely to promote responses to our environmental challenges that are both ecologically adaptive and broadly democratic in character.

8.4 Accountability and Equivocality

A defining characteristic of the Earth System Governance Project has been the recurring analytic focus of accountability. This is due, in part, to the weakness of representative institutions at the global level (Slaughter 2004) and the democratic deficit that an absence of conventional legislative oversight produces. But in addition to raising issues of accountability regarding international bureaucracies, the absence of strong legislative institutions makes especially problematic the heavy reliance on science networks, public–private partnerships, and other nonstate actors in global environmental governance (Biermann and Pattberg 2012; Auld and Gulbrandsen 2014; Dryzek and Pickering 2017).

Some of the accountability innovations applied by the European Union in overseeing the actions of its myriad bureaucracies illustrate that deliberative democratic approaches to administrative accountability are possible (Chapter 6). There is nothing so unique about the issues of environmental governance that they fall outside the reach of democratic deliberation. Watershed partnerships are the best-known examples of stakeholder planning and the coproduction of regulatory implementation. Other well-tested techniques like deliberative polling can readily be used to elicit more reflective public opinion on contending models of environmental policy than currently drives the policy process. A new deliberative technique, juristic modeling, can easily be imagined as a tool for exploring the contours and limitations of normative consensus about both the exploitation and conservation of natural resources and the avoidance or amelioration of the results of that exploitation, extending the process of "juridifying" accountability already under way in earth system governance (Bavinck and Gupta 2014; Boelens and Vos 2014; Conti and Gupta 2014; Kramarz, Cosolo, and Rossi 2017). At each successive step of the process of developing policies of environmental governance, deliberative techniques are readily deployable and they offer significant advantages over less fully participatory approaches. This is particularly true considering that the legitimacy and political durability of deliberative solutions is a result of the equivocal character of the narratives supporting those solutions, which can only be assessed in the broader context of the polity those deliberations serve (Dryzek 2017a).

The fact that democratic deliberation is deployable at each stage of the process of environmental policy development also means that deliberative democracy has potential to add significantly to the political legitimacy of global environmental governance (Sénit, Biermann, and Kalfagianni 2017; Dryzek et al. 2019). This is

160   *Earth System Democracy*

significant because issues of both natural resource management and environmental protection are likely to involve issues of distributive justice (Rusca and Schwartz 2014) and significant levels of political conflict (Dryzek 2011). This dual characteristic of environmental governance makes it more difficult, and more essential, to broaden involvement in the policy process to include representatives of historically underrepresented groups. The realization that every step in the process of environmental governance can include significant citizen participation means that a virtuous circle of public confidence and public involvement can be created that would (when combined with a higher level of distributive justice) legitimize outcomes that are ecologically sound but, for that very reason, frustrate the objectives of some stakeholders (Anderson 2015).

The unidirectional assumptions inherent in the very concept of the policy process, and the role of administrative agencies in it, needs to be overcome. In any broadly participatory political process, arriving at sustainable policy consensus is a recursive proposition as socioenvironmental systems are subject to continuous reconfiguration (Dryzek 2017b). Normative agreement can be unwound, first by political dissent and ultimately by social discord. This, of course, is a second sense in which decisions of democratic governance are (almost inevitably) equivocal. As skilled environmental policy analysts and the experienced public officials who populate administrative agencies know keenly, all conclusions are tentative pending future research findings and the next round of environmental assessments (Haas 2017). That is why these policy actors so often find themselves grappling with challenges of organization development and maintenance rather than the environmental issues that originally concerned them. Genuinely democratic environmental governance is always likely to be at least as much a matter of organization (re)building as it is environmental protection. And a long-recognized strength of deliberative democracy is its tendency to increase the social capital necessary for recursive institution-building by sustaining the politically crucial virtues of transparency and participation (Duyck 2014).

8.5 Access, Allocation, and Equity

Environmental goods are supplied by nature but how they are received is a matter that is decided by people. In order to steer those decisions in more ecologically sustainable directions, an assessment of how these goods are accessed and allocated needs to take account of how people actually benefit from different ecosystem services or, conversely, suffer from the deprivation of those services. The critical question is, what determines the distribution of ecosystem service benefits between different sections of society and equitability of that distribution? Ignoring this question is likely to result in policy lapses that leave large and dangerous gaps in global environmental governance filled with unaddressed social and environmental issues (Lima and Gupta 2013).

In responding to this fundamental question of equity, it is important to understand the development of and subsequent changes in the institutional mechanisms that determine access to ecosystem services and to account for historical changes in rules, norms, and conventions composing those mechanisms (Schroeder, Boykoff, and Spiers 2012). In doing so, it is equally important to acquire the highly particular knowledge of local circumstances in order to assess the scales at which ecosystem services are supplied, demanded, and governed and to discover any scale misfits in relation to historical conflicts over access to ecosystem services – in order to counter the tendency of decision-makers to become preoccupied with global considerations (Di Gregorio et al. 2013).

Over recent decades, the insights gained by pursuing this kind of local knowledge have resulted in a paradigm shift in how natural resource management is conceived. This shift has been away from state-centered control toward approaches that involve local people playing a much more active role – community-based approaches situated in a theoretical framework seeking to empower local communities through decentralization policies (Krause, Collen Wain, and Nicholas 2013). Many case studies have examined the organizational frameworks within which decentralization is implemented. Generally speaking, they find that at the local level there is a complex interface between traditional and modern authority structures, with both complimentary and conflicting jurisdictions and mandates – rendering conventional analytical categories increasingly problematic (Perkins 2013). These complexities not only present challenges for the initial access to environmental goods and for their appropriate allocation over time but also for dealing with the environmental change that inequality itself ultimately produces (Schroeder 2014).

A juristic deliberative model that does not rely on effective legislative oversight has implications for access to and allocation of environmental resources (Baber and Bartlett 2009a). The juristic deliberative model draws on functions that nongovernmental and intergovernmental organizations, as well as average citizens, already perform. It does not rely on new legislative inputs or continuous monitoring by elected officials (Chapter 6). Research on this approach builds on and extends an existing (albeit limited) research literature on the implications of deliberative democratic practices for environmental justice policy and governance (Chapter 1). It provides an investigative procedure that can be used with low transaction costs by networks of policy specialists, civil society activists, or regulated entities (preferably, in partnership) to craft environmental rules (within the present competencies of existing environmental institutions) enjoying a significant level of democratic legitimacy (Baber and Bartlett 2005). Whether conceived of as general principles of law, soft law, well-established norms, or global administrative law, the resulting structure of rules would have the potential to enhance environmental governance by making access to environmental goods more open and the allocation of those goods among various elements of the population more equitable (Chapter 7). Perhaps of even greater importance, this approach to collective will formation presents a concept of equitable allocation to the sphere of political discourse that originates, not in the halls of power, but in the common experience of people like those who will ultimately be called on to respect the governance policies that are developed (Baber and Bartlett 2015).

The process for arriving at substantively equitable access and allocations described in our research represents one particular conceptualization of democratic governance (Baber and Bartlett 2016). It is a form of democratic practice in which people accept an *equivocal* form of citizenship by agreeing to justify themselves to one another by offering reasons for their positions that are (for them) true but not total (Baber and Bartlett 2015). The objective is to allow citizens to interact dialogically, to engage the argument of the other, rather than merely continually assert the self. Moreover, both the mutual respect that democracy requires and the adaptiveness that environmental governance in the Anthropocene demands are best served if these arguments are adjudicated (insofar as possible) through experimentation, by a comparison of peoples' ideas about environmental governance with reliable observations – by the substitution of testing validity claims for the testing of political influence (Baber and Bartlett 2015).

Assuring access to and the equitable allocation of environmental goods will require us to undertake a commitment to refrain from imposing political marginalization on people based on their inability to resist and to resolve disagreement among citizens based on the soundness (and empirical validation) of their arguments. When this is combined with a concept of equal opportunity that guarantees fundamental capacities to all, we will have come as close as we probably can to assuring equity in global environmental governance (Baber and Bartlett 2019).

8.6 Final Thoughts

The research inspired by the first Science Plan of the Earth System Governance Project has confirmed that effective environmental governance in the Anthropocene must attend to the need for *accountability* in governance policy-making, the substantive necessity for environmental policies that are *adaptive* to rapidly changing ecological imperatives, the importance of understanding *access* to and the *allocation* of environmental resources, the significance of *agency* as a central feature of environmental governance, and the challenges of building environmental governance *architecture* that is fit for purpose.

8.6 Final Thoughts

These five analytical elements certainly are critical components of effective environmental governance at the global level. Just as Adam Smith promised only that markets would find their own equilibrium – not that the equilibria eventually found would be morally or politically tolerable – there is no promise that environmental governance decisions will turn out to be sustainable over the long run if they are effective (analytically sound) but not also fundamentally democratic. Thus, a set of avowedly political, normative criteria must be added to the analytical ones just mentioned. In the pursuit of accountability, environmental governance must maintain a level of *equivocality* – a multilayered concept capturing elements of both pluralism and creative obfuscation. For environmental governance to achieve the highest possible level of adaptiveness, an *experimental attitude* must prevail – uniting flexible and collaborative search strategies with a deliberative ethos that rewards evidence-based reasoning while holding all conclusions open to reassessment. Assessment of access to and allocation of environmental resources cannot become dominated by considerations of technical efficiency or political expediency. Distributions of both environmental goods and risks must be governed by a self-conscious commitment to the value of *equity* if they are to ultimately prove sustainable.

Moreover, this argument is closely related to the insight that agency in environmental governance has an irreducible core of moral content – a core that is properly understood as a dedication to the *empowerment* of human beings, both as individuals and as societies. And the architecture of global environmental governance is only truly fit for purpose if its foundation is *embedded* in the human culture that creates and sustains it. There is, in short, no room left in environmental governance for complaints about anthropocentrism. The onset of the Anthropocene has left the distinctions that idea relies on in tatters. Going forward, any defense of the environment that aspires to be both ecologically effective and politically defensible will have to speak directly to environmental human rights (Baber and Bartlett 2020). For better or worse, that is where environmental sustainability ultimately lies.

Afterword

Governance by Uncommon Global Environmental Law?

> What ye will that other men should not do unto you, that do ye not to other men.
>
> *Alfred the Great*

Earth system governance is not for the faint of heart. To a considerable extent, governance is a concept that makes sense only within an established legal framework. A plausible argument can be made that no such framework in its modern, constitutional sense even exists outside the confines of the sovereign nation-state (Rabkin 2005). But international law is a complex system of treaties, institutions, and informal governing arrangements that already does exhibit adaptive self-organizing and emergent properties (Kim and Mackey 2014). Greater adaptive capacity might be found, however, by increased reliance on the development of law that is consciously experimental, equivocal, and embedded – a pattern of international law development based on a legal tradition, no less primitive than is contemporary international law, from which emerged a system of law that built an empire and today governs (in whole or part) the lives of nearly 40 percent of the world's population.[1] This tradition traces the law back, not to scriptural duties or sovereign declarations, but to a gradual and organic accretion of precedent – a process that, more easily than most others, might be imagined as a pattern for the development of global and international law that is truly equivocal, experimental, and embedded.

A.1 Veterem Traditionem

In his *A History of the English-Speaking Peoples*, Winston Churchill traces the traditions of the common law back to the late ninth century and the person of Alfred, King of Wessex from 871 to 899. Referring to the epigram at the start of this chapter, Churchill describes Alfred's inversion of the Golden Rule as "a less ambitious principle" than the biblical original. This limited reach was in keeping with Alfred's own understanding of his *Book of Laws*, which he modestly described as the wisdom handed down to him by his ancestors and kinsmen, to which he had added but little. He declared that "I have not dared to presume to set down in writing many laws of my own, for I cannot tell what will meet with the approval of our successors." Yet he admitted to no failing in this regard because he believed that little in the way of recorded law was actually required. Alfred even went so far as to say that with this one basic precept (described by Churchill as modest) a judge can "do justice to all men" needing "no other law-books" if only he will put himself in the place of the plaintiff (Churchill 1956, 120). This is probably just as well, because the rest of Alfred's *Book of Laws* is so poorly organized that it is nearly useless as a philosophical treatise on the law, much less a practical guide for litigators and judges.

Indeed, it has been argued that the orderly administration of justice was not even the primary objective of Alfred's lawgiving. Alfred's *Book of Laws* may have been intended primarily as a symbolic gesture – an ideological manifesto for kingship designed to press his argument for the greater unification of England (Wormald 2001). Even according to Churchill's appreciative account, there was much that Alfred left for his successors to do. Alfred's laws had to be "continually amplified by his successors" before they grew into that great body of customary practice "administered by the shire and hundred courts," which, with "much manipulation by feudal lawyers," became the common law we know today (Churchill 1956, 120). Yet even this one brief entry in the history of the common law touches on many of the reasons that the institution has proven so enduring.

First, the common law concerns itself with judgment – as did Alfred, who is remembered for his close attention to the decisions of his courts. This might seem to be an obvious point, but it is far from that. From its earliest manifestations, the notion that law would resolve disputes through judgment rather than interest or prejudice was an innovation of fundamental significance to address a tension built into the very heart of the adjudicatory process. Enforcing prejudices or favoring interests are unreflective practices. Often found in close proximity to one another, prejudice is nothing more than an application of existing sentiments and values (prejudgments) to the case at hand, and interest is a heading for all the selfish preoccupations of which prejudgments are so often made. Judgment, on the other hand, is a Janus-faced alternative that presents endless challenges precisely because it is reflective. Hannah Arendt (2005, 102) sums up the dichotomy implicit in judgment by observing that it sometimes means "subsuming the individual and particular under the general and universal, thereby making an orderly assessment by applying standards by which the concrete is identified and according to which decisions are then made." Alternatively, judgment can mean something quite different when "we are confronted with something which we have

166   *Afterword*

never seen before." Under these circumstances, we are able to "appeal to nothing but the evidence of what is being judged ... " After more than a millennium of practical experience, no simple formula has yet been devised to describe this process of balancing the known and the novel that has not been critiqued for importing either prejudice or interest into the act of judgment (Bernstein 2002).

A second feature of common law that bears discussion is closely related to the first. It is a due regard for precedent, reflected in the care Alfred took to acknowledge his dependence on the wisdom and judgment of his ancestors in crafting his *Book of Laws*. To stand by things previously decided – *stare decisis* in Latin – is thought to be a virtue in law for at least two reasons. First, it combines an appropriate modesty about one's own abilities with reverence for tradition in a way that makes one's judgments significantly easier for both the contestants at bar and the community to accept. Moreover, the continuity that *stare decisis* lends to a legal tradition provides a level of predictability to that system's operation. This is useful as both a matter of economy (because it discourages behavior that people reliably expect to be sanctioned, thus reducing the number of disputes that actually arise) and of legitimacy (because it increases predictability of outcomes, making legal sanctions the result of informed choices for which people can justly be held responsible). *Stare decisis*, however, shows evidence of the contradiction inherent in the concept of judgment. As Posner (2008) points out, if fealty to precedent is used as a method to legitimate adjudication, it builds the law on a weak foundation – for it offers no justification for the judges of antiquity, who had no choice but to behave immodestly, willfully, and creatively because they had no precedent to follow.

A third fundamental feature of the common law might best be understood as an answer to the problem of legitimacy remaining after the concepts of judgment and *stare decisis* do what good they can. King Alfred enjoined his magistrates to put themselves in the place of the plaintiffs in their courts – posing to themselves the question of how they would want to be treated under similar circumstances. There is, of course, more to good judging than sympathetic identification. Sympathy, undisciplined by any ability to consider the longer-term systemic consequences of decisions, would result in judicial chaos. After all, Alfred also demanded that his magistrates do justice to all men. A trier of fact, whether judge or jury, must become a sympathetic observer in order to do justice in a given case. This implies "impartiality, possession of relevant knowledge, and powers of imaginative identification" sufficient to assure an accurate response of our natural sympathy (Rawls 1971, 187). The reach of that natural sympathy would have to include not only the plaintiff and the defendant in the instant case but also the plaintiffs and defendants in all future cases. So, judicial sympathy must be tempered by a certain detachment as well as a future orientation that allows for a reflective equilibrium.

This state of affairs, when fully achieved, "is an equilibrium because our principles and judgments coincide; and it is reflective since we know to what principles our judgments conform and the premises of their derivation" (20).[2]

Finally, the common law was understood from its inception to be an organic, growing thing. Alfred justified his dependence on ancient wisdom and his reluctance to set down new laws on his own to his concern for whether his act of lawgiving would find favor with later generations. Alfred's *Book of Laws* follows no internal narrative; it lacks any obvious system of organization. Already noted is one possible explanation that Alfred's *Book of Laws* may have been merely a ploy in his effort to achieve a more united kingdom (with himself and his descendants in the title role). A more charitable view would be that Alfred did not intend his law to be divinely inspired commands or expressions of sovereign will, but a source book for the inevitable future development of the law of his realm. Its somewhat haphazard arrangement could be taken as evidence that he assumed it would undergo a process of progressive development, a possibility that is implicit in the concept of *stare decisis*. The doctrines of supremacy of the law and of judicial discretion, present in the common law from its birth, have turned out to be inherently hostile to divine-right monarchy – as the revolution of 1688 and the flight of King James II eventually demonstrated (Hogue 1966).

Perhaps Alfred was searching for a social and political balance between permanence and change nearly a millennium before the great legal codifications of the eighteenth century. By focusing attention on considered judgment, guided by precedent and tempered by sympathetic observation, Alfred created an opportunity that came to fruition in the modern legal systems that we see today – systems capable of "generalizing and abstracting from the adjudication of cases" without giving up "the participant perspective" (Habermas 1996, 388). To the extent that modern legal systems generally, and the common law in particular, have proven to be durable, it is largely due to the fact that they have been able to create a dynamic equilibrium – bending to the influences of social and economic change without breaking completely from the underlying principles that lend them legitimacy.

A.2 Novus Traditio

A concrete illustration of the reflective and dynamic equilibrium maintained by the common law is not difficult to find. Because so much of the common law's contribution to the law of environmental protection can be traced to tort law – the law governing civil wrongs causing loss or harm – it seems sensible to seek an example of dynamic equilibrium there. The real challenge is to find an instance of the pace of change in the law that is sufficiently rapid that we can perceive the forces driving it. Change at a glacial pace not only taxes our attention span but also

168 *Afterword*

challenges our ability to filter out possible reasons for the change that coincide with it for no better reason than the long timeframe involved. An example that serves is the doctrine of contributory negligence as a defense to a complaint of nuisance.[3]

Unique within the common law tradition is the series of *Restatements of the Law* published by the American Law Institute (ALI). The *Restatements* are essentially codifications of existing US case law, intended to distill the black letter law[4] from cases, indicate the trend of the cases in a particular area of law, and (occasionally) suggest a direction in which the law should proceed. Prepared by teams of legal specialists after extensive analysis of cases and multiple iterations of drafting and critique, these documents are intended to represent the consensus of the American legal community regarding what the law is, often what direction it is taking, and sometimes what direction it ought to take. According to US Supreme Court Justice Benjamin Cardoza (1924), the Restatements are "less than a code but more than a treatise," invested not with the authority to command but with a powerful ability to persuade.

Section 840B of the *Restatement of Torts Second* (American Law Institute 2013) summarized the rule of contributory negligence as follows:

"(1) When a nuisance results from negligent conduct of the defendant,
the contributory negligence of the plaintiff is a defense to the same extent as in other actions founded on negligence."

As with all entries in the *Restatements*, this rule is followed both by Reporter's Comments, exploring various aspects and implications of the rule, as well as hypothetical illustrations showing how the rule would be applied in concrete circumstances. In the case of the defense of contributory negligence, these materials even go so far as to address such questions as the relationship of the rule to the intent of the defendant (indicating that in the case of intentional nuisances, the defense of contributory negligence is not available).

The practical effect of this doctrine was to deny recovery to any plaintiff who had contributed to his or her own injury. If a judge in the time of Alfred the Great had placed himself in the position of such a plaintiff, he might well have concluded (as later judges did) that it would be unreasonable for that plaintiff to expect to be compensated for injuries that he could have avoided through ordinary and reasonable precautions of his own. But as one might imagine, over the course of time this doctrine produced results that were often difficult to justify. Even with the application of *de minimis non curat lex* (the law is not concerned with trivia) as a qualifier, contributory negligence often left a plaintiff who had suffered shocking injuries without any recourse simply because he or she was not entirely blameless in the case. Judgments of this sort achieved equilibrium because the principle from which they derived was clear. But that equilibrium proved temporary because their reflective nature led lawyers to wonder which principle should actually govern cases such as these. The resulting transition from the doctrine of contributory negligence to the rule of comparative responsibility (reducing a plaintiff's recovery by the degree of his or her own responsibility for the injury) shows how this reflection renders law's equilibrium dynamic and, therefore, durable. But it shows even more than this.

The transformation of the contributory negligence was part of a larger evolution in the law of torts. What had been simply a defense to liability, scattered through dozens of nooks and crannies in the *Restatement Second*, became part of a consolidated analytical system in the *Restatement Third of Torts* (American Law Institute 2000). Topic 1 in the new *Restatement* is "Basic Rules of Comparative Responsibility." Contributory negligence is subsumed by a comprehensive system for apportioning responsibility for tortious injury among multiple parties. The plaintiff is now viewed simply as one of these parties. This new approach has allowed the ALI to develop a new analytical structure that categorizes tort rules around the central problem of apportionment of liability. These categories include:

> "(1) the legal effects of different types of plaintiff conduct, such as a plaintiff's intentional self-injury, a plaintiff's negligence, and a plaintiff's voluntary assumption of risk;
> (2) joint and several liability;
> (3) apportionment of damages by causation; and
> (4) contribution and indemnity" (American Law Institute 2000, 6).

The *Restatement Third* places all of the disparate entries on these subjects, which were spread across the previous *Restatement*, into this new schema.

In summarizing the net effect of this new doctrine, the *Restatement Third* (American Law Institute 2000, 5) declares that "the nearly universal adoption of comparative responsibility by American courts and legislatures has had a dramatic impact" on the law of torts. Sometimes this effect is direct, as when comparative responsibility "determines the effect a plaintiff's negligence on his or her recovery." Or the new doctrine can have an indirect effect, as when it affects "the rules of apportionment, which in turn can affect other rules of tort law" such as the effect of joint and several liability. Taking account of all these effects, comparative responsibility requires courts to coordinate liability rules "in ways that transcend the traditional boundaries between various torts," which sets up "tensions between maintaining the distinctions based on different torts and a common comparison of the parties' responsibility in a single lawsuit." In an era of multi-party, multi-theory lawsuits, this kind of doctrinal change signals significant policy shifts, the overall effects of which are "profound" (6). Most significant for our present purpose is the fact that this profound change in the law arose from the accumulation of opinions arising from the resolution of concrete disputes between parties, rather than the determination of a legislature that changes in the law of torts were needed. In fact, the legislatures that did adopt comparative responsibility followed the lead of other public officials whose task it was to deal with the discrete problems arising from the day-to-day activities and practices of the communities that they served.

Is a template for international environmental governance hidden within this ongoing and progressive development of the common law? A significant problem with thinking of the evolution of the common law as a format for the development of international law is simply a matter of numbers. Countries with common law systems consist of federal, state or provincial, and local governments, each of which provide forums in which plaintiffs can pursue relief of their grievances. Polities of this sort can be expected to generate a "data base" of judgments that will sustain generations of Restatement reporters for an eternity. But the global polity includes fewer than 200 legal "persons" and only a handful of tribunals arbitrating disputes. Try as they might, it will take them a very long time to create, from the disparate discourses that currently comprise the best available thinking about international law, a database that will make the process of restatement a worthwhile endeavor.

Alternatives to this passive approach may be available. Hypothetical adjudications can be used in the same way that actual precedent is used in the common law. With sufficient repetition, patterns can be identified in simulations that serve to indicate how concrete environmental disputes ought to be resolved. Much effort would be required to develop a collection of restatements of juristic simulations sufficiently far-reaching to provide the raw material necessary for codification. These adjudicatory decisions can ultimately be summarized through a procedure similar to the restatement process as developed by the American Law Institute (ALI). If this restatement can be accomplished in a way that scholars could agree is accurate and reliable, the result would be a body of global environmental proto-regulation that would be presumptively legitimate because of its populist provenance. Of course, this juristic democracy technique would be merely one element in a broader pattern of policy-making designed to redress the democratic deficit in international law (Baber and Bartlett 2009a).

A.3 Finalis Cogitata

Policies intended to achieve environmental sustainability must be sustainable in two senses of the word – the ecological and the political. No environmental policy will be politically sustainable unless it is fundamentally democratic (Baber and Bartlett 2005) and this is as true of global politics as it is of politics within the nation-state (Baber and Bartlett 2009a). The difficulties in translating the techniques of representative democracy to the global arena are well-known and need not be rehearsed here. A discursive form of democracy, however, might be founded on democratic practices that partake of the participatory rather than the representative (Dryzek 2006). Discursive democracy offers a participatory form of democratic engagement that can be deployed at (at least) two different stages of the policy process.

Discursive mapping can be used to compile an as-complete-as-possible inventory of the varying (and sometimes competing) discourses that average citizens produce in response to an ideal-typical case constructed to represent a larger category of actual environmental disputes. The claims and counter-claims of the hypothetical parties can be used to represent the competing views of problems such as trans-boundary environmental threats posed by multiple parties. In this way, these arguments, charged as they typically are by interest and ideology, can be subjected to a process of sorting and comparison conducted by sympathetic but disinterested representatives of societies anywhere in the world. The results, introduced into international negotiations by the parties at an early stage, would legitimate some potential discourses and de-legitimate others. Disputes over the validity and reliability of results such as these could be easily addressed because the research that produces them is transparent, inexpensive to repeat, and subject to subsequent iterative rounds designed to determine the significance of any disputed details of the scenarios employed (the construction of which by the parties can be, in itself, a consensus-building exercise).

Second, research of this nature can provide decision-makers with an inexpensive means for testing the democratic credentials of any contending policy regimes that their negotiations might produce. The basic arguments in favor of two or more regulatory policies can be placed in the mouths of hypothetical parties to concrete disputes in order to see which line of reasoning people will actually use to resolve the kind of dispute at issue. The goal, and reasonable expectation, is the production of final agreements arrived at by negotiating processes whose multiple rounds of public involvement give the agreements a democratic provenance that probably never can be provided by representative bodies at the international level.

Discursive democracy can do more than simply avoid the representative weaknesses of existing international legislatures. It can draw on the one relative strength of international intergovernmental organizations (IGOs) – their bureaucracies (Slaughter 2004). IGO secretariats across the international stage deploy significant human resources in pursuit of objectives that are often quite limited (through no fault of their own). The technical and analytical skills at their command often exceed those of many member states of the international organizations they serve. Moreover, their connections to nongovernmental international organizations, which could easily be considered a sign of regulatory capture (Carpenter and Moss 2013), can be turned to a useful purpose by involving these interests at an early point in the construction of hypothetical cases and the design of research protocols for their use. This combination of participation by the "organized public" of interest groups with a more direct form of participation by the general public might offer unique strengths of both a conceptual and a practical nature.

Notes

Chapter 1

1 The term and concept "Anthropocene" has become widely used since being coined at the turn of the century (Crutzen and Stoermer 2000) and its definition and implications continue to be debated extensively, in both scholarly and nonscholarly discourses, with no convergence on a singular and universally accepted definition or understanding (Biermann and Lövbrand 2019). Like "democracy" and "sustainability," "Anthropocene" is an ambiguous and essentially contested concept. Nevertheless it has a core meaning that can be usefully deployed without attending to all of the distinctions, variations, qualifications, and complexities found in discourse about it. The vast scholarly literature attending to the "Anthropocene" is certainly of significance for many political and philosophical purposes, but a simple core definition suffices for the purposes of the analysis we undertake in this book. The Anthropocene refers to a reality in which humanity's impact on the environment had become so pervasive that it no longer made sense to distinguish between human and nonhuman nature.

2 The term "earth system governance" came into wider use beginning in March 2007 when the Scientific Committee of the International Human Dimensions Programme on Global Environmental Change (IHDP) mandated a scientific planning committee to draft a science plan for a new IHDP Earth System Governance Project. The Earth System Governance Project and its Science and Implementation Plan were launched in 2008 (Biermann et al. 2009).

3 A second Earth System Governance Science and Implementation Plan, which was adopted ten years after the first (Burch et al. 2019), identified five sets of research lenses that overlapped with the five central analytic problems identified in the first plan: architecture and agency, democracy and power, justice and allocation, anticipation and imagination, and adaptiveness and reflexivity.

Chapter 3

1 One might be forgiven for thinking that all the advent of private regulation has done is to solve the problem of regulatory capture through the expediency of governmental surrender. At a minimum, it is clear that private regulation poses a serious challenge to the democratic credentials of administrative law (Freeman 1999). The role of private governance beyond the state is emerging as a prominent debate in international relations, focusing on the activities of private nonstate actors and the influences of private rules and standards (Pattberg 2006; Green 2014; Bäckstrand et al. 2017; Gulbrandsen 2018).

Chapter 4

1 The concept of governance architecture is fundamental to the study of earth system governance (Biermann 2014). It "stands between two other concepts frequently used in international relations

173

174   *Notes to pages 85–164*

research," the concepts of a "regime" and an "order." Architectures are broader than regimes, which are usually defined as "sets of implicit or explicit principles, norms, rules, and decision-making procedures around which actors' expectations converge in a given area of international relations" (Krasner 1983, 2; Biermann 2014, 81). Architecture, in contrast, focuses on "the overall institutional setting in which distinct institutions exist and interact" (Biermann 2014, 82). Because of its focus on a particular issue area, however, an architecture differs from an order, which is concerned with "overarching governance structures that reach beyond the scope of single regimes" (82).

2 Core themes of *geomorphology* include open systems and connectivity; feedbacks and complexity; spatial differentiation of dominant physical processes within a landscape; and legacy effects of historical human use of resources. Core themes of *ecology* include open systems and connectivity; hierarchical, heterogeneous, dynamic, and context-dependent characteristics of ecological patterns and processes; nonlinearity, thresholds, hysteresis, and resilience within ecosystems; and human effects. Core themes of *environmental governance* include architecture of institutions and decision-making; agency, or ability of actors to prescribe behavior of people in relation to the environment; adaptiveness of social groups to environmental change; accountability and legitimacy of systems of governance; allocation of and access to resources; and thresholds and feedback loops within environmental policy (Wohl et al. 2014).

3 Authorized by the Farmer-to-Consumer Direct Marketing Act of 1946, as amended (7 U.S.C. 3005).

4 United States Department of Agriculture Agricultural Marketing Service. 2018. Local Food Promotion Program. Washington, DC: United States Department of Agriculture Agricultural Marketing Service www.ams.usda.gov/AMSv1.0/ams.fetchTemplateData.do?template=TemplateA&leftNav= WholesaleandFarmersMarkets&page=LFPP&description=Local%20Food%20Promotion%20Program

5 United States Department of Agriculture Agricultural Marketing Service. 2018. Farmers Market Promotion Program. Washington, DC: United States Department of Agriculture Agricultural Marketing Service www.ams.usda.gov/AMSv1.0/ams.fetchTemplateData.do? template=TemplateN&navID=WholesaleandFarmersMarkets&leftNav=WholesaleandFarmersMarkets& page=FMPP&description=Farmers%20Market%20Promotion%20Program&acct=fmpp

6 European Union Commission, Directorate-General for Agriculture and Rural Development, Funding Opportunities under the Common Agricultural Policy. Brussels, Belgium: European Union Commission Directorate-General for Agriculture and Rural Development http://ec .europa.eu/agriculture/cap-funding/funding-opportunities/index_en.htm

7 The term *foodshed* appeared in the literature as early as 1929 (Hedden 1929). It has been employed more recently to provide "a bridge from thinking to doing, from theory to action," suggesting that thinking in terms of foodsheds implies the development of what might be called "foodshed analysis," the posing of particular kinds of questions and the gathering of particular types of information or data (Kloppenburg, Hendrickson, and Stevenson 1996, 35). More recently, food policy councils have been discussed as an institutional form that can be used to pursue objectives associated with food and environmental justice (Purifoy 2014). We have not, however, found any previous suggestion that the concept of a foodshed should form the basis of a stakeholder partnership as is widely found in land use planning. This is the next step, from analysis and advocacy to governance.

Afterword

1 A wide variety of legal orders are associated with the common law tradition. "For most of its history the common law was in the *process* of becoming a common law, and its history is above all one of relations with other laws, themselves also common in considerable measure, both in England and in Europe. This was the case with chthonnic law, its earliest and most significant interlocutor, and then with ecclesiastical law, once the ecclesiastical courts were up and running. In examining the growth of the common law, we have necessarily spoken of unavoidable reciprocal influences and, also, more interestingly, of the underlying harmony of this process . . . Rules are not seen as being in conflict if the rules count for less than the facts" (Glenn 2010, 269). Due in part to worldwide colonization by the British empire (not to mention the English language), there has been "a kind of embedding of common law thinking in a large number of diverse societies around the world" (Glenn 2010, 262). Indeed, the very existence of the Westphalian nation-state was (at least conceptually)

Notes to pages 167–168 175

a Western project, the product of a dynamic interaction between the British common law tradition and the Continental tradition, much of which was also influenced by common law (Landauer 2011). In fact, there is a vast source of international norms – what we might call transnational common law – that has long transcended the nation-state altogether. Judicial globalization, domestic treaty enforcement, transnational criminal prosecution, and international and transnational custom count among the principal areas in which the external pressures of foreign affairs developments are profoundly affected by the internal, social commitments of domestic legal systems (Dryzek 2000; Flaherty 2006).

2 The blinding speed of this progression from Alfred's judicial sympathy to Rawls's reflective equilibrium invites the criticism that we have engaged in some Churchillian style hand-waving of our own. Indeed, an examination of the developmental history we have passed over shows that the problem of impartial judgment in the development of the common law is a history of fits and starts - including many starts that turned out to be false ones. Much of the manipulation by medieval lawyers of which Churchill spoke took place exactly in this corner of the common law. For instance, against this backdrop the proliferation of different kinds of courts is easier to understand. The court of Chancery, for example, provided a place where causes of action relating to the Crown itself could be heard with less fear or favor – a practice which eventually produced the collection of principles that we recognize today as the law of equity (Hardy, 2009 [1890]; Kerly 2016). Moreover, the system of writs was an early effort to spell out the principles with which the judgments of the law might be thought to coincide (Hogue 1966). While this system ultimately proved to be impractically complex, the pattern of complaint and response is still evident in contemporary motions practice. Likewise, the transition of the jury from a twelfth-century collection of sworn witnesses to a thirteenth-century panel of triers of fact was both a reflection of concern for impartiality of judgment and an occasion for new practices designed to promote it. William Blackstone (Blackstone 1979 [1765–1769], v.3, 363, emphasis in the original) distinguishes early challenges to the seating of individual jurors, dividing them into the categories of "a principal challenge" or a challenge "to the favour." A principal challenge alleged a relationship between a particular juror and a party to the case (usually within the ninth degree). A challenge to the favour, on the other hand, alleged a form of bias in the more general sense, involving "some probable circumstance of suspicion, as acquaintance, and the like." Most revealing for our purpose is that the veracity of the challenge was to be heard by two "indifferent persons" named by the court. What is sought is not ignorance of the matter at hand (which would make it impossible to determine the suitability of the challenged juror) but, rather, personal indifference regarding the outcome of the case – in other words, a considered judgment derived from the jurors' sense of justice. Here we close the loop back to the concept of reflective equilibrium. Our judgments cannot be said to conform to our principles (to be considered, in the way that the concept suggests) if those judgments find their derivation in some form of interest or bias unrelated to principle.

3 As the reader may have inferred, the concept of contributory negligence recurs with some frequency throughout the *Restatement Second*. We focus on its use in the area of nuisance simply because that area of tort law has been especially important in the development of environmental law.

4 In the common law tradition, black letter law is a term of art used to refer to what judges and scholars take to be the technical legal rules enunciated in an opinion (or collection of opinions). These expressions of the law are thought to be so well-established that their authority is taken to be beyond dispute.

Bibliography

Adam, Silke and Michaela Maier. 2011. "National Parties as Politicizers of EU Integration? Party Campaign Communication in the Run-Up to the 2009 European Parliament Election." *European Union Politics* 12 (3):431–453.

Agyeman, Julian and Bob Evans. 2006. "Justice, Governance, and Sustainability: Perspectives on Environmental Citizenship from North America and Europe." In *Environmental Citizenship*, edited by Andrew Dobson and Derek Bell, 185–206. Cambridge, MA: MIT Press.

Albrow, Martin. 1996. *The Global Age*. Stanford, CA: Stanford University Press.

Albrow, Martin and Elizabeth King, eds. 1990. *Globalization, Knowledge and Society*. London: SAGE.

Ambrey, Christopher, Jason Byrne, Tony Matthews, Aiden Davison, Chole Portanger, and Alex Lo. 2016. "Cultivating Climate Justice: Green Infrastructure and Suburban Disadvantages in Australia." *Applied Geography* 89:52–60.

Amechi, Emeka Polycarp. 2009. "Poverty, Socio-Political Factors and Degradation of the Environment in Sub-Saharan Africa: The Need for a Holistic Approach to the Protection of the Environment and Realisation of the Right to Environment." *Law, Environment and Development Journal* 5 (2):107–129.

American Law Institute. 2000. *Restatement of the Law, Third, Torts: Apportionment of Liability*. Chicago: American Law Institute.

American Law Institute. 2013. *Restatement of the Law, Second, Torts 2d*. Chicago: American Law Institute.

Anderson, Paul. 2015. "Which Direction for International Environmental Law?" *Journal of Human Rights and the Environment* 6 (1):98–126. https://doi.org/10.4337/jhre.2015.01.05.

Anderton, Karen. 2017. "Understanding the Role of Regional Influence and Innovation in EU Policymaking: Bavaria and Cars and CO2." *Environment and Planning C: Politics and Space* 35 (4):640–660.

Anderton, Karen and Joana Setze. 2018. "Subnational Climate Entrepreneurship: Innovative Climate Action in California and Sao Paulo." *Regional Environmental Change* 18 (5):1273–1284.

Andresen, Steinar and Kristin Rosendal. 2014. "The Role of the United Nations Environment Programme in the Coordination of Multilateral Environmental Agreements." In *International Organizations in Global Environmental Governance*, edited by Frank Biermann, Bernd Siebenhüner, and Anna Schreyögg, 133–150. New York: Routledge.

Bibliography

Angel, David P. and Michael T. Rock. 2005. "Global Standards and the Environmental Performance of Industry." *Environment and Planning A: Economy and Space* 37 (11):1903–1918.

Angel, David P., Trina Hamilton, and Matthew T. Huber. 2007. "Global Environmental Standards for Industry." *Annual Review of Environment and Resources* 32 (1):295–316.

Appalachian Sustainable Agriculture Project. 2018. "ASAP: Local Food, Strong Farms, Healthy Communities." Appalachian Sustainable Agriculture Project, accessed 13 March. http://asapconnections.org/.

Arendt, Hannah. 2005. *The Promise of Politics*. New York: Schocken.

Arias-Maldonado, Manuel. 2019. "The 'Anthropocene' in Philosophy: The Neo-material Turn and the Question of Nature." In *Anthropocene Encounters: New Directions in Green Political Thinking*, edited by Frank Biermann and Eva Lövbrand, 50–66. New York: Cambridge University Press.

Armitage, Derek, Rob de Loë, and Ryan Plummer. 2012. "Environmental Governance and Its Implications for Conservation Practice." *Conservation Letters* 5 (4):245–255.

Arnold, Jennifer S. and Maria Fernandez-Gimenez. 2007. "Building Participatory Capital through Participatory Research: An Analysis of Collaboration on Tohono O'odham Tribal Rangelands in Arizona." *Society and Natural Resources* 20 (6):481–495.

Ashwood, Loka, Noelle Harden, Michael Bell, and William Bland. 2014. "Linked and Situated: Grounded Knowledge." *Rural Sociology* 79 (4):427–452.

Auld, Graeme and Lars Gulbrandsen. 2014. "Learning through Disclosure: The Evolving Importance of Transparency in the Practice of Nonstate Certification." In *Transparency in Global Environmental Governance: Critical Perspectives*, edited by Aarti Gupta and Michael Mason, 271–296. Cambridge, MA: MIT Press.

Baber, Walter F. 1983. *Managing the Future: Matrix Models for the Postindustrial Polity*. University, AL: University of Alabama Press.

Baber, Walter F. 2010. "Democratic Deliberation and Environmental Practice: The Case of Natural Resource Management." *Environmental Practice* 12:195–201.

Baber, Walter F. 2011. "Administrative Law and Discursive Democracy: Toward a Comparative Perspective." *International Journal of Public Administration* 34 (1):297–311.

Baber, Walter F. 2014. "Public Management for Volatile Times: Toward Adaptive, Collaborative, and Deliberative Governance." In *Governance and Public Management: Strategic Foundations for Volatile Times*, edited by Charles Conteh, Thomas J. Greitens, David K. Jesuit, and Ian Roberge, 3–14. New York: Routledge.

Baber, Walter F. and Robert V. Bartlett. 2005. *Deliberative Environmental Politics: Democracy and Ecological Rationality*. Cambridge, MA: MIT Press.

Baber, Walter F. and Robert V. Bartlett. 2009a. *Global Democracy and Sustainable Jurisprudence: Deliberative Environmental Law*. Cambridge, MA: MIT Press.

Baber, Walter F. and Robert V. Bartlett. 2009b. "Race, Poverty, and the Environment: Toward a Global Perspective." *Public Administration Quarterly* 33 (4):457–480.

Baber, Walter F. and Robert V. Bartlett. 2011. "The Role of International Law in Global Governance." In *The Oxford Handbook of Climate Change and Society*, edited by John S. Dryzek, Richard B. Norgaard, and David Schlosberg, 653–665. New York: Oxford University Press.

Baber, Walter F. and Robert V. Bartlett. 2015. *Consensus and Global Environmental Governance: Deliberative Democracy in Nature's Regime*. Cambridge, MA: The MIT Press.

Baber, Walter F. and Robert V. Bartlett. 2016. "Simulations." In *Encyclopedia of Global Environmental Politics and Governance*, edited by Philipp Pattberg and Fariborz Zelli, 156–160. London: Edward Elgar.

Baber, Walter F. and Robert V. Bartlett. 2019. "Democracy and Climate Change: The Unfolding of Tragedy." In *Climate Futures: Re-imagining Global Climate Justice*, edited by Kum-Kum Bhavnani, John Foran, Priya A. Kurian, and Debashish Munshi, 145–151. London: Zed Books.

Baber, Walter F. and Robert V. Bartlett. 2020. *Environmental Human Rights in Earth System Governance: Democracy beyond Democracy*. New York: Cambridge University Press.

Bäckstrand, Karin. 2006. "Democratizing Global Environmental Governance? Stakeholder Democracy after the World Summit on Sustainable Development." *European Journal of International Relations* 12 (4):467–498.

Bäckstrand, Karin. 2011. "The Democratic Legitimacy of Global Governance after Copenhagen." In *Oxford Handbook on Climate Change and Society*, edited by John S. Dryzek, Richard B. Norgaard, and David Schlosberg, 669–684. New York: Oxford University Press.

Bäckstrand, Karin, Jamil Khan, Annica Kronsell, and Eva Lövbrand, eds. 2010. *Environmental Politics and Deliberative Democracy: Examining the Promise of New Modes of Governance*. Northampton, MA: Edward Elgar.

Bäckstrand, Karin, Jonathan Kuyper, Björn-Ola Linnér, and Eva Lövbrand. 2017. "Nonstate Actors in Global Environmental Governance: From Copenhagen to Paris and beyond." *Environmental Politics* 26 (4):561–579.

Bacon, Christopher M., Christy Getz, Sibella Kraus, Maywa Montenegro, and Kaelin Holland. 2012. "The Social Dimensions of Sustainability and Change in Diversified Farming Systems." *Ecology and Society* 17 (4):607–626.

Bartlett, Robert V. 1990. "Comprehensive Environmental Decision Making: Can It Work?" In *Environmental Policy in the 1990s: Toward a New Agenda*, edited by Norman J. Vig and Michael E. Kraft, 235–254. Washington, DC: CQ Press.

Baskin, Jeremy. 2019. "Global Justice and the Anthropocene: Reproducing a Development Story." In *Anthropocene Encounters: New Directions in Green Political Thinking*, edited by Frank Biermann and Eva Lövbrand, 150–168. New York: Cambridge University Press.

Bauer, Steffen. 2009a. "The Ozone Secretariat: The Good Shepard of Ozone Politics." In *Managers of Global Change: The Influence of International Environmental Bureaucracies*, edited by Frank Biermann and Bernd Siebenhüner, 225–244. Cambridge, MA: MIT Press.

Bauer, Steffen. 2009b. "The Secretariat of the United Nations Environment Programme: Tangled Up in Blue." In *Managers of Global Change: The Influence of International Environmental Bureaucracies*, edited by Frank Biermann and Bernd Siebenhüner, 169–201. Cambridge, MA: MIT Press.

Bauer, Steffen and Silke Weinlich. 2011. "International Bureaucracies: Organizing World Politics." In *The Ashgae Research Companion to Non-State Actors*, edited by Bob Reinalda. Aldershot: Ashgate.

Bauer, Steffen, Steinar Andresen, and Frank Biermann. 2012. "International Bureaucracies." In *Global Environmental Governance Reconsidered*, edited by Frank Biermann and Philipp Pattberg, 27–44. Cambridge, MA: MIT Press.

Bavinck, Maarten and Joyeeta Gupta. 2014. "Legal Pluralism in Aquatic Regimes: A Challenge for Governance." *Current Opinion in Environmental Sustainability* 11:78–85.

Beierle, Thomas. 2004. "The Benefits and Costs of Disclosing Information about Risks: What Do We Know about Right to Know?" *Risk Analysis* 24 (2):335–346.

Bell, Daniel. 1976. *The Coming of Post-Industrial Society*. New York: Basic Books.

Berg, Monika and Rolf Lidskog. 2018. "Deliberative Democracy Meets Democratized Science: A Deliberative Systems Approach to Global Environmental Governance." *Environmental Politics* 27 (1):1–20.

Bernstein, Steven. 2002. "Liberal Environmentalism and Global Environmental Governance." *Global Environmental Change* 2 (3):1–16.

Bernstein, Steven and Matthew Hoffmann. 2018. "The Politics of Decarbonization and the Catalytic Impact of Subnational Climate Experiments." *Policy Sciences* 51 (2):189–211.

Betsill, Michele, Tabatha M. Benney, and Andrea K. Gerlak, eds. 2020. *Agency in Earth System Governance*. New York: Cambridge University Press.

Betsill, Michele M. and Matthew J. Hoffmann. 2011. "The Contours of "Cap and Trade": The Evolution of Emissions Trading Systems for Greenhouse Gases." *Review of Policy Research* 28 (1):83–106.

Betsill, Michele M., Philipp Pattberg, and Eleni Dellas. 2011. "Special Issue: Agency in Earth System Governance." *International Environmental Agreements: Politics, Law and Economics* 11 (1):1–6.

Biddle, Jennifer C. and Tomas M. Koontz. 2014. "Goal Specificity: A Proxy Measure for Improvements in Environmental Outcomes in Collaborative Governance." *Journal of Environmental Management* 145:268–276.

Biermann, Frank. 2010. "Beyond the Intergovernmental Regime: Recent Trends in Global Carbon Governance." *Current Opinion in Environmental Sustainability* 2 (4):284–288. https://doi.org/10.1016/j.cosust.2010.05.002.

Biermann, Frank. 2014. *Earth System Governance: World Politics in the Anthropocene*. Cambridge, MA: MIT Press.

Biermann, Frank. 2016. "Politics for a New Earth: Governing in the 'Anthropocene'." In *New Earth Politics: Essays from the Anthropocene*, edited by Simon Nicholson and Sikina Jinnah, 405–420. Cambridge, MA: MIT Press.

Biermann, Frank and Aarti Gupta. 2011. "Accountability and Legitimacy in Earth System Governance : A Research Framework." *Ecological Economics* 70 (11):1856–1864.

Biermann, Frank and Rakhyun E. Kim, eds. 2020. *Architectures of Earth System Governance: Institutional Complexity and Structural Transformation*. New York: Cambridge University Press.

Biermann, Frank and Eva Lövbrand, eds. 2019. *Anthropocene Encounters: New Directions in Green Political Thinking*. New York: Cambridge University Press.

Biermann, Frank and Ina Möller. 2019. "Rich Man's Solution? Climate Engineering Discourses and the Marginalization of the Global South." *International Environmental Agreeements: Politics, Law and Economics* 19 (2):151–167.

Biermann, Frank and Philipp Pattberg. 2012. "Global Environmental Governance Revisited." In *Global Environmental Governance Reconsidered*, edited by Frank Biermann and Philipp Pattberg, 1–24. Cambridge, MA: MIT Press.

Biermann, Frank and Bernd Siebenhüner. 2009. *Managers of Global Change: The Influence of International Environmental Bureaucracies*. Cambridge, MA: MIT Press.

Biermann, Frank, Olwen Davies, and Nicolien Grijp. 2009. "Environmental Policy Integration and the Architecture of Global Environmental Governance." *International Environmental Agreeements: Politics, Law and Economics* 9 (4):351–369.

Biermann, Frank, Michele M. Betsill, Joyeeta Gupta, Norichika Kanie, Louris Lebel, Kiana Liverman, Heike Schroeder, and Bernd Siebenhüner. 2009. *Earth System Governance: People, Places, and the Planet (Earth System Implementation Plan of the Earth System Governance Project)*. Bonn: Earth System Governance Project.

Biermann, Frank, Xuemei Bai, Ninad Bondre, Wendy Broadgate, Chen-Tung Arthur Chen, Opha Pauline Dube, Jan Willem Erisman, Marion Glaser, Sandra van der Hel, Maria

Carmen Lemos, Sybil Seitzinger, and Karen C. Seto. 2016. "Down to Earth: Contextualizing the Anthropocene." *Global Environmental Change* 39:341–350.

Bizzo, Eduardo and Gregory Michener. 2017. "Forest Transparency without Transparency? Evaluating State Efforts to Reduce Deforestation in the Brazilian Amazon." *Environmental Policy and Governance* 27 (6):560–574.

Blackstone William. 1979 [1765–1769]. *Commentaries on the Laws of England*. Chicago: University of Chicago Press.

Bled, Amandine. 2010. "Technological Choices in International Environmental Negotiations: An Actor-Network Analysis." *Business and Society* 49 (4):570–590.

Blumstein, Sabine. 2017. "Managing Adaptation: International Donors' Influence on International River Basin Organizations in Southern Africa." *International Journal of River Basin Management* 15 (4):461–473.

Boelens, Rutgerd and Jeroen Vos. 2014. "Legal Pluralism, Hydraulic Property Creation and Sustainability: The Materialized Nature of Water Rights in User-Managed Systems." *Current Opinion in Environmental Sustainability* 11:55–62.

Bohman, James and Henry S. Richardson. 2009. "Liberalism, Deliberative Democracy, and 'Reasons that All Can Accept'." *Journal of Political Philosophy* 17 (3):253–274.

Bonfazi, Alessandro, Carlo Rega, and Paola Gazzola. 2011. "Strategic Environmental Assessment and the Democratisation of Spatial Planning." *Journal of Environmental Assessment Policy and Management* 13 (1):9–37.

Bonnell, Joseph E. and Tomas Koontz. 2007. "Stumbling Forward: The Organizational Challenges of Building and Sustaining Collaborative Watershed Management." *Society and Natural Resources* 20 (2):153–167.

Boswell, Terry and Christopher Chose-Dunn. 2000. *The Spiral of Capitalism and Socialism: Toward Global Democracy*. Boulder, CO: Lynne Reinner.

Boughey, Janina. 2013. "Administrative Law: The Next Frontier for Comparative Law." *The International and Comparative Law Quarterly* 62 (1):55–95.

Bouteligier, Sofie. 2011. "Exploring the Agency of Global Environmental Consultancy Firms in Earth System Governance." *International Environmental Agreeements: Politics, Law and Economics* 11 (1):43–61.

Boyd, David R. 2012. *The Environmental Rights Revolution: A Global Study of Constitutions, Human Rights, and the Environment*. Vancouver, BC: UBC Press.

Boyd, David R. 2017. *The Rights of Nature: A Legal Revolution that Could Save the World*. Toronto: ECW Press.

Bremer, Scott. 2013. "Mobilizing High-Quality Knowledge through Dialogic Environmental Governance: A Comparison of Approaches and their Institutional Settings." *International Journal of Sustainable Development* 16 (1–2):66–90.

Brondizio, Edwardo S., Karen O'Brien, Xuemei Bai, Frank Biermann, Will Steffen, Frans Berkhout, Christophe Cudennec, Maria Carmen Lemos, Alexander Wolfe, Jose Palma-Oliveira, and Chen-Tung Arthur Chen. 2016. "Re-Conceptualizing the Anthropocene: A Call for Collaboration." *Global Environmental Change* 39:318–327.

Buck, Matthias and Clare Hamilton. 2011. "The Nagoya Protocol on Access to Genetic Resources and the Fair and Equiable Sharing of Benefits Arising from their Utilization to the Convention on Biological Diversity." *Review of European Community and International Environmental Law* 20 (1):47–61.

Bührs, Ton. 2009. *Environmental Integration: Our Common Challenge*. Albany: State University of New York Press.

Buijs, Arjen, Rieke Hansen, Sander van der Jagt, Biana Ambrose-Oji, Birgit Elands, Emily Lorance Rall, Thamos Mattijssen, Stephan Pauleit, Hens Runhaar, Anton Stahl Olafsson, and Maja Steen Mller. 2019. "Mosaic Governance for Urban Green

Bibliography 181

Infrastructure: Upscaling Acitve Citizenship from a Local Government Perspective." *Urban Forestry & Urban Greening* 40:53–62.

Burch, Sarah, Aarti Gupta, Cristina Y.A. Inoue, Agni Kalfagianni, Åsa Persson, Andrea K. Gerlak, Atsushi Ishii, James Patterson, Jonathan Pickering, Michelle Scobie, Jeroen van der Heijden, Joost Vervoort, Carolina Adler, Michael Bloomfield, Riyanti Djalante, John Dryzek, Victor Galaz, Christopher Gordon, Renée Harmon, Sikina Jinnah, Rakhyun E. Kim, Lennart Olsson, Judith van Leeuwen, Vasna Ramasar, Paul Wapner, and Ruben Zondervan. 2019. "New Directions in Earth System Governance Research." *Earth System Governance* 1:1–18.

Burke, Anthony and Stefanie Fishel. 2019. "Power, World Politics, and Thing-Systems in the Anthropocene." In *Anthropocene Encounters: New Directions in Green Political Thinking*, edited by Frank Biermann and Eva Lövbrand, 87–108. New York: Cambridge University Press.

Burrell, Alison. 2011. "'Good Agricultural Practices' in the Agri-Food Supply Chain." *Environmental Law Review* 13 (4):251–270.

Cadman, Tim, Tapan Sarker, Zahrul Muttaqin, Fitri Nurfatriana, Mimi Salminah, and Tek Mraseni. 2019. "The Role of Fiscal Instruments in Encouraging the Private Sector and Smallholders to Reduce Emissions from Deforestation and Forest Degradation: Evidence from Indonesia." *Forest Policy & Economics* 108 (101913):1–10.

Caldwell, Lynton K. 1996. *International Environmental Policy*. 3rd ed. Durham, NC: Duke University Press.

Camilleri, Mark Anthony. 2015a. "Environmental, Social, and Governance Disclosures in Europe." *Sustainability Accounting, Management and Policy Journal* 6 (2):224–242.

Camilleri, Mark Anthony. 2015b. "Valuing Stakeholder Engagement and Sustainability Reporting." *Corporate Reputation Review* 18 (3):210–222.

Campbell-Johnson, Joey ten Kate, Maja Elfering-Petrovic, and Joyeeta Gupta. 2019. "City-level Circular Transitions: Barriers and Limits in Amsterdam, Utrecht and The Hague." *Journal of Cleaner Production* 235:1232–1239.

Caplan, Bryan. 2007. *The Myth of the Rational Voter: Why Democracies Choose Bad Policies*. Princeton, NJ: Princeton University Press.

Cardoza, Benjamin. 1924. *The Growth of the Law*. New Haven, CT: Yale University Press.

Carpenter, Daniel and David A. Moss, eds. 2013. *Preventing Regulatory Capture: Special Interest Influence and How to Limit It*. New York: Cambridge University Press.

Casella, Alessandra. 2001. "Product Standards and International Trade: Harmonization through Private Coalitions?" *Kyklos* 54 (2–3):243–264.

Castree, Noah. 2019. "The "Anthropocene" in Global Change Science: Expertise, the Earth, and the Future of Humanity." In *Anthropocene Encounters: New Directions in Green Political Thinking*, edited by Frank Biermann and Eva Lövbrand, 25–49. New York: Cambridge University Press.

Chan, Sandler and Wanja Amling. 2019. "Does Orchestration in the Global Climate Action Agenda Effectively Prioritize and Mobilize Transnational Climate Adaptation?" *International Environmental Agreements: Politics, Law and Economics* 19 (4–5):429–446.

Chan, Sander, Paula Ellinger, and Oscar Widerberg. 2018. "Exploring National and Regional Orchestration of Non-State Action for a < 1.5 °C World." *International Environmental Agreements: Politics, Law and Economics* 18 (1):135–152. https://doi.org/10.1007/s10784-018-9384-2.

Cheng, Antony S. and Janet D. Fiero. 2005. *The Deliberative Democracy Handbook: Strategies for Effective Civic Engagement in the 21st Century*. San Francisco: John Wiley & Sons.

Christoff, Peter and Robyn Eckersley. 2013. *Globalization and the Environment*. Lanham, MD: Rowman & Littlefield.

Churchill, Winston S. 1956. *A History of the English Speaking Peoples*. New York: Dorset.

Ciplet, David, Kevin M. Adams, Romain Weikmans, and J. Timmons Roberts. 2018. "The Transformative Capability of Transparency in Global Environmental Governance." *Global Environmental Politics* 18 (3):130–150.

Ciplet, David, J. Timmons Roberts, and Mizan R. Khan. 2015. *Power in a Warming World: The New Global Politics of Climate Change and the Remaking of Environmental Inequality*. Cambridge, MA: MIT Press.

Clapp, Jennifer. 2019. "The Rise of Financial Investment and Common Ownership in Global Agrifood Firms." *Review of International Political Economy* 26 (4):604–629.

Clapp, Jennifer and Ryan Isakson. 2018. "Risky Returns: The Implications of Financialization in the Food System." *Development and Change* 49 (2):437–460.

Clark, Jo. 1997. *Strategic Partnerships: A Strategic Guide for Local Conservation Efforts in the West*. Denver, CO: Western Governors' Association.

Cobb, Tanya. 2011. *Reclaiming Our Food: How the Grassroots Food Movement Is Changing the Way We Eat*. North Adams, MA: Storey Publishing.

Coleman, Sarah, Stephanie Hurley, Christopher Koliba, and Asim Zia. 2017. "Crowdsourced Delphis: Designing Solutions to Complex Problems with Broad Stakeholder Participation." *Global Environmental Change* 45 (1):111–123.

Conteh, Charles, Thomas J. Greitens, David K. Jesuit, and Ian Roberge, eds. 2014. *Governance and Public Management: Strategic Foundations for Volatile Times*. New York: Routledge.

Conti, Kirstin I. and Joyeeta Gupta. 2014. "Protected by Pluralism? Grappling with Multiple Legal Frameworks in Groundwater Governance." *Current Opinion in Environmental Sustainability* 11:39–47.

Coolsaet, Brendan. 2015a. "Fair and Equitable Negotiations? African Influence and the International Access and Benefit-Sharing Regime." *Global Environmental Politics* 15 (2):38–56.

Coolsaet, Brendan. 2015b. "Transformative Participation in Agrobiodiversity Governance: Making the Case for an Environmental Justice Approach." *Journal of Agricultural and Environmental Ethics* 28 (6):1089–1104.

Cosmides, Leda and John Tooby. 2008. "Can a General Deontic Logic Capture the Facts of Human Moral Reasoning?" In *Moral Psychololgy, Volume 1 – The Evolution of Morality: Adaptations and Innateness*, edited by Walter Sinnott-Armstrong, 51–119. Cambridge, MA: MIT Press.

Cotton, Matthew. 2013. "Deliberating Intergenerational Environmental Equity: A Pragmatic, Future Studies Approach." *Environmental Values* 22 (3):317–337.

County of San Diego Department of Agriculture, Weights and Measures. 2017. *County of San Diego Crop Statistics and Annual Report*. San Diego: County of San Diego Department of Agriculture, Weights and Measures.

Craig, Paul. 2012. *EU Administrative Law*. 2nd ed. New York: Oxford University Press.

Crawford, Neta C. 2018. *United States Budgetary Costs of the Post-9/11 Wars through FY2019: $5.9 Trillion Spent and Obligated*. Providence, RI: Brown University, Watson Institute for International and Public Affairs.

Cronin, Amanda E. and David M. Ostergren. 2007. "Democracy, Participation, and Native American Tribes in Collaborative Watershed Management." *Society and Natural Resources* 20 (6):527–542.

Crutzen, Paul J. and Eugene F. Stoermer. 2000. "The 'Anthropocene'." *Global Change: International Geosphere–Biosphere Programme (IGBP) Newsletter* 41:17–18.

Curato, Nicole, John S. Dryzek, Selen A. Ercan, Carolyn M. Hendricks, and Simon Niemeyer. 2017. "Twelve Key Findings in Deliberative Democracy Research." *Daedalus* 146 (3):28–38.

Dabbagh, Alya, Rebecca L. Laws, Claudia Steulet, Laure Dumolard, Mick N. Mulders, Katrina Kretsinger, James P. Alexander, Paul A. Rota, and James L. Goodson. 2018. "Progress Toward Regional Measles Elimination – Worldwide, 2000–2017." *Morbidity and Mortality Weekly Report* 67 (47):1323–1329. http://dx.doi.org/10.15585/mmwr.mm6747a6.

Davis, Kenneth Culp. 1969. *Discretionary Justice: A Preliminary Inquiry*. Baton Rouge: Louisiana State University Press.

De Caro, Daniel A., Brian C. Chaffin, Edella Schlager, Ahjond S. Garmestani, and J. B. Ruhl. 2017. "Legal and Institutional Foundations of Adaptive Environmental Governance." *Ecology and Society* 22 (1):778–797.

Dellas, Eleni, Philipp Pattberg, and Michele Betsill. 2011. "Agency in Earth System Governance." *International Environmental Agreeements: Politics, Law and Economics* 11 (1):85–98.

Demartini, Eugenio, Anna Gaviglio, and Alberto Pirani. 2017. "Farmers' Motivation and Perceived Effects of Participating in Short Food Supply Chains: Evidence from a North Italian Survey." *Agricultural Economics (Czech)* 63 (5):204–216. http://dx.doi.org/10.17221/323/2015-AGRICECON.

Dennett, Daniel. 1991. *Consciousness Explained*. Boston: Little, Brown.

Dennett, Daniel. 2003. *Freedom Evolves*. New York: Viking.

Dennett, Daniel. 2006. *Breaking a Spell: Religion as a Natural Phenomenon*. New York: Viking.

Di Gregorio, Monica, Maria Brockhaus, Tim Cronin, Efrian Muharrom, Levania Santoso, Sofi Mardiah, and Mirjam Büdenbender. 2013. "Equity and REDD+ in the Media: A Comparative Analysis of Policy Discourses." *Ecology and Society* 18 (2):39. http://dx.doi.org/10.5751/ES-05694-180239.

Diaz-Kope, Luisa and Katrina Miller-Stevens. 2015. "Rethinking a Typology of Watershed Partnerships: A Governance Perspective." *Public Works Management and Policy* 20 (1):29–48.

Dibden, Jacqui, Clive Potter, and Chris Cocklin. 2009. "Contesting the Neoliberal Project for Agriculture: Productivist and Multifunctional Trajectories in the European Union and Australia." *Journal of Rural Studies* 25 (3):299–308.

Diesing, Paul. 1971. *Patterns of Discovery in the Social Sciences*. New York: Aldine.

Dingwerth, Klaus and Margot Eichinger. 2010. "Tamed Transparency: How Information Disclosure under the Global Reporting Initiative Fails to Empower." *Global Environmental Politics* 10 (3):74–96.

Dingwerth, Klaus and Margot Eichinger. 2014. "Tamed Transparency and the Global Reporting Initiative." In *Transparency in Global Environmental Governance: Critical Perspectives*, 225–247. Cambridge, MA: MIT Press.

Dodge, Jennifer. 2014. "Civil Society Organizations and Deliberative Policy Making: Interpreting Environmental Controversies in the Deliberative System." *Policy Sciences* 47 (2):161–185.

Domingo, José. L. and Jordi Giné Bordonaba. 2011. "A Literature Review on the Safety Assessment of Genetically Modified Plants." *Environment International* 37 (4):734–742.

Dorsch, Marcel J. and Christian Flachsland. 2017. "A Polycentric Approach to Global Climate Governance." *Global Environmental Politics* 17 (21):45–64.

Downing, Jim. 2006. "Olive Oil Turns Golden." *Sacramento Bee*, 10 May, D1.

Dryzek, John S. 1990. *Discursive Democracy: Politics, Policy, and Political Science*. New York: Cambridge University Press.

Dryzek, John S. 1995. "Political and Ecological Communication." *Environmental Politics* 4 (4):13–30.

Dryzek, John S. 2000. *Deliberative Democracy and Beyond: Liberals, Critics, Contestations*. New York: Oxford University Press.

Dryzek, John S. 2006. *Deliberative Global Politics: Discourse and Democracy in a Divided World*. Malden, MA: Polity.

Dryzek, John S. 2011. "Global Democracy and Earth System Governance." *Ecological Economics* 70 (11):1865–1874.

Dryzek, John S. 2014. "Institutions for the Anthropocene: Governance in a Changing Earth System." *British Journal of Political Science* 46 (4):937–956. https://doi.org/10.1017/S0007123414000453.

Dryzek, John S. 2016. "Institutions for the Anthropocene: Governance in a Changing Earth System." *British Journal of Political Science* 46 (4):937–956.

Dryzek, John S. 2017a. "The Forum, the System, and the Polity: Three Varieties of Democratic Theory." *Political Theory* 45 (5):610–636.

Dryzek, John S. 2017b. "The Meanings of Life for Non-State Actors in Climate Politics." *Environmental Politics* 26 (4):789–799.

Dryzek, John S. and Simon Niemeyer. 2008. "Discursive Representation." *American Political Science Review* 102 (4):481–493.

Dryzek, John S. and Jonathan Pickering. 2017. "Deliberation as a Catalyst for Reflexive Governance." *Ecological Economics* 131:353–360.

Dryzek, John S. and Jonathan Pickering. 2019. *The Politics of the Anthropocene*. New York: Oxford University Press.

Dryzek, John S. and Hayley Stevenson. 2011. "Democracy and Global Earth System Governance." *Ecological Economics* 70 (11):1865–1874.

Dryzek, John S., Quinlan Bowman, Jonathan Kuyper, Jonathan Pickering, Jensen Sass, and Hayley Stevenson. 2019. *Deliberative Global Governance*. New York: Cambridge University Press.

Dupont, Claire. 2019. "The EU's Collective Secularization of Climate Change." *Western European Politics* 42 (2):369–390.

Duyck, Sébastien. 2014. "MRV in the 2015 Climate Agreement: Promoting Compliance through Transparency and the Participation of NGOs." *Carbon and Climate Law Review* 3:175–187. http://ssrn.com/abstract=2557175.

Dworkin, Ronald. 2000. *Sovereign Virtue: The Theory and Practice of Equality*. Cambridge, MA: Harvard University Press.

Earth System Governance Project. 2009. *Earth System Governance: People, Places, and the Planet (International Human Dimensions Programme on Global Environmental Change, IHDP Report No. 20)*. Bonn: Earth System Governance Project.

Eckersley, Robyn. 2017. "Geopolitan Democracy in the Anthropocene." *Political Studies* 65 (4):983–999.

Edellenbos, Jurian, Nienke van Schie, and Lasse Gerrits. 2010. "Organizing Interfaces between Government Institutions and Interactive Governance." *Policy Sciences* 43:73–94.

Edwards, Gareth A. S. and Harriet Bulkeley. 2018a. "Heterotopia and the Urban Politics of Climate Change Experimentation." *Environment & Planning D: Society and Space* 36 (2):350–369.

Edwards, Gareth A. S. and Harriet Bulkeley. 2018b. "Urban Political Ecologies of Housing and Climate Change: The 'Coolest Block' Contest in Philadelphia." *Urban Studies* 54 (5):1126–1141.

Elbadawi, Ibrahim and Nicholas Sambanis. 2000. "Why Are There so Many Civil Wars in Africa? Understanding and Preventing Violent Conflict." *Journal of African Economies* 9 (3):244–269.

Ellison, Brian. 2001. "Institutional Controls and Local Autonomy in Land-Use Planning: Balancing Economic Development and Environmental Protection in Jasper County, Missouri." *State and Local Government Review* 21 (1):133–144.

Elmer, Thomas R., Susanne Lutz, and Verena Schuren. 2016. "Varieties of Localization: International Norms and the Commodification of Knowledge in India and Brazil." *Review of International Political Economy* 23 (3):450–479.

Elster, Jon. 2009. *Alexis de Tocqueville: The First Social Scientist*. New York: Cambridge University Press.

European Council. 2000a. Presidency Conclusions, Lisbon European Council, 23–24 March 2000. edited by European Council. Brussels: European Council.

European Council. 2000b. Presidency Conclusions, Nice European Council Meeting, 7–9 December 2000. Brussels: European Council.

European Council. 2005. Presidency Conclusions, European Council Brussels, 22–23 March 2005. Brussels: European Council.

Falck Zepeda, José. 2006. "Coexistence, Genetically Modified Biotechnologies and Biosafety: Implications for Developing Countries." *American Journal of Ecological Economics* 88 (5):1200–1208.

Feagan, Robert. 2007. "The Place of Food: Mapping Out the 'Local' in Local Food Systems." *Progress in Human Geography* 31 (1):23–42.

Feinberg, Matthew and Robb Willer. 2013. "The Moral Roots of Environmental Attitudes." *Psychological Science* 24 (1):56–62.

Ferrara, Enzo. 2017. "Earth System Governance: Ruling Climate Across Society." *Electronic Green Journal* 1 (40):1–9.

Finco, Adele, T. Sargentoni, A. Tramontano, Deborah Bentivoglio, and M. Rasetti. 2013. "Economic Sustainability of Short Food Supply Chain in the Italian Olive Oil Sector: A Viable Alternative for Tunisian Agrifood Market." African Association of Agricultural Economists Fourth International Conference, Hammamet, Tunisia, 22–25 September.

Fisher, Dana R. 2013. "Understanding the Relationship between Subnational and National Climate Change Politics in the United States: Toward a Theory of Boomerang Federalism." *Environment and Planning C: Government and Policy* 31:769–784.

Fishkin, James. 1995. *The Voice of the People: Public Opinion and Democracy* New Haven, CT: Yale University Press.

Fishkin, James S. 2011. *When the People Speak: Deliberative Democracy and Public Consultation*. New York: Oxford University Press.

Flaherty, Martin S. 2006. "Introduction: 'External' versus 'Internal' in International Law." *Fordham International Law Journal* 29:447–456.

Flanagan, Owen, Hagop Sarkissian, and David Wong. 2008. "Naturalizing Ethics." In *Moral Psychology, Volume 1 – The Evolution of Morality: Adaptations and Innateness*, edited by Walter Sinnott-Armstrong, 1–25. Cambridge, MA: MIT Press.

Florini, Ann. 2007. *The Right to Know: Transparency for an Open World*. New York: Columbia University Press.

Florini, Ann and Bharath Jairaj. 2014. "The National Context for Transparency-Based Global Environmental Governance." In *Transparency in Global Environmental Governance: Critical Perspectives*, edited by Aarti Gupta and Michael Mason, 61–80. Cambridge, MA: MIT Press.

Food and Agriculture Organization. 2017. *Climate-Smart Agriculture Sourcebook*. 2nd ed. Rome: Food and Agriculture Organization of the United Nations.

Fowler, Penny and Simon Heap. 2000. "Varieties of Participation in Complex Governance." *Public Administration Review* 66 (1):66–75.

Frank, Jason. 2007. "Aesthetic Democracy: Walt Whitman and the Poetry of the People." *Review of Politics* 69 (3):402–430.

Frantzeskaki, Niki, Timon McPhearson, Marcus Collier, Dave Kendal, Harriet Bulkeley, Adina Dumitru, Claire Walsh, Kate Noble, Ernita van Wyk, Camilo Ordonez, Cathy Oke, and Laszlo Pinter. 2019. "Nature-Based Solutions for Urban Climate Change Adaptation: Linking Science, Policy, and Practice Communities for Evidence-Based Decision-Making." *BioScience* 69 (6):455–466.

Freeman, Jody. 1999. "The Real Democracy Problem in Administrative Law." In *Recrafting the Rule of Law: The Limits of Legal Order*, edited by David Dyzenhaus, 331–370. Portland, OR: Hart Publishing.

Fremaux, Anne and John Barry. 2019. "The 'Good Anthropocene' and Green Political Thinking: Rethinking Environmentalism, Resisting Eco-modernism." In *Anthropocene Encounters: New Directions in Green Political Thinking*, edited by Frank Biermann and Eva Lövbrand, 171–190. New York: Cambridge University Press.

French, Duncan and Louis J. Kotzé. 2019. "Towards a Global Pact for the Environment: International Environmental Law's Factual, Technical, and (Unmentionable) Normative Gaps." *Review of European, Comparative & International Environmental Law* 28 (1):25–32.

Friberg-Fernros, Henrik and Johan Karlsson Schaffer. 2014. "The Consensus Paradox: Does Deliberative Agreement Impede Rational Discourse?" *Political Studies* 62 (1):99–116.

Friedman, Benjamin. 2005. *The Moral Consequences of Economic Growth*. New York: Vintage Books.

Fuerstein, Michael. 2014. "Symposium on Consensus: Democratic Consensus as an Essential Byproduct." *The Journal of Political Philosophy* 22 (3):282–301.

Fukuyama, Francis. 2014. *Political Order and Political Decay*. New York: Farrar, Strauss and Giroux.

Fulponi, Linda. 2006. "Private Voluntary Standards in the Food System: The Perspective of Major Food Retailers in OECD Countries." *Food Policy* 31 (1):1–13.

Fung, Archon, Mary Graham, and David Weil. 2007. *Full Disclosure: The Perils and Promise of Transparency*. New York: Cambridge University Press.

Funtowicz, Silvio and Jerome Ravertz. 1993. "Science for the Post-Normal Age." *Futures* 27 (9):739–755.

Galaz, Victor, Henrik Österblom, Örjan Bodin, and Beatrice Carona. 2016. "Global Networks and Global Change-Induced Tipping Points." *International Agreements: Politics, Law & Economics* 16 (2):189–221.

Gallemore, Caleb and Darla K. Munroe. 2013. "Centralization in the Global Avoided Deforestation Collaboration Network." *Global Environmental Change* 23 (5):1199–1210.

Gaus, Gerald. 2011. *The Order of Public Reason: A Theory of Freedom and Morality in a Diverse and Bounded World*. New York: Cambridge University Press.

Gellers, Joshua C. and Chris Jeffords. 2018. "Toward Environmental Democracy? Procedural Environmental Rights and Environmental Justice." *Global Environmental Politics* 18 (1):99–121.

Gerlak, Andrea K., Tanya Heilkkila, Sharon K. Smolinski, Dave Huitema, and Derek Armitage. 2018. "Learning Our Way Out of Environmental Policy Problems: A Review of the Scholarship." *Policy Sciences* 51 (3):335–371.

Bibliography

Gerlak, Andrea K., Tanya Heilkkila, Sharon K. Smolinski, Dave Huitema, and Brendan Moore. 2019. "It's Time to Learn About Learning: Where Should Environmental and Natural Resource Governance Field Go Next?" *Society and Natural Resources* 32 (9):1056–1064.

Gilio-Whitaker, Dina. 2019. *As Long as Grass Grows: The Indigenous Fight for Environmental Justice from Colonization to Standing Rock*. Boston: Beacon Press.

Glaser, Marion and Rosete de Silva Oliveira. 2004. "Prospects for the Co-Management of Mangrove Ecosystems on the Northern Brazilian Coast: Whose Rights, Whose Duties, and Whose Priorities?" *Natural Resources Forum* 28:224–233.

Glenn, H. Patrick. 2010. *Legal Traditions of the World: Sustainable Diversity in Law*. 4th ed. New York: Oxford University Press.

Gómez-Baggethun, Erik, Eszter Kelemen, Berta Martin-López, Ignacio Palomo, and Carlos Montes. 2013. "Scale Misfit in Ecosystem Service Governance as a Source of Environmental Conflict." *Society and Natural Resources* 26 (10):1202–1216.

Goodin, Robert E. 1992. *Green Political Theory*. Cambridge, MA: Polity Press.

Goodin, Robert E. 1996. "Enfranchising the Earth and Its Alternatives." *Political Studies* 44 (5):835–849,.

Gore, Christopher. 2019. "Agency and Climate Governance in African Cities: Lessons from Urban Agriculture." In *Urban Climate Politics: Agency and Empowerment*, edited by Jeroen van der Heijden, Harriet Bulkeley, and Chiara Certomà, 190–209. New York: Cambridge University Press.

Gould, Carol. 1988. *Rethinking Democracy: Freedom and Social Cooperation in Politics, Economy, and Society*. New York: Cambridge University Press.

Gould, Carol. 2004. *Globalizing Democracy and Human Rights*. New York: Cambridge University Press.

Granvik, Madeleine, Gunnar Lindberg, Karl-Anders Stigzelius, Erik Fahlbeck, and Yves Surry. 2012. "Prospects of Multifunctional Agriculture as a Facilitator of Sustainable Rural Development: Swedish Experience of Pillar 2 of the Common Agricultural Policy (CAP)." *Norwegian Journal of Geography* 66 (3):155–166.

Green, Jessica. 2013. "Order Out of Chaos: Public and Private Rules for Managing Carbon." *Global Environmental Politics* 13 (2):1–25.

Green, Jessica. 2014. *Rethinking Private Authority: Agents and Entrepreneurs in Global Environmental Governance*. Princeton, NJ: Princeton University Press.

Gulbrandsen, Lars. 2006. "Creating Markets for Eco Labelling: Are Consumers Insignificant?" *International Journal of Consumer Studies* 30 (5):477–489.

Gulbrandsen, Lars H. 2018. "Studying Institutions for Nonstate Environmental Governance." In *A Research Agenda for Global Environmental Politics*, edited by Peter Davergne and Justin Alger. Cheltenham: Edward Elgar.

Gunderson, Adolph G. 1995. *The Environmental Promise of Democratic Deliberation*. Madison: University of Wisconsin Press.

Gunningham, Neil. 2009a. "Environmental Law, Regulation and Governance: Shifting Architectures." *Journal of Environmental Law* 21 (2):179–212.

Gunningham, Neil. 2009b. "The New Collaborative Environmental Governance: The Localization of Regulation." *Journal of Law and Society* 36 (1):145–166.

Gupta, Aarti. 2000. "Governing Trade in Genetically Modified Organisms: The Cartagena Protocol on Biosafety." *Environment* 42 (4):23–33.

Gupta, Aarti. 2004. "When Global Is Local: Negotiating Safe Use of Biotechnology." In *Earthly Politics: Local and Global in Environmental Governance*, edited by Sheila Jasanoff and Marybeth Long Martello, 127–148. Cambridge, MA: MIT Press.

Gupta, Aarti. 2010. "Transparency to What End? Governing by Disclosure through the Biosafety Clearing-House." *Environment and Planning C: Government and Policy* 28 (2):128–144.

Gupta, Aarti. 2014. "Risk Governance through Transparency: Information Disclosure and the Global Trade in Transgenic Crops." In *Transparency in Global Environmental Governance: Critical Perspectives*, edited by Aarti Gupta and Michael Mason, 133–156. Cambridge, MA: MIT Press.

Gupta, Aarti and Michael Mason. 2014. "A Transparency Turn in Global Environmental Governance." In *Transparency in Global Environmental Governance: Critical Perspectives*, edited by Aarti Gupta and Michael Mason, 3–38. Cambridge, MA: MIT Press.

Gupta, Aarti and Ina Möller. 2019. "De facto Governance: How Authoritatitve Assessments Construct Climate Engineering as an Object of Governance." *Environmental Politics* 28 (3):480–501.

Gupta, Aarti, Ingrid Boas, and Peter Oosterveer. 2020. "Transparency in Global Sustainability Governance: To What Effect?" *Journal of Environmental Policy & Planning* 22 (1):84–97.

Gupta, Aarti, Steinar Andresen, Bernd Siebenhüner, and Frank Biermann. 2012. "Science Networks." In *Global Environmental Governance Reconsidered*, edited by Frank Biermann and Philipp Pattberg, 69–93. Cambridge, MA: MIT Press.

Gupta, Joyeeta and Karin Arts. 2018. "Achieving the 1.5 °C Objective: Just Implementation through a Right to (Sustainable) Development Approach." *International Environmental Agreements: Politics, Law and Economics* 18 (1):11–28. https://doi.org/10.1007/s10784-017-9376-7.

Gupta, Joyeeta and Louris Lebel. 2010. "Access and Allocation in Earth System Governance: Water and Climate Change Compared." *International Environmental Agreeements: Politics, Law and Economics* 10 (4):377–395.

Gupte, Manjusha and Robert V. Bartlett. 2007. "Necessary Preconditions for Deliberative Environmental Democracy? Challenging the Modernity Bias of Current Theory." *Global Environmental Politics* 7 (3):94–106.

Gutmann, Amy and Dennis Thompson. 2004. *Why Deliberative Democracy?* Princeton, NJ: Princeton University Press.

Haas, Peter M. 2017. "The Epistemic Authority of Solution-Oriented Global Environmental Assessments." *Environmental Science and Policy* 77:221–224. https://doi.org/10.1016/j.envsci.2017.03.013.

Habermas, Jürgen. 1984. *The Theory of Communicative Action, Volume 1: Reason and the Rationalization of Society*. Boston: Beacon Press.

Habermas, Jürgen. 1993. *Justification and Application: Remarks on Discourse Ethics*. Cambridge, MA: MIT Press.

Habermas, Jürgen. 1996. *Between Facts and Norms: Contributions to a Discourse Theory of Law and Democracy*. Cambridge, MA: MIT Press.

Habermas, Jürgen. 1998. *The Inclusion of the Other*. Cambridge, MA: MIT Press.

Habermas, Jürgen. 2001. "From Kant's 'Ideas' of Pure Reason to the 'Idealizing' Presuppositions of Communicative Action: Reflections on the Detranscendentalized 'Use of Reason'." In *Pluralism and the Pragmatic Turn: The Transformation of Critical Theory*, edited by William Rehg and James Bohman, 11–40. Cambridge, MA: MIT Press.

Habermas, Jürgen. 2009. *Europe: The Faltering Project*. Malden, MA: Polity Press.

Hackman, Bernd. 2012. "Analysis of the Governance Architecture to Regulate GHG Emissions from International Shipping." *International Environmental Agreeements: Politics, Law and Economics* 12 (1):85–103.

Haidt, Johathan. 2012. *The Righteous Mind: Why Good People are Divided by Politics and Religion*. New York: Vintage.

Hall, Cheryl. 2007. "Recognizing the Passion in Deliberation: Toward a More Democratic Theory of Deliberative Democracy." *Hypatia* 22 (4):81–95.

Hamilton, Matthew and Mark Lubell. 2018. "Collaborative Governance of Climate Change Adaptation Across Spatial and Institutional Scales." *Policy Studies Journal* 46:222–247.

Hampton, Jean. 1994. "Democracy and the Rule of Law." In *The Rule of Law*, edited by Ian Shapiro, 18–44. New York: New York University Press.

Harden, Noelle M., Loka L. Ashwood, and William L. Bland. 2013. "For the Public Good: Weaving a Multifunctional Landscape in the Corn Belt." *Agriculture and Human Values* 30 (4):525–537.

Hardy, Scott and Tomas Koontz. 2009. "Rules for Collaboration: Institutional Analysis of Group Membership and Levels of Action in Watershed Partnerships." *Policy Studies Journal* 37 (3):393–414.

Hayward, Bronwyn. 2008. "Let's Talk About the Weather: Decentering Democratic Debate About Climate Change." *Hypatia* 23 (3):81–98.

Hayward, Tim. 2005. *Constitutional Environmental Rights*. New York: Oxford University Press.

Hedden, Walter P. 1929. *How Great Cities are Fed*. Boston: D.C. Heath.

Helwig, Niklas. 2013. "EU Foreign Policy and the High Representative's Capacity-Expectations Gap: A Question of Political Will." *European Foreign Affairs Review* 18 (2):235–253.

Henson, Spenser and Matthew Humphrey. 2010. "Understanding the Complexities of Private Standards in Global Agri-Food Chains as They Impact Developing Countries." *Journal of Development Studies* 46 (9):1628–1646.

Herzig, Christian. 2006. "Corporate Sustainability Reporting: An Overview." *Sustainability and Accounting* 21:301–324.

Hickmann, Thomas. 2017a. "The Reconfiguration of Authority in Global Climate Governance." *International Studies Review* 19 (3):430–451. https://doi.org/10.1093/isr/vix037.

Hickmann, Thomas. 2017b. "Voluntary Global Business Initiatives and the International Climate Negotiations: A Case Study of the Greenhouse Gas Protocol." *Journal of Cleaner Production* 169:94 104.

Hickmann, Thomas, Harald Fuhr, Chris Höhne, Markus Lederer, and Fee Stehle. 2017. "Carbon Governance Arrangements and the Nation-State: The Reconfiguration of Public Authority in Developing Countries." *Public Administration and Development* 37(5):331–343.

Hicks, Christina C. and Joshua E. Cinner. 2014."Social, Institutional, and Knowledge Mechanisms Mediate Diverse Ecosystem Service Benefits from Coral Reefs." *PNAS* 111(50):17791–17796.

Higham, John. 1959. "The Cult of the "American Consensus": Homogenizing Our History." *Commentary* 27 (February) 93–100.

Hobolth, Mogens and Dorte Sindbjerg Martinsen. 2013. "Transgovernmental Networks in the European Union: Improving Compliance Effectively?" *Journal of European Public Policy* 20 (10):1406–1424.

Hogue, Arthur. 1966. *Origins of the Common Law*. Bloomington: Indiana University Press.

Holman, Ian P., Calum Brown, Timothy R. Carter, Paula A. Harrison, and Mark Rounsevell. 2019. "Improving the Representation of Adaption in Climate Change Impact Models." *Regional Environmental Change* 19 (3):711–721.

Holmes, Oliver Wendell Jr. 1991 [1881]. *The Common Law*. New York: Dover.

Huitema, Dave, Marleen van De Kerkhof, and Udo Pesch. 2007. "The Nature of the Beast: Are Citizens' Juries Deliberative or Pluralist?" *Policy Sciences* 40 (4):287–311.

Huntington, Samuel. 1965. "Political Development and Political Decay." *World Politics* 17 (3):386–430.

Hurlbert, Margot A. and Joyeeta Gupta. 2019. "An Institutional Analysis Method for Identifying Policy Instruments Facilitating the Adaptive Governance of Drought." *Environmental Science & Policy* 93:221–231.

Hurlbert, Margot A., Joyeeta Gupta, and Hebe Verrest. 2019. "A Comparison of Drought Instruments and Livelihood Capitals: Combining Livelihood and Institutional Analysis to Study Drought Policy Instruments." *Climate & Development* 11 (10):863–872.

Iancu, Bogdan. 2012. *Legislative Delegation: The Erosion of Normative Limits in Modern Constitutionalism*. New York: Springer.

Ignatieff, Michael. 2001. *Human Rights as Politics and Idolatry*. Princeton, NJ: Princeton University Press.

International Maritime Organization. 2018. *Adoption of the Initial IMO Strategy on Reduction of GHG Emissions from Ships and Existing IMO Activity Related to Reducing GHG Emissions in the Shipping Sector*. London: International Maritime Organization.

Isyaku, Usman, Albert A. Arhin, and Adeniyi P. Asiyanbi. 2017. "Framing Justice in REDD+ Governance: Centring Transparency, Equity and Legitimacy in Readiness Implementation in West Africa." *Environmental Conservation* 44 (3):212–220.

Ivanova, Maria. 2012. "Institutional Design and UNEP Reform: Historical Insights on Form, Function and Financing." *International Affairs* 88 (3):565–584.

James, Clive. 2012. *Global Status of Commercialized Biotech/GM Crops 2012*. Ithaca, NY: International Service for the Acquisition of Agri-biotech Applications.

Jamieson, Dale. 2014. *Reason in a Dark Time*. New York: Oxford University Press.

Jansen, Kees. 2008. "The Unspeakable Ban: The Translation of Global Pesticide Governance into Honduran National Regulation." *World Development* 36 (4):575–589.

Jansen, Kees and Milou Dubois. 2014. "Global Pesticide Governance by Disclosure: Prior Informed Consent and the Rotterdam Convention." In *Global Environmental Governance: Critical Perspectives*, edited by Aarti Gupta, 107–131. Cambridge, MA: MIT Press.

Jeffords, Chris and Joshua C. Gellers. 2017. "Constitutionalizing Environmental Rights: A Practical Guide." *Journal of Human Rights Practice* 9:136-145.

Jinnah, Sikina. 2014. *Post-Treaty Politics: Secretariat Influence in Global Environmental Governance*. Cambridge, MA: MIT Press.

Jinnah, Sikina. 2018. "Why Govern Climate Engineering? A Preliminary Framework for Demand-Based Governance." *International Studies Review* 20 (2):272–282.

Jinnah, Sikina, Simon Nicholson, and Jane Flegal. 2018. "Toward Legitimate Governance of Solar Geoengineering Research: A Role for Sub-state Actors." *Ethics, Policy & Environment* 21 (3):362–381.

Jordan, Andrew, Dave Huitema, Harro van Asselt, and Johanna Forster, eds. 2018. *Governing Climate Change: Polycentricity in Action?* New York: Cambridge University Press.

Joseph, Jonathan. 2014. "The EU in the Horn of Africa: Building Resilience as a Distant Form of Governance." *Journal of Common Market Studies* 52 (2):285–301.

Kalfagianni, Agni. 2013. "Addressing the Global Sustainability Challenge: The Potential and Pitfalls of Private Governance from the Perspective of Human Capabilities." *Journal of Business Ethics* 122 (2):307–320.

Kalfagianni, Agni and Onno Kuik. 2017. "Seeking Optimality in Climate Change Agrifood Policies: Stakeholder Perspectives from Western Europe." *Climate Policy* 17:72–92.

Kalfagianni, Agni and Philipp Pattberg. 2013. "Participation and Inclusiveness in Private Rule-Setting Organizations: Does It Matter for Effectiveness?" *Innovation: The European Journal of the Social Sciences* 26 (3):231–250.

Kanie, Norichika, Michele Betsill, Ruben Zondervan, Frank Biermann, and Oran R. Young. 2012. "A Charter Moment: Restructuring Governance for Sustainability." *Public Administration and Development* 32 (3):292–304.

Kanie, Norichika, Michele M. Betsill, Ruben Zondervan, Frank Biermann, and Oran R. Young. 2012. "A Charter Moment: Restructuring Governance for Sustainability." *Public Administration and Development* 32 (3):292–304. https://doi.org/10.1002/pad .1625.

Kaplan, Abraham. 1964. *The Conduct of Inquiry*. San Francisco: Chandler.

Karparowitz, Christopher, Tali Mendelber, and Lee Shaker. 2012. "Gender Inequality in Deliberative Participation." *American Political Science Review* 106 (3):533–547.

Karparowitz, Christopher, Chad Raphael, and Allen S. Hammond. 2009. "Deliberative Democracy and Inequality: Two Cheers for Enclave Deliberation among the Disempowered." *Politics & Society* 37 (4):576–615.

Kashwan, Prakash. 2016. "What Explains the Demand for Collective Forest Rights Amidst Land Use Conflicts?" *Journal of Environmental Management* 183 (3):657–666.

Kates, Robert W., William C. Clark, Robert Corell, J. Michael Hall, Carlo C. Jaeger, Ian Lowe, James J. McCarthy, Joachim Schellnhuber, Bert Bolin, Nancy M. Dickson, Silvie Faucheux, Gilberto C. Gallopin, Arnulf Grübler, Brian Huntley, Jill Jager, Narpat S. Jodha, Roger E. Kaslperson, Akin Mabogunje, Pamela Matson, Harold Mooney, Berrien Moore III, Timothy O'Riordan, and Uno Svedin. 2001. "Sustainability Science." *Science* 292 (5517):641–642.

Kelsen, Hans. 2006 [1949]. *General Theory of Law and State*. New Brunswick, NJ: Transaction Publishers.

Keohane, Robert. 2006. "Accountability in World Politics." *Scandinavian Political Studies* 29 (2):75 87.

Kerly, D. M. 2016. *Historical Sketch of the Equitable Jurisdiction of the Court of Chancery*. South Yarra, Victoria, Australia: Leopold Classic Library.

Key, Suzie, Julian K-C Ma, and Pascal M. W. Drake. 2008. "Genetically Modified Plants and Human Health." *Journal of the Royal Society of Medicine* 101 (6):290–298.

Keyes, Ralph. 2006. *The Quote Verifier: Who Said What, Where, and When*. New York: St. Martin's Griffin.

Kim, Rakhyun E. and Brendan Mackey. 2014. "International Environmental Law As a Complex Adaptive System." *International Environmental Agreements: Politics, Law and Economics* 14:5–24.

Kirsop, Barbara and Leslie Chan. 2005. "Transforming Access to Research Literature for Developing Countries." *Serials Review* 31 (4):246–255.

Kirton, John J. and Michael J. Trebilcock. 2004. *Hard Choices, Soft Law: Voluntary Standards in Global Trade, Environment and Social Governance*. Burlington, VT: Ashgate.

Klinke, Andreas and Ortwiin Renn. 2014. "Expertise and Experience: A Deliberative System of a Functional Divison of Labor for Post-normal Risk Governance." *Innovation: The European Journal of the Social Sciences* 27 (4):442–465.

Kloppenburg, Jack Jr., John Hendrickson, and G. W. Stevenson. 1996. "Coming in to the Foodshed." *Agriculture and Human Values* 13 (3):33–42.

Kolstad, Ivar and Tina Søreide. 2009. "Corruption in Natural Resource Management: Implications for Policy Makers." *Resources Policy* 34 (4):214–226.

Koontz, Tomas M. 2014. "Social Learning in Collaborative Watershed Planning: The Importance of Process Control and Efficacy." *Journal of Environmental Planning and Management* 57 (9010):1572–1593.

Kopela, Sophia. 2017. "Making Ships Cleaner: Reducing Air Pollution from International Shipping." *Review of European, Comparative and International Environmental Law* 26 (3):231–242.

Kotzé, Louis J. 2019. "International Environmental Law and the Anthropocene's Energy Dilemma." *Environmental Policy and Planning Law Journal* 36 (5):437–456.

Kotzé, Louis J. and Duncan French. 2018. "A Critique of the Global Pact for the Environment: A Stillborn Initiative or the Foundation for Lex Anthropocenae?" *International Environmental Agreeements: Politics, Law and Economics* 18 (6):811–838.

Kotzé, Louis J. and Wendy Muzangaza. 2018. "Constitutional International Environmental Law for the Anthropocene?" *Review of European, Comparative & International Environmental Law* 27 (3):278–292.

Kotzé, Louis K. and Rakhyun E. Kim. 2019. "Earth System Law: The Juridical Dimensions of Earth System Governance." *Earth System Governance* 1 (100003):1–2.

Kraft, Michael E., Mark Stephan, and Troy D. Abel. 2011. *Coming Clean: Information Disclosure and Environmental Performance*. Cambridge, MA: MIT Press.

Kramarz, Teresa and Susan Park. 2016. "Accountability in Global Environmental Governance: A Meaningful Tool for Action?" *Global Environmental Politics* 16 (2):1–21. https://doi.org/10.1162/GLEP_a_00349.

Kramarz, Teresa, David Cosolo, and Alejandro Rossi. 2017. "Judicialization of Environmental Policy and the Crisis of Democratic Accountability." *Review of Policy Research* 34 (1):31–49. https://doi.org/10.1111/ropr.12218.

Krasner, Stephen. 1983. *International Regimes*. Ithaca, NY: Cornell University Press.

Krause, Torsten, Collen Wain, and Kimberly A. Nicholas. 2013. "Evaluating Safeguards in a Conservation Incentive Program: Participation, Consent, and Benefit Sharing in Indigenous Communities of the Ecuadorian Amazon." *Ecology and Society* 18 (4):1. http://dx.doi.org/10.5751/ES-05733-180401.

Kronsell, Annica and Dalia Mukhtar-Landgren. 2018. "Experimental Governance: The Role of Municipalities in Urban Living Labs." *European Planning Studies* 26 (5):988–1107.

Lakoff, George and Mark Johnson. 1999. *Philosophy in the Flesh: The Embodied Mind and Its Challenge to Western Thought*. New York: Basic Books.

Landauer, Carl. 2011. "Regionalism, Geography, and the International Legal Imagination." *Chicago Journal of International Law* 11 (2):557–595.

Larson, Anne M. and Fernanda Soto. 2008. "Decentralization of Natural Resource Governance Regimes." *Annual Review of Environment and Resources* 33 (1):213–239.

Lasswell, Harold. 1936. *Politics: Who Gets What, When, How*. New York: Whittlesey House.

Lautensach, Sabina W. and Alexander K. Lautensach. 2014. "Environmental Security: International, National and Human." In *Routledge Handbook of Global Environmental Politics*, edited by Paul G. Harris, 246–258. New York: Routledge.

Leach, William D. and Neil W. Pelky. 2001. "Making Watershed Partnerships Work: A Review of the Empirical Literature." *Journal of Water Resources Planning and Management* 127:378–385.

Lebel, Louis. 2013. "Local Knowledge and Adaptation to Climate Change in Natural Resource-Based Societies of the Asia-Pacific." *Mitigation & Adaptation Strategies for Global Change* 18 (7):1057–1076.

Lebel, Louis, Torsten Grothmann, and Bernd Siebenhüner. 2010. "The Role of Social Learning in Adaptiveness: Insights from Water Management." *International Environmental Agreements: Politics, Law and Economics* 10 (4):333–353.

Lebel, Phimphakan, Louis Lebel, Darunee Singphonphral, Chatta Duangsuwan, and Yishu Ahou. 2019. "Making Space for Women: Civil Society Organizations, Gender and Hydropower Development in the Mekong Region." *International Journal of Water Resources Development* 35 (2):305–325.

Lee, Maria. 2018. "Brexit and Environmental Protection in the United Kingdom: Governance, Accountability and Law Making." *Journal of Energy & Natural Resources Law* 36 (3):151–159.

Lima, Mairon G. Bastos and Joyeeta Gupta. 2013. "The Policy Context of Biofuels: A Case of Non-Governance at the Global Level?" *Global Environmental Politics* 13 (2):46–64. https://doi.org/10.1162/GLEP_a_00166.

Lin, Kuo-ming. 2014. "Deliberative Inequality: Discursive Interactions in Taiwan's Citizen Conferences." *Taiwanese Sociology* 27:1–50.

Linnér, Björn-Ola and Victoria Wibeck. 2019. *Sustainability Transformations: Agents and Drivers across Societies*. New York: Cambridge University Press.

Llewellyn, Sue and Emma Tappin. 2003. "Strategy in the Public Sector: Management in the Wilderness." *Journal of Management Studies* 40 (4):955–982.

Lövbrand, Eva and Jamil Kahn. 2014. "The Deliberative Turn in Green Political Theory." In *Environmental Politics and Deliberative Democracy: Examining the Promise of New Modes of Governance*, edited by Karin Bäckstrand, Jamil Kahn, Annica Kronsell, and Eva Lövebrand, 47–64. Northampton, MA: Edward Elgar.

Lowi, Theodore. 1969. *The End of Liberalism: Ideology, Policy, and the Crisis of Public Authority*. New York: W.W. Norton.

Lubell, Mark, Mark Schneider, John T. Scholz, and Mihriye Mete. 2002. "Watershed Partnerships and the Emergence of Collective Action Institutions." *American Journal of Political Science* 46 (1):148–163.

Machlup, Fritz. 1962. *The Production and Distribution of Knowledge in the United States*. Princeton, NJ: Princeton University Press.

Maciel, Carolina Toschi and Bettina Bock. 2013. "Modern Politics in Animal Welfare: The Changing Character of Governance of Animal Welfare and the Role of Private Standards." *International Journal of Sociology of Agriculture & Food* 20 (2):219–235.

MacIntyre, Alasdair. 2006. *Ethics and Politics: Selected Essays*, Volume 2. New York: Cambridge University Press.

Mah, Daphne Ngar-yin, Guihua Wang, Kevin Lo, Michael K. H. Leung, Peter Hills, and Alex Y. Lo. 2018. "Barriers and Policy Enablers for Solar Photovoltaics in Cities: Perspectives from Potential Adopters in Hong Kong." *Renewable & Sustainable Energy Reviews* 92:921–936.

Marion Suiseeya, Kimberly R. 2014. "Negotiating the Nagoya Protocol: Indigenous Demands for Justice." *Global Environmental Politics* 14 (3):102–124.

Martinez de Anguita, Pablo, Maria Martin, and Abbie Clare. 2014. "Environmental Subsidiarity as a Guiding Principle for Forestry Governance: Application to

Payment for Ecosystem Services and REDD+ Architecture." *Journal of Agriculture and Environmental Ethics* 27 (4):617–631.

Mason, Michael. 2014. "So Far but No Further? Transparency and Disclosure in the Aarhus Convention." In *Transparency in Global Environmental Governance: Critical Perspectives*, edited by Aarti Gupta and Michael Mason, 83–106. Cambridge, MA: MIT Press.

Mason, Michael. 2020. "Transparency, Accountability and Empowerment in Sustainability Governance: A Conceptual Review." *Journal of Environmental Policy and Planning* 22 (1):98–111.

Mastronardi, Luigi, Davide Marino, Aurora Cavallo, and Agostino Giannelli. 2015. "Exploring the Role of Farmers in Short Food Supply Chains: The Case of Italy." *International Food and Agribusiness Review* 18 (2):109–130.

Matsumoto, Ken'ichi, Kanako Morita, Dimitrios Mavrakis, and Popi Konidari. 2017. "Evaluating Japanese Policy Instruments for the Promotion of Renewable Energy Sources." *International Journal of Green Energy* 14 (8):724–736.

May, Candace. 2019. "Governing Resilience through Power: Explaining Community Adaptations to Extreme Events in Coastal Louisiana." *Rural Sociology* 84 (3):489–515.

Mburu, John and Regina Birner. 2007. "Emergence, Adoption, and Implementation of Collaborative Wildlife Management or Wildlife Partnerships in Kenya: A Look at Conditions of Success." *Society and Natural Resources* 20:379–395.

McGeer, Victoria. 2008. "Varieties of Moral Agency: Lessons from Autism (and Psychopathy)." In *Moral Psychology, Volume 3 – The Neuroscience of Morality, Brain Disorders, and Development*, edited by Walter Sinnott-Armstrong, 227–257. Cambridge, MA: MIT Press.

Meadowcroft, James and Daniel J. Fiorino, eds. 2017. *Conceptual Innovation in Environmental Policy*. Cambridge, MA: MIT Press.

Mees, Helen, Niels Tijhus, and Carel Dieperink. 2018. "The Effectiveness of Communication Tools in Addressing Barriers to Municipal Climate Change Adaptation: Lessons from the Netherlands." *Climate Policy* 18 (10):1313–1326.

Mert, Ayşem. 2019. "Democracy in the Anthropocene: A New Scale." In *Anthropocene Encounters: New Directions in Green Political Thinking*, edited by Frank Biermann and Eva Lövbrand, 128–149. New York: Cambridge University Press.

Meyer, John M. 2015. *Engaging the Everyday: Environmental Social Criticism and the Resonance Dilemma*. Cambridge, MA: MIT Press.

Milkoreit, Manjana. 2017. *Mindmade Politics: The Cognitive Roots of International Climate Governance*. Cambridge, MA: MIT Press.

Miller, David. 1992. "Deliberative Democracy and Social Choice." *Political Studies* 40 (Special Issue):54–67.

Miller, David. 2003. "Deliberative Democracy and Social Choice." In *Debating Deliberative Democracy*, edited by James S. Fishkin and Peter Laslett, 182–199. Malden, MA: Blackwell Publishing.

Miller, Joshua Louis. 2011. "A New 'Democratic Life' for the European Union? Administrative Lawmaking, Democratic Legitimacy, and the Lisbon Treaty." *Contemporary Politics* 17 (3):321–334.

Miller, Michael. 2006. "Biodiversity Policy Making in Costa Rica: Pursuing Indigenous and Peasant Rights." *Journal of Environment and Development* 15 (4):359–381.

Mitchell, Ronald B. 2011. "Transparency for Governance: The Mechanism and Effectiveness of Disclosure-Based and Education-Based Transparency Policies." *Ecological Economics* 70 (11):1882–1890.

Mol, Arthur. 2014. "The Lost Innocence of Transparency in Environmental Politics." In *Transparency in Global Environmental Governance: Critical Perspectives*, edited by Aarti Gupta and Michael Mason, 39–59. Cambridge, MA: MIT Press.

Monheim, Kai. 2015. *How Effective Negotiation Management Promotes Multilateral Cooperation: The Power of Process in Climate, Trade, and Biosafety Negotiations.* New York: Routledge.

Moore, Alfred and Kieran O'Doherty. 2014. "Deliberative Voting: Clarifying Consent in a Consensus Process." *The Journal of Political Philosophy* 22 (3):302–319.

Morin, Jean-Frederic and Chatal Blouin. 2019. "How Environmental Treaties Contribute to Global Health Governance." *Globalization and Health* 15 (1):1–8.

Morin, Jean-Frederic and Sikina Jinnah. 2018. "The Untapped Potential of Preferential Trade Agreements for Climate Governance." *Environmental Politics* 27 (3):541–565.

Morin, Jean-Frederic, Dominique Blumer, Clara Brandl, and Axel Berger. 2019. "Kick-starting Diffusion: Explaining the Varying Frequency of Preferential Trade Agreements' Environmental Provisions by Their Initial Conditions." *World Economy* 42 (9):2602–2628.

Morseletto, Piero, Frank Biermann, and Philipp Pattberg. 2017. "Governing by Targets: Reductio ad Unum and Evolution of the Two-degree Climate Target." *International Environmental Agreements: Politics, Law and Economics* 17 (5):655–676.

Moseley, William, Matthew Schnurr, and Rachel Bezner Kerr. 2015. "Interrogating the Technocratic (Neoliberal) Agenda for Agricultural Development and Hunger Alleviation in Africa." *African Geographic Review* 34 (1):1–7. http://dx.doi.org/10.1080/19376812.2014.1003308.

Munaretto, Stefania and Dave Huitema. 2012. "Adaptive Comanagement in the Venice Lagoon? An Analysis of Current Water and Environmental Management Practices and Prospects for Change." *Ecology and Society* 17 (2):272–288.

Murphree, David W., Stuart A. Wright, and Helen Ebaugh. 1996. "Toxic Waste Siting and Community Resistance: How Cooptation of Local Citizen Opposition Failed." *Sociological Perspectives* 39 (4):447–463.

Nedergaard, Peter. 2009. "There Are Coalitions Everywhere: Coalitions and Side Payments in the Committees under the Open Method of Coordination in the European Union." *European Societies* 11 (5):649–671.

Neilson, Jeff. 2008. "Global Private Regulation and Value-Chain Restructuring in Indonesian Smallholder Coffee Systems." *World Development* 36 (9):1607–1622.

Nemarundewe, Nontokozo. 2004. "Social Charters and Organization for Access to Woodlands: Institutional Implications for Devolving Responsibilities for Resource Management to the Local Level in Chivi District, Zimbabwe." *Society and Natural Resources* 17 (4):279–291.

Netting, Robert McC. 1972. "Of Men and Meadows: Stategies of Alpine Land Use." *Anthropological Quarterly* 45 (3):132–144.

Netting, Robert McC. 1976. "What Alpine Peasants Have in Common: Observations on Communal Tenure in a Swiss Village." *Human Ecology* 4 (2):135–146.

Newall, Peter, Olivia Taylor, and Charles Touni. 2018. "Governing Food and Agriculture in a Warming World." *Global Environmental Politics* 18 (2):53–71.

Newell, Peter and Harriet Bulkeley. 2017. "Landscape for Change? International Climate Policy and Energy Transitions: Evidence from Sub-Saharan Africa." *Climate Policy* 17 (5):650–663.

Niemeyer, Simon. 2004. "Deliberation in the Wilderness: Displacing Symbolic Politics." *Environmental Politics* 13 (2):347–372.

Niemeyer, Simon and John S. Dryzek. 2007. "The Ends of Deliberation: Metaconsensus and Inter-Subjective Rationality as Ideal Outcomes." *Swiss Political Science Review* 13:497–526.

Nilsson, Måns and Åsa Persson. 2012. "Can Earth System Interactions Be Governed? Governance Functions for Linking Climate Change Mitigation with Land Use, Freshwater and Biodiversity Protection." *Ecological Economics* 81:10–20.

Nin-Pratt, Alejandro and Linden McBride. 2014. "Agricultural Intensification in Ghana: Evaluating the Optimist's Case for a Green Revolution." *Food Policy* 153–167.

Nussbaum, Martha. 2000. *Women and Human Development: The Capabilities Approach.* New York: Cambridge University Press.

Nussbaum, Martha. 2001. *Upheavals of Thought: The Intelligence of Emotion.* New York: Cambridge University Press.

Nussbaum, Martha. 2006. *Frontiers of Justice: Disability, Nationality, Species Membership.* Cambridge, MA: Harvard University Press.

Nussbaum, Martha. 2011. *Creating Capabilities: The Human Development Approach.* Cambridge, MA: Belknap Press of Harvard University Press.

Oberthür, Sebastian and Lisanne Groen. 2018. "Explaining Goal Achievement in International Negotiations: The EU and the Paris Agreement on Climate Change." *Journal of European Public Policy* 25 (5):708–727.

Oberthür, Sebastian and Justyna Pożarowska. 2013. "Managing Institutional Complexity and Fragmentation: The Nagoya Protocol and the Global Governance of Genetic Resources." *Global Environmental Politics* 13 (3):100–118.

Obradovic-Wochnik, Jelena and Anneliese Dodds. 2015. "Environmental Governance in a Contested State: The Influence of European Union and Other External Actors on Energy Sector Regulation in Kosovo." *Environment and Planning C: Government and Policy* 33 (5):935–949.

Olwig, Kenneth R. 2011. "The Earth Is Not a Globe: Landscape Versus the 'Globalist' Agenda." *Landscape Research* 36 (4):401–415.

Orr, Shannon K. 2013. *Environmental Policymaking and Stakeholder Collaboration: Theory and Practice.* New York: Routledge.

Orsini, Amandine. 2016. "The Negotiation Burden of International Interactions: Non-state Organizations and the International Negotiations on Forests." *Cambridge Review of International Affairs* 29 (4):1421–1440.

Orsini, Amandine, Sebastian Oberthür, and Justyna Pożarowska. 2014. "Transparency in the Governance of Access and Benefit Sharing from Genetic Resources." In *Transparency in Global Environmental Governance: Critical Perspectives*, edited by Aarti Gupta and Michael Mason, 157–180. Cambridge, MA: MIT Press.

Orts, Eric. 1995. "A Reflexive Model of Environmental Regulation." *Business Ethics Quarterly* 5 (4):779–794.

Orwin, Alexander. 2014. "Can Humankind Deliberate on a Global Scale? Alfarabi and the Politics of the Inhabited World." *American Political Science Review* 108 (4):830–839.

Ostrom, Elinor. 1990. *Governing the Commons: The Evolution of Institutions for Collective Action.* New York: Cambridge University Press.

Ostrom, Elinor. 2005. *Understanding Institutional Diversity.* Princeton, NJ: Princeton University Press.

Overdevest, Christine and Jonathan Zeitlin. 2014a. "Assembling an Experimentalist Regime: Transnational Governance Interactions in the Forest Sector." *Regulation and Governance* 8 (1):22–48.

Bibliography

Overdevest, Christine and Jonathan Zeitlin. 2014b. "Constructing a Transnational Timber Legaity Assurance Regime: Architecture, Accomplishments, Challenges." *Forest Policy and Economics* 48 (1):6–15.

Paavola, Jouni. 2008. "Governing Atmospheric Sinks: The Architecture of Entitlements in the Global Commons." *International Journal of the Commons* 2 (2):313–336.

Page, Edward A. 2012. "The Hidden Costs of Carbon Commodification: Emissions Trading, Political Legitimacy and Procedural Justice." *Democratization* 19 (5):932–950.

Park, Susan and Teresa Kramarz, eds. 2019. *Global Environmental Governance and the Accountability Trap*. Cambridge, MA: MIT Press.

Parkinson, John and Jane J. Mansbridge, eds. 2012. *Deliberative Systems: Deliberative Democracy at the Large Scale*. New York: Cambridge University Press.

Parsons, Meg, Johanna Nalau, and Karen Fisher. 2017. "Alternative Perspectives on Sustainability: Indigenous Knowledge and Methodologies." *Challenges in Sustainability* 5 (1):7–14. http://dx.doi.org/10.12924/cis2017.05010007.

Pattberg, Philipp. 2006. "Private Governance and the South: Lessons from Global Forest Politics." *Third World Quarterly* 27 (4):579–593.

Patterson, James J. and Dave Huitema. 2019. "Institutional Innovation in Urban Governance: The Case of Climate Change Adaptation." *Journal of Environmental Planning and Management* 62 (3):374–398.

Pelizzo, Riccardo and Frederick Stapenhurst. 2013. *Government Accountability and Legislative Oversight*. New York: Routledge.

Perkins, Richard. 2013. "Sustainable Development and the Making and Unmaking of a Developing World." *Environment and Planning C: Politics and Space* 31 (6):1003–1022. https://doi.org/10.1068/c12286.

Petrie, Murray. 2018. "Reversing the Degradation of New Zealand's Environment through Greater Government Transparency and Accountability." *Policy Quarterly* 14 (2):32–39.

Petts, Judith and Catherine Brooks. 2006. "Expert Conceptualisations of the Role of Lay Knowledge in Environmental Decisionmaking: Challenges for Deliberative Democracy." *Environment & Planning A* 38 (6):1045–1059.

Pinker, Steven. 2012. *The Better Angels of Our Nature: Why Violence Has Declined*. New York: Viking.

Pisupati, Balakrishna. 2007. *Access to Genetic Resources, Benefit Sharing and Bioprospecting (UNU-IAS Pocket Guide)*. Yokohama: United Nations University Institute of Advanced Studies.

Pitt, Damian and Ellen Bassett. 2014. "Innovation and the Role of Collaborative Planning in Local Clean Energy Policy." *Environmental Policy and Governance* 24 (6):377–390.

Plato. 1952. *The Dialogues of Plato*. Chicago: Encyclopedia Britannica.

Posner, Richard A. 2008. *How Judges Think*. Cambridge, MA: Harvard University Press.

Purifoy, Danielle M. 2014. "Food Policy Councils: Integrating Food Justice and Environmental Justice." *Duke Environmental Law and Policy Forum* 24 (2–3):375–398.

Rabitz, Florian. 2018. "Regime Complexes, Critical Actors and Institutional Layering." *Journal of International Relations and Development* 21 (2):300–321. https://doi.org/10.1057/jird.2016.16.

Rabkin, Jeremy A. 2005. *Law Without Nations? Why Constitutional Government Requires Sovereign States*. Princeton, NJ: Princeton University Press.

Rajão, Raoni and Yola Georgiadou. 2014. "Blame Games in the Amazon: Environmental Crises and the Emergence of a Transparency Regime in Brazil." *Global Environmental Politics* 14 (9):97–115.

Rangan, Haripriya and Marcus B. Lane. 2001. "Indigeneous Peoples and Forest Management: Comparative Analysis of Institutional Approaches in Australia and India." *Society and Natural Resources* 14 (2):145–160.

Raufflet, Emmanuel, Luciano Barin Cruz, and Luc Bres. 2014. "An Assessment of Corporate Social Responsibility Practices in the Mining and Oil and Gas Industries." *Journal of Cleaner Production* 84:256–270.

Rawls, John. 1971. *A Theory of Justice*. Cambridge, MA: Harvard University Press.

Reed, Maureen G. and Paivi Abernethy. 2018. "Facilitatiing Co-Production of Transdisciplinary Knowledge for Sustainability: Working with Canadian Biosphere Reserve Practitioners." *Society and Natural Resources* 31 (1):39–56.

Reinalda, Bob and Bertjan Verbeck, eds. 2004. *Decision Making Within International Organisations*. London: Routledge.

Reynolds, Laura T. 2012. "Fair Trade Flowers: Global Certification, Environmental Sustainability, and Labor Standards." *Rural Sociology* 77 (4):493–519.

Robertson, Chistina and Jennifer Westerman, eds. 2015. *Working on Earth: Class and Environmental Justice*. Reno: University of Nevada Press.

Rorty, Richard. 1989. *Contingency, Irony, and Solidarity*. New York: Cambridge University Press.

Rosenbloom, David. 2014. *Administrative Law for Public Administrators*. Boulder, CO: Westview Press.

Roskies, Adina. 2014. "Can Neuroscience Resolve Issues of Free Will?" In *Moral Psychology, Volume 4: Free Will and Responsibility*, edited by Walter Sinnott-Armstrong, 103–126. Cambridge, MA: MIT Press.

Rumsfeld, Donald. 2002. DoD News Briefing. In *U.S. Department of Defense News Transcript*. Washington, DC: US Department of Defense.

Runhaar, Hens, Runhaar Piety, Machiel Bouwmans, Simon Vink, Arjen Buijs, and David Kleijn. 2019. "The Power of Argument: Enhancing Citizen's Valuation of and Attitude Towards Agricultural Biodiversity." *International Journal of Agricultural Sustainability* 17 (3):231–242.

Runhaar, Hens, Nico Polman, and Marijke Dijkshoorn-Dekker. 2018. "Self-initiated Conservation by Farmers: An Analysis of Dutch Farming." *International Journal of Agricultural Sustainability* 16 (6):486–497.

Rusca, Maria and Klaas Schwartz. 2014. "'Going With the Grain': Accommodating Local Institutions in Water Governance." *Current Opinion in Environmental Sustainability* 11:34–38.

Sabatier, Paul A., Will Focht, Mark Lubell, Zev Trachtenberg, Arnold Vedlitz, and Marty Matlock. 2005. *Swimming Upstream: Collaborative Approaches to Watershed Management*. Cambridge, MA: MIT Press.

Sarkar, A. N. 2011. "Global Climate Governance: Emerging Policy Issues and Future Organisational Landscapes." *International Journal of Business Insights and Transformation* 4 (2):67–84.

Savaresi, Annalisa. 2016. "A Glimpse into the Future of the Climate Regime: Lessons from the REDD+ Architecture." *Review of European Community and International Environmental Law* 25 (2):186–196.

Scharpf, Fritz. 1999. *Governing in Europe: Effective and Democratic?* New York: Oxford University Press.

Schlosberg, David and Luke Craven. 2019. *Sustainable Materialism; Environmental Practice and the Politics of Everyday Life*. New York: Oxford University Press.

Schroeder, Heike. 2010. "Agency in Earth System Governance: The Case of International Forest Governance." *Conference Papers – International Studies Association* 1.

Schroeder, Heike. 2014. "Governing Allocation and Access in the Anthropocene." *Global Environmental Change* 26:A1–A3. https://doi.org/10.1016/j.gloenvcha.2014.04.017.

Schroeder, Heike and Nidia Gonzalez. 2019. "Bridging Knowledge Divides: The Case of Indigenous Ontologies of Territoriality and REDD+." *Forest Policy & Economics* 100:198–206.

Schroeder, Heike, Maxwell T. Boykoff, and Laura Spiers. 2012. "Equity and State Representations in Climate Negotiations." *Nature Climate Change* 2 (12):834–836.

Schuster, Monica and Miet Maertens. 2013. "Do Private Standards Create Exclusive Supply Chains? New Evidence from the Peruvian Asparagus Export Sector." *Food Policy* 43:291–305.

Schwarze, Jürgen. 2012. "European Public Law in the Light of the Treaty of Lisbon." *European Public Law* 18 (2):285–304.

Scobie, Michelle. 2018. "Accountability in Climate Change Governance and Caribbean SIDS." *Environment, Development and Sustainability* 20 (2):769–787.

Sekhri, Sheetal and Paul Landefeld. 2013. Agricultural Trade, Institutions, and Depletion of Natural Resources. *Virginia Economics Online Papers* 405.

Sellitto, Miguel Afonso, Luis Antonio Machado Vial, and Cláudia Viviane Viegas. 2018. "Critical Success Factors in Short Food Supply Chains: Case Studies with Milk and Dairy Producers from Italy and Brazil." *Journal of Cleaner Production* 170:1361–1368. http://dx.doi.org/10.1016/j.jclepro.2017.09.235.

Sen, Amartya. 1992. *Inequality Reexamined*. Cambridge, MA: Harvard University Press.

Sen, Amartya. 2001. *Democracy as Freedom*. New York: Oxford University Press.

Sen, Amartya. 2003. "Democracy and Its Global Roots: Why Democratization is Not the Same as Westernization." *New Republic*, October 6, 28–35.

Sen, Amartya. 2009. *The Idea of Justice*. Cambridge, MA: Belknap Press of Harvard University Press.

Sénit, Carole-Anne, Frank Biermann, and Agni Kalfagianni. 2017. "The Representativeness of Global Deliberation: A Critical Assessment of Civil Society Consultations for Sustainable Development." *Global Policy* 8 (1):62–72.

Setiadi, Rukuh and Alex Y. Lo. 2019. "Does Policy Research Really Matter for Local Climate Change Policies?" *Urban Policy and Research* 37 (1):111–124.

Shandas, Vivek and W. Barry Messer. 2008. "Fostering Green Communities through Civic Engagement: Community Based Environmental Stewardship in the Portland Area." *Journal of the American Planning Association* 74 (4):408–418.

Shane, Peter M. 2010. "Legislative Delegation, the Unitary Executive, and the Legitimacy of the Administrative State." *Harvard Journal of Law & Public Policy* 33 (1):103–110.

Shaw, Malcolm. 2003. *International Law*. New York: Cambridge University Press.

Shinn, Jamie E. 2016. "Adaptive Environmental Governance of Changing Socio-Ecological Systems: Empirical Insights from the Okavango Delta, Botswana." *Global Environmental Change* 40:50–59.

Slaughter, Anne-Marie. 2004. *A New World Order*. Princeton, NJ: Princeton University Press.

Snell, Chelsea, Aude Bernheim, Jean-Baptiste Bergé, Marcel Kuntz, Gérard Pascal, Alain Paris, and Agnès E. Ricroch. 2012. "Assessment of the Health Impact of GM Plant Diets in Long-term and Multigenerational Animal Feeding: A Literature Review." *Food and Chemical Toxicology* 50 (3–4):1134–1148.

Sovacool, Benjamin K. and Marie-Claire Brisbois. 2019. "Elite Power in Low-Carbon Transitions: A Critical and Interdisciplinary Review." *Energy Research and Social Science* 57:1–10.

Spruijt, Pita, Anne B. Knol, Arthur C. Peterson, and Etik Lebret. 2016. "Differences in Views of Experts About Their Role in Particulate Matter Policy Advice: Empirical Evidence from an International Expert Consultation." *Environmental Science & Policy* 59:44–52.

Steger, Manfred B. 2001. *Globalism: The New Market Ideology*. Lanham, MD: Rowman & Littlefield.

Steger, Manfred B. 2017. *Globalization: A Very Short Introduction*. 4th ed. New York: Oxford University Press.

Stevens, Casey and Norichika Kanie. 2016. "The Transformative Potential of the Sustainable Development Goals (SDGs)." *International Environmental Agreements: Politics, Law and Economics* 16 (3):393–396.

Stevenson, Hayley. 2016. "The Wisdom of the Many in Global Governance: An Epistemic-Democratic Defense of Diversity and Inclusion." *International Studies Quarterly* 60 (3):400–412.

Stokke, Olav. 2012. *Disaggregating International Regimes: A New Approach to Evaluation and Comparison*. Cambridge, MA: MIT Press.

Sun, Daxin, Saixing Zeng, Hogquan Chen, Xiaohua Meng, and Zhizhou Jin. 2019. "Monitoring Effect of Transparency: How does Government Environmental Disclosure Facilitate Corporate Environmentalism?" *Business Strategy and the Environment* 28 (8):1594–1606.

Sundararajan, Louise. 1995. "Echoes after Carl Rogers: 'Reflective Listening' Revisited." *The Humanistic Psychologist* 23 (2):259–271.

Suškevičs, Monika. 2012. "Legitimacy Analysis of Multi-Level Governance of Biodiversity: Evidence from 11 Case Studies across the EU." *Environmental Policy & Governance* 22 (4):217–237.

Sword-Daniels, Victoria, Christine Eriksen, Emma E. Hudson-Doyle, Ryan Alaniz, Carolina Adler, Todd Schenk, and Suzanne Vallence. 2018. "Embodied Uncertainty: Living with Complexity and Natural Hazards." *Journal of Risk Research* 21 (3):290–307.

Szasz, Andrew and Michael Meuser. 1997. "Public Participation in the Cleanup of Contaminated Military Facilities: Democratization or Anticipatory Cooptation." *International Journal of Contemporary Sociology* 34 (2):211–233.

Tallontire, Anne, Maggie Opondo, and Valerie Nelson. 2014. "Contingent Spaces for Smallholder Participation in GlobalGAP: Insights from Kenyan Horticulture Value Chains." *Geographical Journal* 180 (4):353–364.

Tan, Yeling. 2014. "Transparency without Democracy: The Unexpected Effects of China's Environmental Disclosure Policy." *Governance,* 27 (1):37–62.

Tapela, Barbara N. 2008. "Livelihoods in the Wake of Agricultural Commercialisation in South Africa's Poverty Nodes: Insights from Small-Scale Irrigation Schemes in Limpopo Province." *Development Southern Africa* 25 (2):181–198.

Tarr, G. Alan. 2001. "Laboratories of Democracy? Brandeis, Federalism, and Scientific Management." *Publius* 31 (1):37–46.

Taylor, Charles. 1985. *Human Agency and Language*. New York: Cambridge University Press.

Taylor, Dorceta E. 1999. "Mobilizing for Environmental Justice in Communities of Color: An Emerging Profile of People of Color Environmental Groups." In *Ecosystem Management: Adaptive Strategies for Natural Resources Organizations in the Twenty-First Century*, edited by Jennifer Aley, William R. Burch, Beth Conover, and Donald Field, 33–67. Philadelphia: Taylor & Francis.

Tewari, Meenu and Poonam Pillai. 2005. "Global Standards and the Dynamics of Environmental Compliance in India's Leather Industry." *Oxford Development Studies* 33 (2):245–267.

Thaler, Thomas and Sebastian Seebauer. 2019. "Bottom-up Citizen Initiatives in Natural Hazard Management: Why They Appear and What They Can Do?" *Environmental Science & Policy* 94:101–111.

Themnér, Lotta and Peter Wallensteen. 2014. "Armed Conflicts, 1946–2013." *Journal of Peace Research* 51 (4):541–554.

Thiel, Andreas and Christine Moser. 2018. "Toward Comparative Institutional Analysis of Polycentric Social-Ecological Systems Governance." *Environmental Policy & Governance* 28 (4):269–283.

Thissen, Wil, J. Kwakkel, M. Mens, J. van der Sluijs, S. Stemberger, A. Wardekker, and D. Wildschut. 2017. "Dealing with Uncertainties in Fresh Water Supply: Experiences in the Netherlands." *Water Resources Management* 31 (2):703–725.

Thistlewaite, Jason. 2011. "Counting the Environment: The Environmental Implications of International Accounting Standards." *Global Environmental Politics* 11 (2):75–97.

Toffler, Alvin. 1991. *Powershift: Knowledge, Wealth, and Violence at the Edge of the 21st Century*. New York: Bantam.

Toje, Asle. 2008. "The Consensus-Expectations Gap: Explaining Europe's Ineffective Foreign Policy." *Security Dialogue* 39 (1):121–141.

Torney, Diarmuid. 2019. "Climate Laws in Small European States: Symbolic Legislation and Limits of Diffusion in Ireland and Finland." *Environmental Politics* 28 (6):1124–1144.

Toulmin, Stephen. 2001. *Return to Reason*. Cambridge, MA: Harvard University Press.

Tribe, Laurence. 1988. *American Constitutional Law*. 2nd ed. Mineola, NY: Foundation Press.

Trilling, Lionel. 1965. *Beyond Culture: Essays on Literature and Learning*. New York: Basic Books.

Turnhout, Esther, Katja Neves, and Elsa de Lijster. 2014. "'Measurementality' in Biodiversity Governance: Knowledge, Transparency, and the Intergovernmental Science-Policy Platform on Biodiversity and Ecosystem Services (IPBES)." *Environment & Planning A: Economy and Space* 46 (3):581–597.

Tyfield, David. 2012. "A Cultural and Political Economy of Research and Innovation in an Age of Crisis." *Minerva* 50 (2):149–167.

Urrutia, Isabel, Goretty M. Dias, and Jennifer Clapp. 2019. "Material and Visceral Engagements with Household Food Waste: Towards Opportunities for Policy Interventions." *Resources, Conservation & Recycling* 150:1–8.

van Asselt, Harro, and Fariborz Zelli. 2014. "Connect the Dots: Managing the Fragmentation of Global Climate Governance." *Environmental Economics and Policy Studies* 16 (2):137–155.

van den Brandler, Francine, Joyeeta Gupta, and Michaela Hordijk. 2019. "Megacities and Rivers: Scalar Mismatches between Urban Water Management and River Basin Management." *Journal of Hydrology* 573:1067–1074.

van der Heijden, Jeroen, Harriet Bulkeley, and Chiara Certomà, eds. 2019. *Urban Climate Politics: Agency and Empowerment*. New York: Cambridge University Press.

van der Hel, Sandra. 2016. "New Science for Global Sustainability? The Institutionalisation of Knowledge Co-Production in Future Earth." *Environmental Science & Policy* 61:165–175.

van der Hel, Sandra. 2018. "Science for Change: A Survey on the Normative and Political Dimensions of Global Sustainability Research." *Global Environmental Change* 52:248–258.

van der Hel, Sandra, and Frank Biermann. 2017. "The Authority of Science in Sustainability Governance: A Structured Comparison of Six Science Institutions Engaged with the Sustainable Development Goals." *Environmental Science and Policy* 77:211–220. https://doi.org/10.1016/j.envsci.2017.03.008.

van der Loos, Hendrick, Agni Kalfagianni, and Frank Biermann. 2018. "Global Aspirations, Regional Variation? Explaining the Global Uptake and Growth of Forestry Certification." *Journal of Forestry Economics* 33 (1):41–50.

van der Ven, Hamish. 2019. "Private Accountability in Global Value Chains." In *Global Environmental Governance and the Accountability Trap*, edited by Susan Park and Teresa Kramarz, 63–86. Cambridge, MA: MIT Press.

van der Ven, Hamish, Steven Bernstein, and Matthew Hoffman. 2017. "Valuing the Contributions of Nonstate and Subnational Actors to Climate Governance." *Global Environmental Politics* 17 (1):1–20.

VanDeveer, Stacy D. 2015. "Consumption, Commodity Chains, and Global and Local Environments." In *The Global Environment: Institutions, Law, and Policy*, edited by Stacy D. VanDeveer and Regina Axelrod, 350–372. Los Angeles: CQ Press.

Vijge, Marjanneke. 2013. "The Promise of New Institutionalism: Explaining the Absence of a World or United Nations Environment Organization." *International Environmental Agreements: Politics, Law and Economics* 13 (2):153–176.

Vos, Jeroen and Rutgerd Boelens. 2014. "Sustainability Standards and the Water Question." *Development and Change* 45 (2):205–230.

Vukić, Nikolina Markota, Renata Vuković, and Donato Calace. 2017. "Non-Financial Reporting as a New Trend in Sustainability Accounting." *Journal of Accounting and Management* 7 (2):13–26.

Walzer, Michael. 2007. *Thinking Politically: Essays in Political Theory*. New Haven, CT: Yale University Press.

Wapner, Paul. 2014. "The Changing Nature of Nature: Environmental Politics in the Anthropocene." *Global Environmental Politics* 14 (4):36–54.

Ward, John and David Kaczan. 2014. "Challenging Hydrological Panaceas: Water Poverty Governance Accounting for Spatial Scale in the Niger River Basin." *Journal of Hydrology* 519:2501–2514.

Ward, Sarah, Chad Staddon, Laura De Vito, Adriana Zuniga-Teran, Andrea K. Gerlak, Yolandi Schoeman, Aimee Hart, and Giles Booth. 2019. "Embedding Social Inclusiveness and Appropriateness in Engineering Assessment of Green Infrastructure to Enhance Urban Resilience." *Urban Water Journal* 16 (1):56–67

Weiner, James F. and Katie Glaskin, eds. 2011. *Customary Land Tenure and Registration in Australia and Papua New Guinea: Anthropological Perspectives*. Canberra: ANU E Press.

Welford, Richard and Richard Starkey. 2001. *The Earthscan Reader in Business and Sustainable Development*. New York: Routledge.

West, Tom E. R. B. 2012. "Environmental Justice and International Climate Change Legislation: A Cosmopolitan Perspective." *Georgetown International Environmental Law Review* 25 (1):129–174.

Whelan, James and Kristen Lyons. 2005. "Community Engagement or Community Action: Choosing Not to Play the Game." *Environmental Politics* 14 (5):596–610.

Whitfield, Stephen, Helmut Geist, and Antonio Ioris. 2011. "Deliberative Assessment in Complex Socioecological Systems: Recommendations for Environmental Assessment in Drylands." *Environmental Monitoring & Assessment* 183 (1–4):465–483.

Whitman, Darrell. 2008. "'Stakeholders' and the Politics of Environmental Policymaking". In *The Crisis of Global Environmental Governance: Towards a New Political Economy of Sustainability*, edited by Jacob Park, Ken Conca, and Matthias Finger, 163–192. New York: Routledge.

Whitney, Kristoffer. 2019. "It's About Time: Adaptive Resource Management, Environmental Governance, and Science Studies." *Science, Technology, & Human Values* 44 (2):263–290.

Wiber, Melanie, Fikret Berkes, Anthony Charles, and John Kearney. 2004. "Participatory Research Supporting Community-Based Fishery Management." *Marine Policy* 28 (6):459–468.

Widerberg, Oscar and Philipp Pattberg. 2015. *Harnessing Company Climate Action beyond Paris*. Study 2015: 6. Stockholm: Fores.

Willis, Alan. 2003. "The Role of the Global Reporting Initiative's Sustainability Reporting Guidelines in the Social Engineering of Investments." *Journal of Business Ethics* 43 (3):233–237.

Wilson, Edward O. 1998. *Consilience: The Unity of Knowledge*. New York: Knopf.

Winkler, Harald, Niklas Höhne, Guy Cunliffe, Takeshi Kuramochi, Amanda April, and Maria Jose de Villafranca Casas. 2018. "Countries Start to Explain How Their Climate Contributions Are Fair: More Rigour Needed." *International Environmental Agreements: Politics, Law and Economics* 18 (1):99–115. https://doi.org/10.1007/s10784-017-9381-x.

Wironen, Michael B., Robert V. Bartlett, and Jon D. Erickson. 2019. "Deliberation and the Promise of a Deeply Democratic Sustainability Transition." *Sustainability* 4 (1023):1–18

Wirth, David A. 2009. "The International Organization for Standardization: Private Voluntary Standards and Swords and Shields." *Boston College Environmental Affairs Law Review* 36 (1):79–102.

Wohl, Ellen, Andrea Gerlak, N. Poff, and Anne Chin. 2014. "Common Core Themes in Geomorphic, Ecological, and Social Systems." *Environmental Management* 53 (1):14–27.

Wolff, Robert Paul. 1977. *Understanding Rawls: A Reconstruction and Critique of John Rawls's "A Theory of Justice"*. Princeton, NJ: Princeton University Press.

World Health Organization. 2017. *WHO Report on the Global Tobacco Epidemic, 2017*. Geneva: World Health Organization.

Wormald, Patrick. 2001. *The Making of English Law: King Alfred to the Twelth Century*. London: Wiley-Blackwell.

Young, Oran. 2017. *Governing Complex Systems: Social Capital for the Anthropocene*. Cambridge, MA: MIT Press.

Young, Oran R. 1989. *International Cooperation: Building Regimes for Natural Resources and the Environment*. Ithaca, NY: Cornell University Press.

Young, Oran R. 1998. *Creating Regimes: Arctic Accords and International Governance*. Ithaca, NY: Cornell University Press.

Young, Oran R. 2008. "The Architecture of Global Environmental Governance: Bringing Science to Bear on Policy." *Global Environmental Politics* 8 (1):14–32.

Young, Oran R. 2010. "Institutional dynamics: Resilience, Vulnerability and Adaptation in Environmental and Resource Regimes." *Global Environmental Change* 20 (3):378–385.

Young, Oran R., Leslie A. King, and Heike Schroeder, eds. 2008. *Institutions and Environmental Change: Principal Findings, Applications, and Research Frontiers*. Cambridge, MA: MIT Press.

Zelli, Fariborz and Harro van Asselt. 2013. "The Institutional Fragmentation of Global Environmental Governance: Causes, Consequences, and Responses." *Global Environmental Politics* 13 (3):1–13.

Zelli, Fariborz, Ina Möller, and Harro van Asselt. 2017. "Institutional Complexity and Private Authority in Global Climate Governance: The Cases of Climate Engineering, REDD+ and Short-Lived Climate Pollutants." *Environmental Politics* 26 (4):669–693.

Zelli, Fariborz, Tobias Nielsen, and Wilhelm Dubber. 2019. "Seeing the Forest for the Trees: Identifying Discursive Convergence and Dominance in Complex REDD+ Governance." *Ecology and Society* 23 (1):433–448.

Zimring, Carl. 2016. *Clean and White: A History of Environmental Racism in the United States*. New York: New York University Press.

Index

Aarhus Convention on Access to Information, Public Participation in Decision-Making and Access to Justice in Environmental Matters, 30
access, 2, 13–14, 21, 24, 30, 41–44, 65, 72, 86, 88, 109, 117, 130, 139–141, 143–149, 151–152, 158, 161–163, 174
accountability, 13, 15–17, 20, 22, 24, 31–32, 38, 40, 44–45, 56, 62, 80, 83–84, 123–125, 127–129, 131–133, 135–136, 145, 152, 155, 159, 162, 174
adaptive comanagement, 121
adaptiveness, 13–15, 17, 21, 24, 31, 35, 37, 104, 108, 115, 149, 152, 157–158, 162–163, 174
Administrative Procedures Act, 30
administrative professionals, 105–107, 112, 115, 119, 121–122, 157–158
Africa, 93–94, 120, 139
agency, 8, 13–15, 17, 19, 21, 31, 45, 47–50, 52, 55, 61–63, 65–72, 74–76, 79, 101, 119, 121, 135, 152–155, 162–163, 173–174
aggregative democracy, 2, 4, 6–7, 9, 12, 108
agonistic democracy, 6–7
Agreement on Technical Barriers to Trade, 57
air pollution, 7
allocation, 2, 13–14, 19, 21, 24, 31, 41–42, 45, 139, 142–145, 147–149, 151–152, 161–163, 173–174
American Consensus, 27
American experience, 15
American founders, 15
American Law Institute, 115, 168–170
anthropocentrism, 11, 163
Appalachian Mountains, 90
Appalachian Sustainable Agriculture Project, 90–91, 98
Aquaculture Stewardship Council, 64
architecture, 13–16, 19, 21, 24, 31–32, 42, 50, 55, 78, 80, 82–86, 88–93, 95–96, 100–103, 125, 147, 152, 155–156, 162–163, 173
Arizona, 3
Australia, 86, 109, 143

autonomy, 6, 15, 53–54, 66, 69, 71–72, 74, 76, 142, 153, 155

biodiversity, 26, 39, 42–43, 53, 92, 125
biodiversity policy, 26, 43
Brazil, 3
bureaucracies, international, 52–54, 118, 159

California, 8, 91, 97–99
capabilities, 2, 13, 15, 22, 71–75, 118, 146, 148, 153–155
capital, 20, 55, 65, 106–107, 121, 123, 133–134, 160
carbon, 16, 25, 56, 80, 84, 100, 140, 156
Cartagena Protocol on Biosafety, 35–38
caveat emptor, 32, 37
certification, 33–34, 54, 63–64, 84–85, 125
China, 85
citizen jury, 25
civil society, 14, 31, 39, 60–61, 66, 86, 105, 118–119, 130, 161
Clean Development Mechanism, 100
climate, 3, 11, 15–17, 30, 56, 60, 79–82, 84, 87, 89, 96, 98, 104, 118, 139, 155–158
collaborative governance, 96
collaborative planning, 81
Colorado River, 99
Comitology, 129
Common Agricultural Policy, 89, 91, 174
common law, 47, 114, 164–168, 170, 174–175
common property resources, 18, 111, 144
community supported agriculture, 88–89
consensus, 5, 9, 12, 20, 23–30, 32–34, 36–39, 42–44, 60, 74, 108–109, 115, 120, 133–134, 147, 150–151, 158–160, 168, 171
constitutionalism, 151
Convention on Biological Diversity, 41, 54
cooptation, 8, 11, 14, 22
Copenhagen Accord, 16
corporate social responsibility, 56, 126

205

corporation, 14, 27, 39, 48, 51, 55, 57, 61, 66, 88–89, 146

corruption, 145

Council of Ministers, 129, 135

deep ecology, 22

deforestation and forest degradation, 83

deliberative polling, 25, 133, 159

democratic deficit, 115, 131, 135–136, 159, 170

Earth Summit, 34

Earth System Governance Project, 13, 19, 24, 159, 162, 173

eco-labels, 34

ecological rationality, 2, 124

ecosystem services, 83, 140, 160–161

Ecuador, 64

embedded, 10–13, 15, 63, 69, 78, 86, 93, 95, 97, 102–103, 157, 163–164

embeddedness, 2, 7, 11, 13, 15, 86–88, 91, 93, 152

empowerment, 2, 10–11, 13–15, 21, 31, 65–67, 152, 163

Endangered Species Act, 4, 26

environmental impact assessment, 21

environmental justice, 4, 7, 11, 14–15, 21, 40, 147, 149–150, 161, 174

environmental racism, 22

environmental rights, 30, 150–151

environmentalism, 14, 21–22, 75, 125

equality, 2, 7, 71, 74

equitable, 2, 8, 11–13, 17, 20–21, 25, 41–42, 87, 133, 136, 139, 148–149, 151–152, 162

equity.*See* equitable

equivocal, 1, 9, 12–13, 19–20, 149, 159–160, 162, 164

EU. *See* European Union

EU Commission, 127, 130, *See* European Commission

European Commission, 129–132, 135

European Council, 129–130, 135

European Parliament, 129, 132, 135

European Union, 20, 37, 56, 89, 91, 120, 124–125, 127, 129, 159, 174

experimental, 1, 6, 12–15, 17, 28, 58, 123, 125, 157–158, 163–164

Farmers Marketing and Local Food Promotion Program.*See* FMLFPP

federal systems, 15, 96

FLEGT, 84–85, 125

FMLFPP, 88–89

food, 4, 17, 36, 38, 60–63, 87, 89–91, 93–96, 98–99, 102, 105, 113, 126, 146, 157

Food and Agriculture Organization, 34

foodshed, 97–99

Forest Law Enforcement Governance and Trade.*See* FLEGT

Forest Stewardship Council, 34

forestry, 82–84, 143

Friend of the Sea, 64

GAP principles.*See* good agricultural practices

genetically modified organisms, 35–38

Germany, 65

Ghana, 94

Global Aquaculture Alliance, 64

Global Environmental Facility, 53

global governance, 17, 23, 27–28, 30, 47, 54, 64, 83, 85, 95, 102, 104, 120, 124, 128, 136, 152–153, 157

Global Governance Project, 53

Global Reporting Initiative, 38–40

GlobalGAP, 64

globalism, 81, 108

globalization, 20, 55, 107, 119, 123–124, 131, 143, 152, 175

good agricultural practices, 61–62

governance-by-disclosure, 31–33, 35, 37–38, 40–42, 44

governmental agency, 52

Green Revolution, 93

greenhouse gas, 16, 80, 82, 114, 155–156

greenwashing, 54

health, 4, 17, 22, 37, 56, 73, 90–91, 105, 141, 157

hubris, 103

human rights, 15, 70, 72, 74, 80–81, 146, 150–151, 163

India, 65, 143–144

indigenous and local communities, 41–42

Indonesia, 63

information society, 106–107

International Accounting Standards Board, 57

international law, 115, 118, 164, 170

International Maritime Organization, 53, 82

ISO, 57

Italy, 26, 77, 86, 89, 98, 121

juristic deliberation, 25, 133

juristic modeling, 159

justice, 4, 8, 11, 13–16, 19, 21, 24, 43, 66, 71–73, 76, 80, 114, 128, 133, 139, 143, 147, 152, 155, 160, 165–166, 175

Kenya, 3, 62, 140

Kosovo, 126

Kyoto Protocol, 16, 56, 79, 155

labor, 5, 56, 61, 65, 91, 94, 106

learning, 2, 18, 26, 30, 35, 56, 84–85, 96, 105, 121, 125, 130, 132, 136, 158

legal agency, 47, 51, 66

legislative oversight, 13, 20, 123–124, 127–130, 136, 159, 161

liberalism, 20

Lima-Paris Action Agenda, 158

Lisbon Treaty, 131

local knowledge, 2–3, 6, 10, 145, 151, 158, 161

Index

Marine Stewardship Council, 34, 64
modernity, 1, 48, 51
Montreal Protocol, 53–54
moral agency, 67–69, 71, 75, 154–155

Nagoya Protocol on Access to Genetic Resources and the Fair and Equitable Sharing of Benefits Arising from their Utilization, 41
natural resources management, 26, 141
NGOs, 16, 34–35, 43, 55, 80, 126, 153, 156
Niedersachsen, 96
Non-State Actor Zone for Climate Action, 158
norm, 9, 17, 19, 33, 42–43, 100, 134, 137
North American Free Trade Agreement, 57
North Carolina, 90

Ohio, 96
open method of coordination, 127, 130
Organisation for Economic Co-operation and Development, 53, 61, 64

Pacific, 3, 97
Pantheon, 77–78, 102
Paris Agreement, 16, 79, 140, 155
path dependency, 100, 119, 140
Peru, 63
pesticides, 32, 93
political agency, 50
polycentric governance, 82, 125
polycentricity, 126
post-industrial, 106–107
poverty, 4, 17, 95, 105, 139, 144–145, 157
principal/agent, 40, 48–49, 51, 66
prior informed consent, 31–32, 36, 42–44
private governance, 14, 31, 54, 64–65, 151, 173
private regulation, 47, 57, 63, 153
private standards initiatives, 62–63, 65
problematique, 1, 22–23, 67

Queensland, 86, 109

REDD+, 83–85
reflexivity, 1, 38, 131, 136, 151–152, 173
regime complexes, 55, 82
regime theory, 118
regimes, 15, 17, 25, 31–32, 35–37, 39–40, 45, 51, 55–56, 64, 81–82, 84–85, 88, 101, 104–105, 114–115, 118, 125–126, 141–143, 145, 147, 150–151, 156–157, 171, 174
representation, 3, 6, 10, 48, 51, 70
right-to-know, 30
risk, 1, 4, 8, 11, 30, 32, 35–38, 61, 69, 96, 100, 115, 120, 123, 129, 169
Rotterdam Convention on the Prior Informed Consent Procedure for Certain Hazardous Chemicals and Pesticides in International Trade, 31–32
Rural Development Policy, 89

San Diego, 97–99
science, 14, 17, 23–24, 32–34, 37, 45, 47, 58, 60, 117, 142, 147, 151, 153, 159, 173
secretariats, 53, 118, 122, 171
security, 4, 15–17, 21, 78, 80, 87, 93–96, 98, 100, 105, 138–139, 142–146, 148–149, 156–157
short food supply chains, 89, 96, 98, 100
slave, 48, 50–51
social contract theory, 50
South Africa, 94
sovereignty, 33, 36, 83, 100, 127, 141
stakeholder partnerships, 26–27, 95, 112, 174
Strategic Environmental Assessment, 86
subsidiarity, 83–84, 111
sustainability, 4, 10, 15, 18, 38, 54, 58, 64, 81, 90–92, 101, 111, 151, 158, 163, 170, 173
Switzerland, 110–111
symbolic politics, 27, 29, 109, 112, 120–121

Tasmania, 143
tragedy of the commons, 87
transformation, 1, 17, 21, 81, 156
transparency, 16, 29–31, 33–45, 57, 80, 86, 90, 118, 125, 155, 160

UN General Assembly, 79, 151
United Kingdom, 125
United Nations, 16, 53–54, 79, 83, 101, 124, 155
United Nations Convention to Combat Desertification, 53
United Nations Development Programme, 54
United Nations Environment Programme, 53–54, 79, 100–101
United Nations Framework Convention on Climate Change, 16, 53, 79–80, 83, 155–156
United Nations Industrial Development Organization, 54
United States, 30, 36, 97, 99, 112, 115, 128, 138, 174
US Department of Defense, 8

Venice, 121
Vienna Convention for the Protection of the Ozone Layer, 53

water management, 3, 63, 96
water systems, 17, 96, 105, 157
watershed management, 3
watershed partnerships, 26, 95–96, 100, 112, 133–134, 159
Westphalian nation-state, 20, 107, 174
WikiLeaks, 30
World Bank, 53–54
World Environment Organization, 79, 119
World Summit for Sustainable Development, 95
World Trade Organization, 57, 62
World Wide Fund for Nature, 34

Printed in the United States
by Baker & Taylor Publisher Services